RASTAFARI AND OTHER AFRICAN-CARIBBEAN WORLDVIEWS

Rastafari and Other African-Caribbean Worldviews

Edited by

Barry Chevannes

Rutgers University Press
New Brunswick, New Jersey

First published in Great Britain 1995 by
MACMILLAN PRESS LTD
Houndmills, Basingstoke, Hampshire RG21 6XS
and London

First published in the United States 1998 by
RUTGERS UNIVERSITY PRESS
New Brunswick, New Jersey

This book is printed on paper suitable for recycling and made from fully managed and sustained forest sources.

Printed in Malaysia

Library of Congress Cataloging-in-Publication Data
Rastafari and other African-Caribbean worldviews / edited by Barry Chevannes.
p. cm.
Papers presented at a workshop sponsored by the Institute of Social Studies in The Hague, 1989.
Originally published: Houndmills, Basingstoke, Hampshire : Macmillan, 1995.
Includes bibliographical references and index.
ISBN 0–8135–2411–3 (cloth : alk. paper). — ISBN 0–8135–2412–1 (pbk. : alk. paper)
1. Rastafari movement—Congresses.   2. Afro-Caribbean cults––Congresses.   3. Caribbean Area—Religion—Congresses.
I. Chevannes, Barry.   II. Institute of Social Studies (Netherlands)
[BL2532.R37R385 1997]
299'.676—dc21   97–464
                                                                      CIP

To Derek

Contents

Preface

The publication of this paperback edition is a most welcome development in the brief history of a book that is in increasing demand. Widening interest in the cultures of the Caribbean peoples, generally, and in the global impact of the Rastafari movement in particular, is undoubtedly the main reason for this demand. Their social and cultural influence in the main metropolitan centres of Europe, North America and Japan make the study of their worldviews an important necessity. Especially in the United States where new religious movements have been springing up rapidly, and where Caribbean nationals have made their own contribution to the social landscape, the availability of this collection will be most timely.

The focus on worldviews, and by some of the leading scholars in Caribbean anthropology, is yet another reason for the interest displayed in *Rastafari and Other African-Caribbean Worldviews*. That it was nominated for the 1995 Katherine Briggs Prize is a vindication of the approach adopted.

Barry Chevannes
Mona

Acknowledgements

I am deeply indebted to the Institute of Social Studies for the Visiting Senior Research Fellowship that made this collection possible in the first place, and to its staff for their critical exchanges, collegiality and encouragement. In particular I must single out Ken Post, Valpy Fitz-Gerald, Sipko de Boer and Els Mulder. I also acknowledge the professional hands of Gary Debus, Linda McPhee, Joy Misa and Michelle Williams of the ISS and Belinda Holdsworth of Macmillan, in guiding the manuscript through its several stages. I thank the anonymous readers for their valuable comments, without which the present volume would have been the poorer. Thanks also to Koos van Wieringen for the sketches appearing on page 106. The encouragement of my wife was particularly cherished, coming as it did from across the Atlantic ocean and Caribbean sea.

B.C.

Notes on Contributors

Jean Besson was Head of the Department of Anthropology at the University of Aberdeen. She has also taught at the University of Edinburgh, Scotland, and the Johns Hopkins University, Baltimore, USA. The author of many publications on the Caribbean peasantry, she has undertaken fieldwork in Jamaica, Trinidad and Tobago, is co-editor of *Land and Development in the Caribbean* (Macmillan, 1987) and editor of *Caribbean Reflections* (Karia Press, 1989). She is currently Senior Lecturer in Anthropology at Goldsmiths' College, University of London, England.

E. Ellis Cashmore has held positions in sociology departments at the Universities of Hong Kong, Washington, USA and Tampa, USA and is currently at the University of Aston in England. He is the author of several books, including *Rastaman* (George Allen & Unwin, 1979 and 1983) and *The Logic of Racism* (George Allen & Unwin, 1987).

Barry Chevannes has published extensively on Rastafari and Revival religions. His research interests include the study of religion and identity as well as the sexual values and sexuality of Jamaicans. He is Dean of the Faculty of Social Sciences at the University of the West Indies.

John (Jake) Homiak is an anthropologist who started fieldwork in Jamaica in 1980-81. Throughout the 1980s he travelled frequently to Jamaica to continue research on the Rastafari Movement, publishing on eldership and the production of ideology. More recently, he has helped to sponsor Rastafari cultural programmes in the USA designed to familiarize a wider public with Rastafarianism. He is presently Director of the Human Studies Film Archives in the Department of Anthropology, National Museum of Natural History, Smithsonian Institution, Washington, DC, USA.

Roland Littlewood has published extensively in the fields of cultural psychiatry and social anthropology. He is the author of *Pathology and Identity: The Work of Mother Earth In Trinidad* (1992), joint author of *Aliens and Alienists: Ethnic Minorities and Psychiatry*

(1982) and joint editor of *Inter-cultural Therapy: Themes, Interpretations and Practice* (1992). He is Professor of Anthropology at University College, London, Consultant Psychiatrist and Joint Director of the University College Centre for Medical Anthropology.

H.U.E. Thoden van Velzen has recently retired as Professor of Anthropology at the University of Utrecht and as Member of the Faculty of the Graduate School of Social Science in Amsterdam. He is a member of the Royal Academy of Sciences in The Netherlands and the author of many publications including one jointly authored with W. van Wetering, *The Great Father and the Danger* (Foris, 1988).

Wilhelmina van Wetering is Lecturer in the Department of Anthropology and Religion at the Free University in Amsterdam. She is the author of many publications on Surinamese Creoles and Maroons.

Introduction

Barry Chevannes

The present volume is the fruit of a Workshop sponsored by the Institute of Social Studies in The Hague in September 1989. On a six-month Visiting Senior Research Fellowship, the editor was asked to present some aspects of his work while at the Institute for discussion by colleagues in his field. The only guideline was that due to budgetary constraints only scholars from Europe, and a limited number at that, could be supported. Fortuitously, the Annual Conference of the Society for Caribbean Studies at Hoddesdon, England, in July 1989 provided an opportunity to promote the Workshop among Caribbeanists, while in The Netherlands itself the main contacts were made through the University of Utrecht and the University of Amsterdam, both of which have had an internationally highly respected tradition in Caribbean studies.

The interest generated by the idea of the Workshop on the Rastafari was so great that two scholars from North America funded their own travel across the Atlantic, while others shifted previously made commitments in order to attend. In the end, thirteen scholars came together on 24 and 25 September 1989 and ten made presentations. Apart from the several authors included in this collection, the other participants were Dr Carole Yawney from Queens University in Canada, the most experienced of the younger scholars who have carried out original anthropological fieldwork on the Rastafari in Jamaica; Dr Carolyn Cooper from the University of the West Indies, well-known as a lyrical critic of reggae music; Dr Chris de Beet, an expert on Caribbean maroon resistance, from the University of Amsterdam; Mr Herman Lauwerysen, a development expert in The Netherlands who, as a doctoral candidate in the Applied Anthropology programme at Columbia University, carried out extensive fieldwork among Haitian peasants; and two staff members of the Institute: Mr Sipko de Boer, expert in development studies, and Professor K.W.J. Post, the foremost international scholar on the development and political role of the Jamaican working class in the 1930s.

Nine of the thirteen participants were anthropologists, two sociologists, one a political scientist and one a literary critic, a mix which contributed in no small measure to a most stimulating encounter. Hopefully, the chapters included here do convey some of that excitement, which, regrettably for the reader, is somewhat diminished by the fact that presentations from Yawney, Cooper and Lauwreysen were unable to be included.

Why was interest so great? By way of preparation for the Workshop, the participants were invited to use as stimulant for their own ideas any or all of the three papers presented by myself, whose underlying theme is the continuity of and changes in the worldview of Jamaicans. For some of us, though much original research had been carried out, and even more written, on the Rastafari, this was the first time the movement was the focus of an international meeting of scholars. This fascinating socio-religious movement, which, from an obscure colonial origin has spread its influence among Black people all over the world, provided the scholars who came together, most of whom have contributed to this volume, with much to think and write about.

At the same time, this collection is not an attempt to follow up that first pioneering collection put out by the journal *Caribbean Quarterly* in 1980. Whereas the latter pulled together the ideas of Rastafari and non-Rastafari scholars on the Rastafari, the ISS Workshop was rather concerned with exploring some underlying themes suggested by research on the movement. This surely was the second reason for the interest generated. Drawing upon the extensive fieldwork experiences of Homiak, Yawney, Chevannes and Cashmore among the Rastafari in Jamaica and the United Kingdom, but benefitting from the ethnographic works of Besson in Jamaica, Thoden van Velzen in Suriname, van Wetering among Surinamese in Amsterdam and Littlewood in Trinidad, the Workshop revealed the existence of subterranean linkages, like so many different wells springing up here and there, the burden of the same aquifer. The scope is thus Caribbean, but the themes general.

Foremost among the themes being explored is the concept of 'worldview', although this is nowhere explicitly defined except by Thoden van Velzen. In my use of the term, worldview encompasses (a) cosmology, or the systematic beliefs about the nature and origin of the world, the ordering of its constituent parts, and theory of causation; (b) ethics, or the principles and values guiding daily life and relations between people; and (c) the system of meaning and symbols. Revival and Rastafari religious beliefs, such as the ideas on God, the spirits, man and nature discussed by Besson, Homiak, van Wetering and myself, would fall mainly under cosmology, but they also span ethical principles such as inter-community solidarity, and the system of meaning attached to colours, and to natural and artificial objects, for example. Similarly, Littlewood's journey into the oppositional ideology of radical Puritanism, which he finds quite similar to Rastafari ideology, is to my mind a journey into the ethical values of radical Christianity but also into its creation of symbols in opposition, and its beliefs about God and the world. Thoden van Velzen, on the other hand, is explicit in confining his use of worldview to: ideology, which he defines as 'a set of ideas guiding and justifying actions within the socio-economic arena'; ethos, which he defines as 'the norms and values that govern interaction in a social group'; and collective fantasy or a symbolic system comprising visionary images and a '"philosophy" that ranges over and beyond the sphere of practical action'. It seems to me that what I would call ethics coincides with ethos and ideology as used by Thoden van Velzen, and what he calls collective fantasy with much of what I would call cosmology and semiotics. But there is a great deal of overlapping, and it is clear that Thoden van Velzen's intention is not to set up discrete categories, but, to find a fruitful way of examining a worldview, which he does by analysing it along the 'three axes'.

The richness of the worldview approach taken by the authors in this collection is revealed only in a comparative framework encompassing Jamaican, Trinidadian and Surinamese religions. The two religions which provide the main basis of comparison are Revivalism and Rastafari, both indigenous to Jamaica. Summary descriptions of these are presented in Chapter 1, immediately following, in order to facilitate readers who may be unfamiliar with either or both.

Revivalism, or simply Revival, is a native creation of the descendants of the Africans in Jamaica, with historical roots in slavery. It has many of the features of African traditional religions, including polytheism, and is generally designated African-Caribbean by all scholars who have studied it, in recognition of its origins. Rastafari, on the other hand, the sixty year old creation of Black nationalists, rejects polytheism and other features associated with African-Caribbean religion. Identifying a living person as the Godhead, or Jah, and expecting the repatriation of all new world Africans, to be effected by divine intervention, Rastafari has had all the appearances of a millenarian cult instead of a traditional African folk religion.

Yet, I argue in Chapter 2, Rastafari may be more fruitfully studied from the point of view of its impact on the traditional worldview of the Jamaicans than as a revolutionary, political, millenarian or messianic

cult, as has been the general approach of scholars. To be sure, the tenets of Rastafari members and their ritualized aggressiveness lent themselves to these essentially structural approaches. Instead Chapter 2
draws attention to how Rastafari is a cultural continuum of its historically antecedent, Revivalism, as well as a deviation from it. Hence the
title 'A New Approach'. It is here that I compare the worldview of these
two native religions, pointing out their most important similarities in ritual structure, ritual instruments, notions about humanity and other beliefs.

The immediate implications of adopting this approach is the treatment of Rastafari as one of the African-derived religions of the Caribbean, whose distance from folk traditions is not as great as first im-
agined. But Rastafari is different, it is argued, because it is engaged in
reshaping the Revival worldview with respect to deficiencies revealed in
a more modern context. In other words, Rastafari represents both continuity and change.

The chapter by Besson, 'Religion as Resistance in Jamaican Peasant
Life', draws on the author's extensive fieldwork in the parish of Trelawny, which supports the thesis of continuity and change advanced by
Chevannes. Focusing on the theme of cultural resistance, Besson first
establishes the historical context within which the Baptist and Revival
religions functioned and flourished. The parish with the largest number
of sugar plantations and slaves by the late eighteenth century, Trelawny
became the focus of slave rebellions, marronage and new cultural forms.
It was the vanguard parish of Nonconformist anti-slavery struggles in
Jamaica and of the free village movement after emancipation, both led
by the Baptist missionary William Knibb. By their example, the free villages provided the setting for a wide range of cultural and social forms
of resistance.

This wide agenda is, however, not the author's immediate concern.
Instead, she sets about isolating the central role of land in forming of a
sense of belonging and identity among the peasantry counter to the imposed social organization and values of plantation society. Besson also
focuses on the role of women in this resistance. The task of effecting this
belongs to the three religions, the Baptist denomination, Revival and
Rastafari, which are interwoven in the socio-cultural fabric of the five
Trelawny villages researched, where women are central actors. How the
three religions link together is the main concern of her chapter.

Demonstrating how the establishment of free villages in the 1830s
and 1840s by the Baptist church was itself an act of resistance to plantation society, Besson goes on to explain how the peasants then trans-

formed the pattern of land ownership transmitted by the Baptists into
one of their own creation, the institution known as 'family land', a folk
system of tenure whereby land passed down jointly to all one's male and
female descendants is designated for their use and cannot be alienated.
Except where the state overrules, all members of the lineage have the
right to be buried on family land. The burial plot is a common feature of
family land in the Trelawny villages. It not only symbolizes family lines
going back to the establishment of the free villages, but reflects as well
the 'embedding of the Revival worldview and the peasant culture of resistance'. For, as Besson explains, the mortuary rituals in these Baptist
villages are Revival, not Baptist.

Among the Rastafari, as with the Revivalists and Baptists, land remains the central theme of ideological significance. In the Trelawny villages, this centrality makes it possible for the Rastafari to be integrated
in village life, despite the greatly diverging lifestyles of these communities, for they too are a variant on the family land theme.

Thus, underlying Besson's discussion is the concept of land as a symbol and source of identity. Besson implies in her chapter that Jamaican
peasants, as far as family land is concerned, place the symbolic above
the utility aspect of land. Of course, a different attitude might have prevailed had land been available in limitless quantities, but the point is
that given the conditions of time, of place and the separation from Africa, the memory of which, as Besson shows, is still cherished in some
family histories, we can infer from her chapter that land as symbol provided the Jamaican peasants with a useful tool with which to reorder
their cosmos in a way that allowed them the space to develop and to
protect a new humanism, free from the constricting and alienating plantation system.

The next two chapters, 4 and 5 (by Chevannes), deal with the attempt of the Rastafari to reorder the world in the face of changing situations. Chapter 4, 'The Origin of the Dreadlocks', traces the process of
reformation undertaken by the Dreadlocks, and is followed in Chapter 5
by a discussion of the wider significance of the symbolism behind the
new hair culture.

Fresh evidence points to the tradition of dreadlocks as an innovation
of young Rastafari bent on purging the movement of its traceable linkages to Revivalism, in the period beginning in the late 1940s. Calling
themselves the Youth Black Faith, their main aim was to present an oppositional image of the Rastafari, and this they symbolized by adopting
an illegal substance (*ganja*) as a sacrament, a new speech pattern, a different life-style, and, above all, a different presentation of self, epi-

tomized by the dreadlocks. These measures gave them an identity in opposition, so to speak – opposition not just to White definitions of social
reality but also to those aspects of that definition which were incorporated into African-Jamaicans' definition of their own.

That Jamaicans incorporated aspects of White racism into their own
cosmology points to the limitations of the Revival worldview, and nothing brings this out more clearly than the traditional hair culture and
symbolism. Focusing a substantial part of Chapter 5 on gender differences in hair culture in Jamaica, I show the sort of binary oppositions
which obtained in the 1950s in Jamaica, largely, but not solely, in response to the prevailing racial ideology. Thus the two main determi-
nants of hair aesthetics in Jamaica were race and gender. From ideas
about race came the valuation of hair as good (European) or bad (African). From gender came clear norms about self-presentation, for
example: male hair should be natural but cut short, female hair uncut,
long and cultured. In the face of these differences, the only norm common to both male and female was the combing of hair as a prerequisite
for the presentation of self. It was precisely this norm which the Dreadlocks violated with their uncut, ungroomed hair, and in so doing succeeded in putting themselves symbolically outside the pale of society.
They made themselves outcasts. Deliberately.

But they succeeded also in another direction. Because the dreadlocks became the main, if not the only, visible outward sign of the new
Rastafari, thus differentiating him from the earlier 'combsome' type, the
dreadlocks also symbolized another difference, namely the ritual avoidance of sexual relations with women. Dreadlocks became a phallic symbol. The chapter ends with the suggestion that we may be looking here
at two sides of a coin, in that the ritualized anti-feminism of the early
Dreadlocks could be the rationalization of a perception of women as a
force for social conformity. Such a conclusion is not a contradiction to
Besson's line on the role of women in cultural resistance, for, as noted
in Chapter 3, the Jamaican folk perception of women is ambivalent. The
Dreadlocks, it seems, seized on the negative aspects in that perception.

Many of the points presented here are reinforced and corroborated
by John Homiak's fascinating 'dub version' in Chapter 6, which should
put to rest certain speculations about the origins of dreadlocks. For
though his version makes the dreadlocks an innovation of another group
calling itself the I-gelic House or Ites of Rastafari, Homiak shows that
this was but one aspect of a wider range of beliefs and practices being
inserted into the movement by young Rastas beginning in the late 1940s,
in revolt against their older colleagues. The change was processual and

complex. One key point in the process was the acquisition of literacy by the younger brethren, enabling them to shift from exclusive dependency on the Bible to other sources and eventually to 'a process of signifying upon the authorized social codes that upheld the everyday common-sense legitimacy of the system (i.e. physical appearance, dress, speech, gender relations)'. The name they gave the emergent life-style is *livity*.

Livity, as Homiak shows, includes a range of ideas and codes centred around naturality, an ascetic life-style involving the rejection of material comforts, and of manufactured and processed things, the avoidance of meat, salt and sexual relations with women, on the one hand; and the substitution on the other hand of a life-style involving the incorporation of things in as close to a state of nature as possible – hammocks for beds, calabashes and fired clay for bowls and pots, food without salt or sugar. '[B]arefoot, with matted hair, cloaked in crocus bags, and armed with large rods', these Rastafari brethren became feared not only for their appearance, which they called 'Higes Knots', but also for their verbal aggression, aimed particularly at the police and the Roman Catholic churches and clergy. They claimed also to have developed the I-talk of Rastafari.

The theme of women's subordination provides striking contrast to their central role in cultural resistance and identity, as Jean Besson in Chapter 3 and Wilhelmina van Wetering in Chapter 9 underscore. Here, drawing on a suggestion by Yawney that the Rastafari 'have co-opted the strengths of traditional Jamaican women's culture' and on Ortner's male-female and culture-nature oppositional categories, Homiak provides an explanation for Rastafari female subordination by showing the necessary link between the concept of *i-tal* (naturalness) and Rastafari patriarchal dominion over the domestic sphere, the context in which the *i-tal* ideas were reproduced.

What emerges quite clearly from the chapters by Homiak and the preceding two by myself is the fact that the changes codified by the generation of Dreadlocks Rastafari in the late 1940s and the 1950s were aimed at creating an entirely new definition of a world corrupted against the will of God by racism and injustice, and of the Black man's place in it. It is this redefinition which I believe so impressed itself on young people throughout the Caribbean as to make them converts and sympathizers of Rasta ideas and practices. And not only the Caribbean, but the industrialized countries of the West also, where by the 1970s Black youth were already sporting dreadlocks and proclaiming a belief in Jah. In Britain, second generation Caribbean immigrants faced with the need to articulate and protect their ethnic identity in a society in

which racism was pronounced, found in the Rastafari just the right instrument. We are therefore quite fortunate to be able to include in the
collection a discussion of the Rastafari in Britain (Chapter 7) by Ellis
Cashmore, whose *Rastaman* (1979) remains one of the most widely-
read accounts of the movement there, and whose authoritative testimony proved instrumental in getting the state to shift its view of Rastafari from that of a radical nationalist and anti-social force in British
society to that of a respectable ethnic group against whose members it is
now unlawful to discriminate. How, but especially why, that shift came
about is the subject of Cashmore's chapter.

'The De-Labelling Process' is a story of mutual accommodation between the Rastafari, on the one hand, and British society on the other,
which Cashmore analyses from the point of view of factors external and
internal to the Rastafari. Among external ones are the preoccupation
with bigger threats such as the youth revolts of the 1980s; AIDS and
other 'new panics'; and the incorporation into the mainstream of British
thought of ideas which bear Rasta parallels. Internal factors include a
toning down of Rasta radicalism and their integration in the social system through the unavoidable links with its many and varied institutions.
The result is a new perception by British society and a new status by the
Rastafari.

How much of all this is real rather than apparent change is still too
early to tell, but Cashmore argues that with British racism having mutated into less perceptible but no less intractable forms, the future of
Blacks could take one of two directions: greater conservatism or greater
radicalism, or both. Whatever the outcome, he believes there will be no
return to Rastafari militancy of the 1970s.

With H.U.E. Thoden van Velzen's paper, Chapter 8, the collection
turns from direct focus on the Rastafari to a comparative look at other
Caribbean religions. Using an episode in the turn of the century history
of the Ndyukas, one of the largest maroon tribes of Suriname, Thoden
van Velzen demonstrates the fruitfulness of the worldview approach, in
the discovery of similarities between the Rastafari and the *Gaan Gadu*
cult. Hence the title of his chapter, 'African-American Worldviews in
the Caribbean'. By carefully and clearly situating the construction of a
Gaan Gadu worldview within the socio-economic context of the need of
a rising class of Ndyuka entrepreneurs to protect their achieved status
through a puritanic *ethos*, Thoden van Velzen introduces a valuable and
welcome addition to the discussion. Until the appearance of *Gaan
Gadu*, witchcraft accusations for most of the nineteenth century were
aimed primarily at economically successful men. Now, however, under

Gaan Gadu a 'poor person has a motive for committing the crimes of witchcraft; a rich man has not'. The victims were primarily those who, as the least able to share in the monopoly over the lucrative river transport, were the most dependent on the Ndyuka boat men. Women were thus a principal target.

Gaan Gadu in effect signalled a change in the class structure of maroon society, as the cult made inroads into other tribes, creating divisions between rich and poor. The cult evolved its own ethos, overturning the traditional. Trustworthiness, for example was now seen as a characteristic not of kinship and ethnic affiliation as in the past but as a vestige of a (traditional) poison ordeal (ritual/practice) meant to demonstrate innocence of the eye of envy. The concepts of witchcraft and of God were redefined also. Witchcraft was considered a state of mind, rather than an attribute, a conceptualization that allowed for ideas of sin, self-examination and forgiveness. Consistent with these collective fantasies, the concept of *Gaan Gadu* was of a vindictive God ready to mete out punishment to the guilty. In the *Gaan Gadu* cult it was the dead who must establish their innocence. Although by nature difficult to grasp, this area of *collective fantasy* has potential for yielding the greatest reward, for here, Thoden van Velzen suggests, may be found parallels which could be pan-African-American, and not specifically Rastafari or *Gaan Gadu*, for example the attitude towards death as a contaminating force, and the attitude towards women.

The theme of women as agents of cultural resistance and continuity and their subordinate relations with men surfaces also in Wilhelmina van Wetering's fascinating case study of the *Winti* worldview among Surinamese Creole immigrants in the Bijlmermeer quarter of Amsterdam, where, comprising a subculture, these working class immigrants strive to preserve their ethnic identity in the midst of the pressure to jettison certain aspects of their traditional practices and beliefs. The resulting ambivalence finds expression in the *home rituals*, through which women become the main agents for the adaptation, maintenance and transmission of the community's cosmology and value system.

Old beliefs are highly adaptable in the modern world, van Wetering argues, supporting observations made in Chapter 1 with respect to Revivalism in Jamaica. As an African-Caribbean folk religion *Winti* shares much in common with the Revivalism discussed by both Chevannes and Besson. The *Winti* pantheon comprises various classes of invading spirits without any clear hierarchical order. Of particular interest are the *Bakru*, those demons which play such a central role in the day to day life of the individual. In Surinamese Creole cosmology illness and mis-

fortune are the work of the *Bakru*: a woman who dresses inappropriate-
ly, a man who is caught stealing and killed, a woman who faces down-
ward social mobility, or 'little Cynthia' who faces demotion to kindergarten. From her field notes of a home ritual performed to appease
Cynthia's *Bakru*, van Wetering presents us with a worldview easily understandable to other African-Caribbean peoples: libations to Mother
Earth, herbal baths, dreams as medium of communication with the
spirit world. Another important demon is the *Ampuku*, a forest spirit
which sometimes appears in dreams as an incubus, a phenomenon little
seen or reported in the literature on Revivalism. But the author leaves
us no doubt that women 'do not regard themselves as the helpless victims of demons' any more than they regard themselves as the powerless
victims of male superiority.

With the final chapter we come full circle, so to speak, as Roland
Littlewood, whose contact with African-Caribbean religions was made
through the Earth People of Trinidad, refocuses the reader's attention
on the question of how best to view the Rastafari. In Chapter 2 I raised
the issue of its continuity with Revival, a theme picked up by Besson and
Thoden van Velzen. Here, in Chapter 8, Littlewood presents us with a
well-considered argument for continuity, but from a different angle: the
European millennial tradition. Critical of the Herskovitsian school
which explains Caribbean culture in terms of continuities with the African past but lacks authority primarily because of its 'failure to consider
how and why retentions may be actively selected at specific historical
moments', he advances, instead, the argument that Rastafari values and
ideology are but the most recent resurfacing of an undercurrent of radical utopian and apocalyptic ideas forged in opposition to established
power in Western society since the beginning of Christianity, and repli-
cating itself throughout the history of European domination. The neologisms, homonyms, inversions, reversals, substitutions and other linguistic innovations of the Rastafari; their taboos and attitudes towards
nature; the identification of Rome as the anti-Christ; their this-world
orientation; even the name of their deity – all these represent threads of
continuity in the radical counter tradition in the West, but a tradition
recreated anew in each generation.

Littlewood is not unmindful of the methodological problem posed
by his argument, namely the difficulty of actually proving a radical Puritan pedigree in Rastafari. He argues that while the dominant tradition
may be traced through linear historical continuity, the sub-dominant
tradition owes its continuity not to a lineage but to a 'perverse affinity'
to the dominant tradition itself. The existence in the Caribbean of both

dominant and sub-dominant traditions makes it unlikely 'that there was no explicit 'underground' continuity in the repeated response to established power'.

Notwithstanding its hypothetical nature, the argument produces two effects. It forces a re-examination of the historical factors shaping worldviews, in the way Thoden van Velzen has done for the *Gaan Gadu* cultists, instead of the crude folkloric comparisons which Littlewood charges are the norm in studies of African-Caribbean religion. But secondly – and there is no question that this is intended – it stakes a claim for the '*active* creation by African-Americans of a complex of values and behaviour specifically concerned with the White domination'.

The concluding chapter (11) addresses these and other implications of the themes presented in this collection, which the reader is now invited to share.

1 Introducing the Native Religions of Jamaica

Barry Chevannes

The late Sir Arthur Lewis once remarked that the Caribbean has made an impact on world culture far in excess of the size of its population. Apart from personalities of the order of the economist and Nobel laureate himself, the region is known for producing writers of international reputation, top class athletes and reggae and calypso music. It is also known for giving birth to the Dreadlocks, the Rastafari. In truth, it might be said that from the day the Europeans enslaved Africans, turning the islands into sugar factories, the Caribbean began having an impact on the world.

Jamaica, the small Caribbean island of 2.2 million people, where the Rastafari movement began, is credited with one of the highest rates of slave revolts and conspiracies in the history of any slave society (Patterson 1970). It certainly had the highest number in the anglophone colonies, including the decisive rebellion of 1831-32 which hastened the abolition of slavery by Britain in 1834. It was one of the few slave colonies where an enslaving power was forced into a treaty of accommodation with maroons – slaves who had simply taken and defended their freedom and independence. And in the aftermath of slavery, a very costly peasant rebellion in 1865 ended the career of a governor and forced the local ruling White planter class to relinquish its own democracy. Jamaica, thus, has a long tradition of resistance, nurtured in the deep isolated recesses of its rugged interior, where after emancipation a new class of peasant freeholders fashioned their life and culture.

The most central institution to the tradition of resistance in Jamaica has been religion. Whether resistance through the use of force, or resistance through symbolic forms such as language, folk-tales and proverbs, or resistance through the creation of alternative institutions, religion was the main driving force among the Jamaican peasants. Even in those areas of socio-cultural life where resistance has lost meaning, having

1

successfully brought colonial domination to an end, religion still flourishes as the guardian of public and private morality.

According to contemporary census figures, there are seventeen named denominations functioning in the country, plus a large, undetermined number of small ones, of such insignificant magnitude as to be grouped together under 'Other'. All these religions I would classify into three categories. The first comprises those of European origins, which established themselves as late as the nineteenth century, accounting for 30 per cent of the affiliated church-going population. According to figures published in the 1982 Census, it includes denominations such as the Anglican, Baptist, Methodist, United (Presbyterian and Congregational), Roman Catholic and Moravian churches. Their middle- and upper-class membership gives them much influence and power in the society, particularly through the education system which they played a major role in establishing. The second category comprises those of North American origin, which have been establishing themselves throughout the twentieth century. The leading denominations are Pentecostalism, Church of God, Seventh-day Adventism and African Methodist Episcopalian (AME) Zion, which together have been growing at a fast pace, from a mere 9 per cent in 1960 to 33 per cent in 1982.

It is from the third category, those of Jamaican origin, or Jamaican examples of African-derived religion, that the subject of this chapter is drawn. Here, but for ethnographic and other sociological studies, one might conclude on the basis of the Census that these do not exist. Only Rastafari (0.6 per cent or a little over 14,000 persons) receives attention in the 1982 Census, the first time in four censuses since 1943. Of Revival, Kumina, and Convince, nothing. It is possible that these have been subsumed under the category 'Other' (5.7 per cent), but the more likely explanation for their absence lies first in the phenomenon known as dual membership. Because of their low status, on the one hand, arising from colonial attempts at suppressing them, and because of the power and influence of the European Christian churches, on the other hand, people seek nominal membership in the latter, but active participation in the former. Dual membership, which has been practised from as long ago as late eighteenth century, and which may also be found in other parts of the Caribbean, is far-reaching in its significance, for it implies that the native religions mean much more to the people than a mere head count would suggest, and alternatively that formal Christianity has not been as successful in changing the people's worldview as its long history and its large share of members suggest. Secondly, as the reader will see below, Revival, the largest of its kind, has been undergoing incorporation into the second category of churches, so that many of those described as AME Zion or Pentecostal are in fact Revival groups in disguise. Thus, African-derived religions have survived in Jamaica, as well as other countries of the Caribbean where conditions were similar, in a sort of underground existence.

Revivalism

As late as the 1950s in rural Jamaica, it was a regular, sometimes weekly, occurrence for a small band of people, usually dressed in white, heads wrapped in white or madras, to march silently into a village in the early evening. The leader of the band was usually female, but sometimes male, while most of the members were women. They would bear with them two drums, the larger of the two called the bass, the smaller called the rattler, a Bible, some flowers, and a lantern. This was a Revival band. If they continued through the village square, they were on their way somewhere else; if they stopped, it was a sign they were going to 'jump poko', that is, dance and hold a meeting, there that night. A table, a chair and a glass of water would be the main items borrowed from the villagers, and while these preparations were underway, the bass, like the pealing bell of the Methodists or the Baptists, summoned other Revivalists, onlookers and other participants from the surrounding districts. The bass was played either from a sitting position on the thigh or hung from the shoulder and struck with a wooden hammer wrapped in cloth. The rhythm was three strikes of a 4/4 beat, with the fourth silent. This would continue for an hour or so before the rattler joined in. The rattler, always hanging from the shoulder and clutched in the crook of the player's arm, would rattle out the polyrhythms struck by two sticks. Members of the band, gathering in a semicircle around the table bearing the flowers, a glass of water, some salt, the Bible and hymnbook, would signal the beginning of a Revival street meeting with their lively singing and swaying. Revival choruses were simple and very popular.

> I am going home on the morning train,
> I am going home on the morning train,
> For the evening train will be too late,
> I am going home on the morning train.
>
> Believers, walk right in and take your seat,
> Believers, walk right in and take your seat,

For the evening train will be too late,
I am going home on the morning train.

Or,

O, let the Spirit fall on me, O Lord,
Let the Spirit fall on me.
O, let the Spirit from heaven fall on me,
Let the Spirit fall on me.

Songs like these would be sung on and on scores of times. At a certain point in the meeting, the drums would stop and songs called 'sankeys', from the collection by Ira D. Sankey, would be intoned. This would be followed by preaching and testifying, and a money collection. Depending on the particular night of the week, the crowd of onlookers and participants could number in the scores. A good meeting would turn out a couple of hundred.

The Revival street meeting of the type described above has more or less disappeared. What has remained are the rituals which are confined to the small churches and tabernacles – prayer meeting or divine service, healing service and tables, and the baptismal rites performed in the rivers. These have been amply described by scholars (Simpson 1956; Hogg 1964; Seaga 1969; Chevannes 1978; Wedenoja 1978).

Churches are generally sited in the Revival leader's home, which is sometimes called a 'balm yard', if he or she is noted for healing powers, or simply a church or tabernacle. By whatever name, the yard is a sacred place, usually recognized by a flag aloft a bamboo pole. At the foot of the pole may be planted sacred herbs and flowers, depending on the particular spirit which hovers there, or there may be a separate garden planted with foliage such as croton or herbs such as mint which are sacred to the spirits. A basin of water may complete this *seal*, as all sacred spots are called. Seals may be found all around the yard. Among the ritual objects distinguishing them are water, stones, bottled beverages, candles, vases of flowers and planted shrubs, such as the croton or the basle. At night all seals are lit with burning lamps or candles. Other structures, apart from the leader's dwelling quarters, may include accommodation for the leader's personal assistant, a client undergoing protracted healing, or a novice under spiritual guidance by a spirit.

Within the tabernacle itself, one may find other seals, but here the main seal is usually a very ornately decorated three-tiered altar, with candles, bottles of aerated water, flowers, fruits and, perhaps, a picture of Jesus.

All Revival meetings begin in more or less the same manner as the street meeting, but, unlike the street meeting, spirit possession or 'getting in the spirit' invariably takes place. This is involuntary, on the part of the member. Spirit possession is a sign that one already has a special relationship with the particular identified spirit involving mutual obligations. As soon as possession takes place, the person is attended by two or three members who guide him or her in 'labouring' (or groaning or 'trumping'). Labouring refers to an activity in which those involved hyperventilate to a rhythmic stomping while bending at the waist.

The second part of the ritual is distinguished by the sankeys, which are 'tracked' (that is, read line by line) by the secretary and sung with slow, mournful stress, beginning with prayers to God or Jesus, followed by reading of the sacred scriptures, usually from the Psalms of David. Then follows the preaching, if the meeting is divine worship; or testimonies, if the meeting is a testimonial one; or healing, if a healing one. In other words, not until the second part is the difference between types of Revival meetings manifested ritually.

Healing at Revival meetings is performed by the 'laying on' of hands, rubbing the affected areas of the body and giving consecrated water to drink. Where the leader is a renowned healer, healing is a more elaborate affair and performed in daytime. Clients, assembling from far and wide – even from abroad – must participate in a ceremony of singing and praying, before being treated. Treatment may consist of a 'reading', in which the healer diagnoses the condition not by deduction but by prescience or divination; a ritual bath; the application of especially prescribed oils and potions; or a prescription of spiritual activities such as daily reading of biblical texts or fasting. A healer of some repute does not ask questions – he or she describes for the client the latter's ailment. The range of problems for which people seek out the expertise of Revival healers spans the physical, such as ulcers that won't heal, the psychological, such as neurological disorders, and the social areas of life, such as bad luck or unrequited love. To the Jamaicans there are two causes of disease and illness, 'evil or displeased spirits and germs' (Simpson 1956:383), both operating on the same plane in so far as physical and social ills may also have spiritual causes.

Sometimes closely associated with, but quite distinct from, healing is the practice of *obeah*, the use of fetishes, oils and powders to achieve personal ends such as success in ventures, debilitating an enemy, winning a case in court, winning the affection of a potential lover. The *obeahman* is a sorcerer.

Undoubtedly the most elaborate Revival ritual is the *Table*. This feast is held for any of a variety of reasons: thanksgiving, anniversaries, petitions, fundraising, destruction, memorials. The ceremony acquires its name from the centrepiece of the ritual, a table adorned with candles of various colours, flowers, fruits, coconuts, aerated water, bread, uncooked rice and so on, around which the dancing takes place. Tables always attract visitors from other Revival bands as well as the interested public looking for good entertainment. The ritual follows the divine worship in its inclusion of all the features of the latter, but differs profoundly in the quality of the dancing, which is more intense and protracted, and, of course, in the particular purpose of the Table, which entails additional rites. For example, a thanksgiving to mark the successful initiation of a novice would include a testimony of her journeys, that is her visions and experiences while under the control of the spirit. A Table is considered 'broken' when, the climax passed, the fruits and bread on the table are shared and devoured.

Origins

The reader would have gathered from passing references above that Revivalism combines European and African religious traditions, for example the belief in Jesus along with a pantheon of lesser spirits. The main elements in the Revival belief system being the subject of the ensuing chapter, I shall confine my remaining remarks on this religion to its origins.

Revivalism, as I have described it, is really the end result of a historical development of religious ideas and practices influenced by three different sources. The first became evident in the Tacky rebellion of 1760, when, for the first time in the history of the slaves, a rebellion was planned and staged, incorporating people of different tribal origins. Up to that time revolts were tribal, generally Akan, based. Schuler (1979b) was the first to attribute the new development to the rise of an apparently new, Pan-African religion called Myal. No one has yet been able to convincingly trace the origin of the word Myal, but Schuler believes it may have had Central African roots, given what she identifies as its great capacity to absorb alien influences, ostensively characteristic of Central African religions as well. Apparently, no one also has been able to reconstruct the ritual landscape of mid-eighteenth century Myal, but the description of Taki and his comrades drinking blood sacrifice and exacting oaths of secrecy from their conspirators parallels very closely the development of *vodun* in the Bois Caiman in Haiti. Both went on to play revolutionary roles in the struggle against slavery, indicating that Wedenoja (1978:41) is quite correct in identifying Myal as a revolutionary movement.

An important aspect of Myal was healing. Given a belief in the spiritual cause of disease and social disorder, Myal was also anti-obeah. '[T]he doctor, or Myal-man, is resorted to, that he may neutralize the power of the Obeah-man. Sometimes his remedies are of a very simple character, particularly if his object be to cure some local disease' (Blyth 1851:174). The Myalman or Myalwoman, thus, operated like a practitioner treating a patient, one to one. But there were times when anti-obeah campaigns reached the height of hysteria. In the most remarkable of these outbreaks, the Great Myal Procession of 1842, groups led by Myal men would gather at night singing and dancing in circles and undergoing possession, and then would follow their leaders as they discovered and destroyed obeahs, or released the shadows of those bewitched. The multiple concept of the soul is still found in Jamaica: the soul, which goes to hell or heaven; the spirit, which can journey during sleep; and the shadow, or inner self, of which the visible shadow is but a reflection. Through obeah it is possible to hurt one by attacking one's shadow.

There is no religion in Jamaica today to which the name Myal applies, nor is the name used in reference to healers. Indeed, due to colonial prejudices, the generic designation of obeahman has come to refer, incorrectly of course, to all traditional healers. Where the word still has currency is in Kumina. There the ritual is sometimes called 'dancing myal', and possession as 'getting myal'.

The second source of influence in the development of Revivalism is Christianity, whose roots among the African-Caribbean population began in the last quarter of the eighteenth century. Although the Moravians were already proselytizing from mid-century, it was to some casualties of the American Revolution that the Christian movement among the Africans owed the greater debt. Some Loyalists who had fled to Jamaica brought with them their slaves, among whom were Baptist preachers. The most prominent were George Lisle and George Lewis. Their labours bore fruit, though not quite what they and their masters had expected. The Africans took rapidly and in large numbers to the new religion, but in doing so absorbed it into the Myal framework. The result, the Native Baptist Movement, so distressed Lisle that early in the nineteenth century he wrote pleading to the London Missionary Society

in England for missionaries to stem the flow if not to reverse the spread
of a proliferating religion calling itself Christian but recognizably pagan.
'The grand doctrine of these people was the Spirit's teaching .... The
spirit was sought in dreams and visions of the night, which thus became
the source of their spiritual life' (see Waddell 1863). African water rituals resurfaced in Christian baptism and missionaries had to wage theological battle to convince the people that John the Baptist was not
greater than Jesus and should not be worshipped.

The Native Baptist Movement was able to flourish for three reasons.
First was the relative autonomy and charismatic authority of the cate-
chists or class leaders on the fringe of the orthodox Protestantism. One
of these was Sam Sharpe, the leading organizer of the Great Rebellion
of 1831-32, which was instrumental in speeding up the abolition of
slavery in 1834. The second reason was that conditions favoured the
retention of membership in the orthodox Baptist church while at the
same time belonging to the independently functioning post-Myal
groups. Dual membership has remained a feature ever since and is only
now changing as Revival groups acquire greater social prestige.

The third reason was the one which gave Revival its name, the Great
Revival. Starting in Ireland, this spiritual revival spread to Britain and
the United States before reaching Jamaica in 1860. It swelled the congregations of all the Christian denominations, eliciting public thanks
from religious leaders in the country for this outpouring of the Spirit of
God. The euphoria did not last long, however, for African elements
such as convulsions and other expressions of spirit possession crept into
the Revival. Denounced as the work of Satan, these practices found a
home outside the churches in the small bands we know today.

The Great Revival evolved two traditions: Zion Revival and Pukumina, sometimes referred to by Revivalists themselves as the '60' and '61'
orders, respectively. As the Revival of 1860 progressed into 1861, as it
separated itself from orthodox Christianity, more explicitly African beliefs and practices came to the fore. Both worship the sky-bound spirits,
the triune God, angels and archangels, but whereas Zion worships only
the apostles and prophets among the earth-bound spirits, Pukumina ap-
peases and pays homage to satanic spirits, such as the fallen angels. The
Pukumina variant is seldom practised today.

Post-1860

Revival flourished throughout the remainder of the nineteenth century
and into the first two decades of the twentieth. During the second half

of this period the course of its development was greatly influenced by the activities of a remarkable prophet and healer, Alexander Bedward. Two things stand out in his long career: his arrest for sedition, for preaching that Blacks should rise up and overthrow White domination; and his prophecy declaring the end of the world and assumption into heaven of all true believers. The first marked the start of his career in 1895, the second its end in 1920. Bedward died in a mental asylum ten years later, within days of an event which was to inspire the birth of a new religion, Rastafari.

Despite my earlier argument about the demise of Revivalism (Chevannes 1978a), the religion has entered into a new, modernizing phase. The main feature of this development, which is yet to be fully documented and analysed, is the affiliation by the small groups and bands with overseas churches, almost entirely North American, and most of them Pentecostal, Church of God or AME Zion. Some Revival groups have had to sacrifice certain practices, but in general the move has served to enhance their social standing, allowing upwardly mobile people to join or remain as members. In a repetition of history, then, one is tempted to argue, Myalism has once more shed its garb and is now wearing Pentecostal clothes.

Rastafari

The year, 1930; the month, November. In the remote kingdom of Ethiopia, then also known as Abyssinia, kings, princes and heads of state from all over the Western world assemble to witness the elevation of Prince Tafari Makonnen as the new Emperor of Ethiopia, Haile Selassie I. 'Haile Selassie' means 'power of the Trinity'.

The event was for Africans, both on the continent and in the Americas, a significant event. Not only is Ethiopia one of the earliest countries to have adopted Christianity, but a part of the Ethiopian nobility, including the Makonnens, had at least since the middle ages claimed descent from King Solomon of Judah and the Queen of Sheba. Self-consciously, therefore, the new Emperor in appropriating as his title 'King of Kings', 'Lord of Lords', 'Conquering Lion of the Tribe of Judah', was reaffirming the ancient roots of Ethiopian civilization and its independent place in Judaeo-Christian traditions.

In Jamaica the coronation occasioned the rise of a new religion, the Rastafari – from *Ras*, the Ethiopian for 'prince' and *Tafari*. Haile Selassie's appellations were thought to have biblical references. The 'Conquering Lion of Judah' was imagery used by the prophet Isaiah, to refer to the messiah, as also was the description 'King of Kings' and 'Lord of Lords' by the apocalyptic visionary in the Book of Revelation.

That some Jamaicans could regard this man as the promised messiah, as Jesus Christ in fact, is insufficiently explained by the biblical references. It required other pre-determining factors. Among the most important of these was the impact of the work and ideas of Marcus Garvey in the form of a heightened Black, pan-African consciousness.

Garvey's strategy for achieving the economic advancement and liberation of Africans, 'at home and abroad', was the building up of a powerful and united Africa. To achieve this he looked to the skills and professions of New World Africans. This was the essence of his 'Back-to-Africa' scheme. Blocked by the colonial powers, the scheme failed, but not before Garvey had succeeded in galvanizing millions of Black people in the United States, the Caribbean, Central America and Africa into his Universal Negro Improvement Association (UNIA), and in influencing millions more with his concepts of Black pride, entrepreneurship, and identity based on race. His newspaper, *The Negro World*, which enjoyed a very wide readership, served not only as the main vehicle for his ideas, but also as a means of educating Blacks about their African past and thus of correcting racial prejudices and stereotypes of inferiority, some of which had been internalized. *The Negro World* was banned in most colonies, on pain of death in French West Africa. In the context of a world quickened, as far as Blacks were concerned, with White racism, Garveyism was a liberating philosophy. It denied the innateness of White supremacy and its converse, Black inferiority, fashioned a sense of national identity out of being Black, and gave to its adherents a perspective through which to view the economic and social development of Blacks.

The Afrocentricity of Garveyism would of itself have made his followers in Jamaica turn their attention to the momentous event in Ethiopia. But, regarding Garvey as a prophet, they claimed that he had indeed prophesied about it when he had told the people to 'look to Africa for the crowning of a king to know that your redemption is nigh'. Looking to Africa, looking also to the Bible, a few followers of Garvey concluded that Ras Tafari must be the messiah come back to redeem his people. The titles he bore, the homage paid by the White world through the heads and representatives of state, the antiquity of Ethiopia and its mention in both Old and New Testaments of the Bible, the Solomonic claim – like so many rivulets building up into a mighty river, all swept them away with the powerful conviction that Ras Tafari was none other than Jesus Christ. And he was Black. Now did the Song of Solomon (1:5-6) make sense:

> I *am* Black, but comely, O ye daughters of Jerusalem, as the tents of Kedar, as the curtains of Solomon.
> Look not upon me, because I *am* Black, because the sun hath looked upon me.

If Solomon was Black, so was the Christ. Both were descendants of David. Redemption of the African race was therefore at hand.

Three men are credited with being the first to begin preaching that Ras Tafari, or Haile Selassie, was God, having arrived at this conclusion independently of one another: Leonard Howell, Archibald Dunkley and Joseph Hibbert. These three, plus Robert Hinds, whose first days in the new faith were spent as an associate of Howell, were the main architects of the Rastafari movement for the first twenty years. Stretching Garvey's Back-to-Africa programme, they all saw redemption as 'Repatriation', the return of all Africans to Africa.

Phases of Growth

Since its founding the Rastafari movement has gone through three distinct phases of growth. The first phase lasted through the 1930s and most of the 1940s. Theologically, the main impetus was given to propagating the idea of a Black God among a people whose image of God was of a bearded White father in the sky and of a White man on a cross. Pictures of the Black Christ, circulated at street meetings, acted as a powerful instrument of conversion. The idea of a Black God had been a part of the Garvey movement, but to the Rastafari, God was more. He was not only Black, but physically living among men. They even went further, to argue that if being Black was a divine attribute, then the African race, by being Black, shared in divinity.

Early in the movement's development, as will become clearer in Chapter 4, a most significant practice developed among the Rastafari, namely the wearing of facial hair by adult males, which they sacralized by claiming biblical precepts as well as emulation of the Godhead, Tafari, who was pictured with a full beard. These beliefs and practices had one common underlying motif: they were anti-establishment. Not surprisingly, the early Rastafari encountered considerable hostility, and not every male member wore a beard.

Socially, the message found fertile ground among the urban masses. This was a period which saw an intensification of internal migration, as the most destitute stratum of the peasantry flocked to the city of Kingston. Not only were the avenues of external migration to Cuba and the United States closed off but also many returning migrants preferred to settle in Kingston. Those returning from Cuba were especially receptive to the message of the Rastafari, because of their firsthand experience of racism there and the vitality of the Cuban UNIA branches. Cuba boasted the largest number of UNIA branches outside of the United States. The early preachers, thus, found a most ready audience among the uprooted peasantry (Chevannes 1989a). Early Rastafari made great headway among this section of the urban population, which provided recruits right up to the time when George Eaton Simpson conducted the first study of the brethren, in 1953. Simpson (1955) remained the only source for other writers, such as Lanternari (1963), until the Report by Smith, Augier and Nettleford (1960) which came as a result of developments in the next phase of growth.

The second phase began among second-generation converts who entered the movement in the 1940s but who were in revolt against practices they thought were compromising. The innovations and practices they instituted were to become the hallmarks of the new image of the Rastafari: dreadlocks, ganja-smoking, Rasta talk (sometimes called 'I-talk' because of the pivotal concept of *I*, the personal pronoun). Haile Selassie, who to the earlier generation was simply the King, was now praised as *Jah* or *Jah-Jah*. They intensified their practical opposition to the colonial state, using such forms as repatriation activities, illicit street marches, disruption of the court and defiance of the police. These ideas need not be amplified here, since they are more fully developed in Chapter 4 by this writer and in Chapter 6 by John Homiak. Here it is important to trace, however briefly, the millenarian activities which the Rastas carried out during the 1950s.

Against the background of migration to the United Kingdom, Repatriation marches and other forms of agitation started. In 1958 one young leader, Prince Emmanuel Edwards, issued a successful call for an all Rasta convention. For two weeks Rastafari from all over Jamaica converged on Back-o-Wall, a notorious slum adjacent to Kingston's largest market, which hosted many a migrant fresh from the country. At the end of two weeks they marched to the central square of the city, planted a flag and symbolically 'captured' the city. It was alleged that many had sold off their belongings in the confident expectation that at the end of the convention they would be transported to Africa.

The Prince Emmanuel convention had no serious impact on either the Rastafari or the society, except that Prince lost credibility among the Rasses (or the brethren, as Rastas often style themselves) and retreated with his group into a sect known as Bobos. The millenarian activity which did have an impact, however, was led by a visionary named Claudius Henry. A returned migrant from the United States, Henry quickly established himself as the leader of a Rastafari church, with a branch in Kingston and one in the sugar belt of the parish of Clarendon.

In 1958 Henry took a bold step. He proclaimed 5 October as 'Decision Day' when all of Israel's scattered flock would return to Africa, and towards this distributed for the price of one shilling a blue card, on which he declared that possession of the card rather than a passport was all that was needed. Hundreds of Rastafari brethren flocked to Kingston in anticipation of repatriation. There was much suffering when this prophecy also failed, but Henry managed to keep his following intact. A year and a half later, quite suddenly, news broke that a police raid on Reverend Henry's headquarters in Kingston had uncovered an arms cache and copies of a letter written by Henry and several others addressed to the new leader of neighbouring Cuba, Fidel Castro, inviting him to take over Jamaica before their departure for Africa, which the writers claimed was imminent. Henry, his wife and several other leading members were charged with treason. Before the case could be heard, however, news of yet another serious development swept the country. Two British soldiers were killed in an ambush by guerillas led by Henry's son, Ronald. Aware of untoward activities in and around the church, the police had infiltrated the group, only to discover a guerilla training camp in the Red Hills overlooking the city. The army was called in when the police contact disappeared. His body was later discovered buried near the parade ground of the camp.

These developments were to have a profound effect on Jamaica's Eurocentric middle class and on the Rastafari. Both were thrown together in a headlong confrontation long in the making. The middle class, shocked as much by the concatenation of events as by its own sense of guilt, was forced, after first reacting with expressions of hostility towards the Rastas, whom it saw as representing the very antithesis of all it aspired to, to think seriously about its own African heritage. The Rastafari, for their part, caught as they were by the aggressive posture they had cultivated over the past decade, had to act quickly to inform the public of their essentially peaceful intentions. This they were successful in doing, by appealing to the University College of the West Indies, then a college of London University, for a study of the movement.

The first recommendation of the resulting study (Smith *et al.* 1961), namely, that Government sponsor a fact-finding mission to Africa to investigate the possibilities for migration of Jamaican nationals there, was quickly accepted and implemented. An unofficial nine-man mission was constituted, including one Dreadlock, and dispatched to Ghana, Nigeria, Ethiopia and several other countries. On its return the majority and minority (Rastafari) reports were both published in the press.

The whole Claudius Henry affair, the *University Report*, the Mission and its reports, were together the subject of intense public debate for months. They marked a new stage in the development both of the Rastafari itself and of Jamaican society; both were set on a course of forced mutual accommodation and change, which later gained momentum from the visit in 1966 of His Imperial Majesty Haile Selassie I, and the Black Power Movement started by University lecturer, Walter Rodney, in 1968 (Nettleford 1970). Through these events the Rastafari were able to effect an exorcism of the racial and colour prejudices that had possessed the middle classes from colonial times (Chevannes 1990), with the result that middle-class men and women, mulatto and Black, could feel free enough to form their own Rastafari group known as the Twelve Tribes of Israel (van Dijk 1988).

During the second phase, one other development of far-reaching import was the absorption into the movement of the urban youth, who brought with them many of their social characteristics (Chevannes 1981). This, for example, was how the Rastafari came to be associated with the development of reggae music. The youth of the 1960s, like Bob Marley, Peter Tosh, Bunny Wailer, Bob Andy, Clancy Eccles, Dennis Brown and members of such groups as the Abyssinians, forged their careers as popular artists using reggae to express Rastafari ideas, yearnings and critique (Davis 1983).

The popularity of reggae artistes was itself a measure of the popularity of the Rastafari among the masses throughout the 1970s and the main avenue of its spread abroad. The 1972 general election was contested around the use of a Rastafari symbol, a rod the Emperor had presented as a gift to one of the leaders of the two contesting parties, Michael Manley. Manley not only won, but the vote of the Rastafari-influenced youth proved decisive (Stone 1974). The 1970s also saw the growth of Rastafari throughout the other islands of the Caribbean, due in part to the influence of reggae artistes, in part to the movement throughout the region of Caribbean nationals, including students of the regional University of the West Indies. In Dominica, Grenada, Trinidad they played significant roles in radical left-wing politics (Campbell 1980). Rastafari influence in Trinidad was apparent also among the Earth People, as cited by Roland Littlewood in Chapter 10 of this volume. The Rastafari movement also spread to the United Kingdom, Canada, the United States, several European countries, Africa, Australia and New Zealand. Its development in these parts of the world has not yet been the subject of serious study, with the exception of the UK, where second-generation Blacks found in Rastafari a ready vehicle of expression of their own search for identity (Cashmore 1983). Here too, both British society and Rastafari have had to find mutual accommodation, and with it change, a process described and analysed by Ellis Cashmore in Chapter 7 of this book.

The third, and still current, phase of Rastafari development in Jamaica dates from the 1980s and is characterized by far-reaching changes, the result of an onset of routinization. First, the pervasiveness of Rastafari ideology among the urban youth has waned. Up to the end of the 1970s ghetto youth provided the main recruitment ground for Rastafari. The surest sign of this was the fact that most promising young reggae artistes would begin sprouting dreadlocks as soon as they began to hit the popularity charts. Now, the most successful popular musicians, the DJ artistes, manifest no Rastafari influence, neither in their lyrics nor in their hair culture. Instead, North American hair styles and bawdy lyrics predominate. Most of the young Rastas one now sees at Rastafari gatherings are the children of older Dreads.

Another noticeable development is the increasing vocality of women in the movement. As noted in Chapter 2 and more fully discussed in Chapters 5 and 6, one peculiarity of the Rastas is their ideological and ritual subordination of women. Women are considered essentially incapable of receiving the fullness of divine knowledge directly and must acquire this through their male spouses, their 'king-man'. They do not play any function in rituals (though their presence is not forbidden), must cover their locks at all times and must show deference to males. Menstruating women may not cook, and in one group are secluded from social contact. As a sign of change, Rastafari women have become quite vocal against these beliefs and practices, and some have defied such conventions as covering their dreadlocks, or wearing only ankle-length dress in public.

Finally, a secularization process has been underway since the 1980s, whereby identifying symbols of the Rastafari are being shorn of their religious and ethical significance and diffused to the non-Rastafari population. The most easily observable is the Rasta tricolour, the red, gold and green, which the Rasta movement adopted from the Ethiopian flag but which in part coincided with the UNIA emblem. The black in Garvey's UNIA flag stood for the African peoples, the red for their blood and the green for the verdant wealth of the continent. By substituting the gold for the black the Rastafari forged a closer sense of identity with Ethiopia while retaining the Garveyite connection. Every Rasta tam is woven and every Rasta banner, poster, rod or other artifact painted, in red, gold and green colours. Now these colours are worn by all and sundry, without reference to any ideological commitment. The dreadlocks, also, have suffered a similar fate. While it is true that dreadlocks have been used as a symbol of defiance and rebellion in many parts of the world, it is also a fact that they have become part of 'hair couture'. A short visit to a hair stylist and one may emerge with dreadlocks either styled or woven in. Thus, especially in the tourist zones of the country, one cannot always be sure that the proud display of dreadlocks one frequently sees belongs to the genuine Rastafari believer, and not to the male prostitute locally known as the 'Rent-a-Dread'.

Notwithstanding these recent developments, the Rastafari movement in Jamaica retains great moral authority, due to its pioneering stance on issues of racial identity and colour prejudice in Jamaica and due also to its role in the development of Jamaican culture.

Organization

Rastafari is by and large an acephalous movement. Except for two highly organized groups, most brethren do not belong to a formal organization. They do, however, consider themselves members of the 'House'. The concept of House seemed to have originated in the second phase of the movement's development when, as a result of the reform activities of the emerging Dreadlocks, the movement split into two orders or Houses: the House of Dreadlocks and the House of Combsomes, that is, those who comb their hair. Since the 1960s Combsomes have all but disappeared, leaving only the House of Dreadlocks. Thus, the main distinguishing mark of members of the House today is their dreadlocks. Any Dreadlocks Rastafari, therefore, is entitled to participate in the formal rituals and deliberations of the House. An assembly of 'Elders', in truth Rastafari who show initiative, meet regularly to plan the activities of the House, such as the celebration of the Emperor's coronation, or its affairs, such as a delegation abroad.

The two organized groups are the Bobos and the Twelve Tribes of Israel. The Bobos, led by Prince Emmanuel Edwards, are the only Rastafari group living a truly communal life, on the outskirts of the city of Kingston. Distinguished from other Rastafari by their robe and turban attire and by their production and hawking of brooms, the Bobos place all their daily earnings in one central fund, from which all their material needs are met. Meals, for example, are prepared in, and shared out from, the single kitchen in the commune. The Twelve Tribes is, as indicated earlier, mainly a middle-class organization, headed by Prophet Gad. Members, organized into the twelve biblical tribes of Israel, pay dues.

Rituals

For the majority of Rastafari members rituals are of two kinds: reasonings and the 'binghi', both sometimes referred to as a 'grounding' or a 'grounation', from which has come the verb 'to grounds', meaning to get along well. The reasoning is an informal gathering at which a small group of brethren share in the smoking of the holy weed, ganja, and in a lofty discussion. As the brethren sit around in a circle, the host cuts up the *ganja*, mixing into it a small quantity of tobacco from a cigarette. The matter is stuffed into the chillum of a water pipe (called a 'huka' by the East Indians), from whom the whole *ganja* complex was borrowed (Rubin and Comitas 1975), but called a chalice or cup by the Rastafari, who compare this ritual to the sacred communion of the Christians. He whose honour it is to light the pipe, or chalice, pauses and recites a short prayer before, while all participants bare their heads. Once lit, the chalice is moved counter-clockwise around the circle, until all have 'supped'. Reasoning ends, not formally, but when the participants one by one don their tams or caps and depart.

The 'nyabinghi', or 'binghi' for short, is a dance held on special occasions throughout the year, to mark the coronation of His Imperial Majesty (2 November); His Majesty's ceremonial birthday (6 January); His Majesty's visit to Jamaica (25 April), His Majesty's personal birthday (23 July), Emancipation from Slavery (1 August) and Marcus Garvey's birthday (17 August). The word itself is thought to be of colonial African origin, originally referring to a secret order vowed to bring 'death to White oppressors'. During the Dreadlocks era, Rastafari would on occasion 'dance nyabinghi' to bring 'death to Black and White oppressors'. Today these dances are purely ceremonial celebrations, lasting for several days, depending on the resources of the House.

Rotated from parish to parish, the binghi brings together scores, even hundreds, of Dreadlocks from all over Jamaica. They camp in tents and makeshift lodgings on land owned by the Dreadlocks member playing host. Formal dancing takes place at night in a tabernacle especially set up for the occasion, and to a bank of Rasta drums. These are of three kinds: the bass, struck on the first of four beats and muffled on the third; the *funde*, which plays a steady one-two beat; and the repeater or *akete* (*kete* for short), which plays the improvised syncopations. The Rastas sing and dance to their distinctive beat long into the morning. In the daytime they rest and 'reason'.

The relative dearth of religious ritual among the Rastafari, compared to Revival, is balanced by ritualization in private life. The Rastafari observe a number of personal ritual taboos and practices. The most significant of these govern food, nature and the environment, and Africa. Among foods, pork and crustaceans are universally avoided, but many Rastafari refrain from all meat and fish products. Salt is also taboo. Food cooked without salt is referred to as *ital*, that is, natural. Rastafari rejects, as much as possible, all artificial things and celebrates the use of the natural: manure instead of artificial fertilizers and sprays; herbs and barks instead of pharmaceuticals. Rastafari life is centred on Africa. Every Rasta home is adorned with photographs of Haile Selassie, sometimes referred to as 'King Alpha', his wife, known as 'Queen Omega', maps of Africa and posters with African themes and the Ethiopian colours. Every Rasta man possesses an array of decorative buttons with replicas of Emperor Haile Selassie or some other African leader, which he proudly wears in public.

Conclusion

Revival is an outgrowth of the Jamaican people, whose roots extend through the slavery period and beyond to Africa. Specifically which African people or peoples has not yet been conclusively established, though Monica Schuler (1979b) notes some similarity between Myal and Congolese religions, in particular in their capacity to absorb elements from other religions. Rastafari, on the other hand, is a more modern creation, which sprang up in the city of Kingston. It too has undergone changes from its beginning in the early 1930s, the most significant being the cultivation of the dreadlocks as a symbol of identity. Like Revival, Rastafari has had a great impact. The nature of that impact, however, is debatable. While most scholars emphasize its political role, I identify its main impact as cultural.

Note

1. Both Kumina and Convince are ancestral cults. On Kumina, see Moore (1953). Its main concentration is in the easternmost of Jamaica's fourteen parishes, St Thomas, where membership is confined to certain families. Convince, which has 'a small scattered following' (Hogg 1960:3), is concentrated in the parish of St Mary.

2   New Approach to Rastafari[1]

Barry Chevannes

The Rastafari movement has been described variously as escapist, nativist, millenarian, visionary, revitalist – all terms that reflect the impulse in our discipline towards scientific generalization. However, in only a very few cases of the many works written on the Rastas in Jamaica is the use of the particular terminology based on original field research, as opposed to secondary sources, and on the considered attempt therefrom to classify.

One notable example is that of Klaus de Albuquerque (1977), who makes the strongest case, of which I am aware, that the Rastafari is a millenarian movement. His approach is first to construct a theoretical model of millenarian movements and to test it using the Rastafari movement. To establish the relationship between any millenarian movement and the wider society, he says, one has to examine the 'prerequisites' and the 'conditions' which give rise to it. In practical terms this requires an understanding of four distinct factors. The first is the form: whether the millenarian movement is a religious or a secular one. According to de Albuquerque, what determines the form is the level of development of the society. In industrialized societies the political structure is sharply differentiated from the religious; in pre-industrial and 'modernizing' societies this is not so. As a result, millenarian movements occur mainly in the latter and are generally religious. They are not unknown in the former, but there, he says, they depend on the *locus* of the origin of oppression.

Thus, a second factor is the type of society. Industrialized societies are characterized by political structures that have developed the 'capacity to absorb and deflect protest', or to mobilize and so defuse revolutionary threats. Pre-industrial societies are lacking in this capacity.

A third factor is whether the religious belief system of the society is given to strong or weak eschatological expectations. If these are weak, the millenarian movement will likely take a secular, non-revolutionary and passive form; but if strong, the movement is more likely to be religious, revolutionary and active.

Finally, there is the aetiological origin itself. Here, de Albuquerque argues, the factors may be exogenous or endogenous. In an industrialized society endogenous factors condition the movement to be passive and escapist, appealing to bourgeois elements, whereas in pre-industrialized societies exogenous factors of origin lead to revolutionary millenarian movements, with appeals to the 'external proletariat' – external, that is, in the sense of being marginal to the system. Endogenous factors may also have the same effect, if the political structures are at the same time well-developed, even if the society as a whole is not.

With a model constructed of these elements, de Albuquerque situates Jamaican society within the ranks of the pre-industrialized, or modernizing, societies, but one which also has a well-developed political structure. After examining the Rastafari, he concludes:

> Given the existence of oppression . . . and the above specifying conditions, we would expect the Rastafari movement to assume a revolutionary character and appeal to the external proletariat (landless peasants and urban unemployed). The case study of the movement bears this out, with the exception that the movement had initially, and continues to have, very little impact on the Jamaican peasantry, landless or otherwise. (de Albuquerque 1977:358-9)

Apart from the fact that the theory tends to rule out the possibility of revolutionary millenarian movements in industrialized societies, the main difficulty it presents is not even so much the one acknowledged by the author in the above passage, namely that after nearly fifty years of existence the movement still lacked appeal to the external proletariat (for, it is possible to bring forward evidence to show that it is precisely this sector to which the movement has appealed), but the definition of the Rastafari as a revolutionary movement. De Albuquerque, unfortunately, does not define his use of the word 'revolutionary', so one is not absolutely sure of what he means. In the context of the discussion that would make no sense, since any movement that is radically different from the mainstream could qualify as revolutionary. However, it seems to me, given the context of the discussion, in which he defines politics as participation in some goal seeking, and in which he accords a high place in the paradigm to an activity-passivity dichotomy, that he is using the concept revolutionary in much the same way Professor Hobsbawm used it in relation to the 'primitive rebels' of Sicily: people who, in reaction to existing social and other conditions, actively take measures in pursuit of a radical transformation. If this is so, one would have to concede that the Rastafari movement is revolutionary, not just because it consistently preaches a doctrine about a new order, in which every Black man will have his own 'vine and fig tree', thus reversing the order of Black people at the bottom of society, but because it has in the past (1934, 1956 and, the most notable of all, 1959) taken measures to bring about repatriation to Africa. If one reads de Albuquerque correctly, one cannot be revolutionary and passive at the same time.

But is the Rastafari a revolutionary movement? Is that what it is all about? In what follows I wish to advance a different way of looking at the religion, one which departs from a purely social structure type of perspective and tries to see it rather in the context of cultural continuity. Specifically, I raise two issues without trying at this time to resolve them: the relationship of Rastafari to Revivalism, and the structure of the movement itself.

The Revival Past

As I have already explained in the preceding chapter, Revival grew out of Myal. One of the features of African religion, according to Alleyne (1988:59), is its receptivity to external influences. As an African-derived religion, therefore, Myal was easily able to adopt Christianity, as well as to be adopted by Christianity, as soon as the Black Baptists from the United States (George Lisle, Moses Baker and others) began preaching to the slaves late in the century. Sometimes this religion appeared under its proper name Myal, but it was content to thrive under the name Native Baptist, a development Robotham (1988:35) calls critical, because it constructed 'the synthesis for consciousness in which traditional ethnicities were dissolved' and 'established a new ethical code for the people not only in the religious but also in the *cultural* sense'.

Revival Zion is indeed a religion, and underlying its expression is a coherent worldview, which I refer to as Revivalism, or simply Revival. Briefly summarized, this worldview has three central features, which I shall briefly discuss.

God, Spirits and the Dead

The Jamaicans, like their African forebears, believe in a Supreme Being, a Creator, called God, or Maasa Gad, or the Father. Though He knows and sees all, God is, nevertheless, distant from human affairs. The acts of the elements are His, such as earthquake, lightening, thunder, storm and floods, and swearing by God or by the elements, particularly lightening, is regarded as a grave and solemn act, for which reason it is seldom done.

As God is distant, so are the Spirits near: in and around, and even within. In recognition of this, children used to be taught when eating always to leave a small portion by the edge of their plates, and (rum) drinkers, even today, will pour a libation before drinking. Of all spirits, Jesus is the greatest. His role in dying to save all humanity has imbued him with special powers. Jesus is the object of supplication and prayer, and is often called, Father Jesus or Pupa Jesus. The most central shrine or seal in the tabernacle is devoted to him, but he never possesses anyone as Jesus. His Spirit, though, or the Dove or Messenger, may possess devotees.

Lesser spirits include angels and archangels such as Michael, Gabriel and Raphael; prophets such as Isaiah, Jeremiah and John the Baptist; and apostles. The spirit world also includes the very powerful fallen angels, Satan being the highest among them. They too can be supplicated, especially for material favours, but they are dangerous.

Spirits of the dead, *duppies*, complete the Jamaican pantheon. The elaborate death rituals are characterized by great mourning and displays of grief among near relatives, a compulsive need to show respect for the deceased and solidarity with the bereaved, and by elaborate precautions to prevent the duppy from returning across the threshold separating the worlds of the living and the dead. Duppies are thought to roam abroad at nights, frightening and terrorizing the living. They may also be used by *obeahmen* to harm people. The most feared are East Indian, Chinese and baby duppies. To relatives, however, duppies may assume protective roles, communicating with them in sleep. Such communications from the spirit world are called visions, to distinguish them from ordinary dreams.

A function of the spirits is the possession of the living. Spirits are not feared on account of this, and spirit possession is considered not only a normal part of religious worship but an honour. It is the way some people are chosen for a higher life.

Man, Nature and Magic

Nature represents a zone which interfaces the material and spirit worlds, thus establishing a continuum of universal existence. Nature is material, but it is also spiritual. The same croton which makes a beautiful hedge also symbolizes the Prophet Jeremiah, and adorns graves because it is thought to keep duppies within the graves. Herbs, such as mint and sage, trees, such as the majestic cottonwood, rivers and certain species of animals, such as frogs and large moths, all have both sacred and profane identities. One never kills large moths, or bats as they are called; they are believed to represent the ancestors.

But if nature is one threshold across which the spirit world crosses into the world of the living, it is also a zone whereby one can acquire the power of the spirits and control both worlds. Here, even inanimate things may be used: a pinch of salt and a swig of rum, for example, are all the guarantees grave-diggers need. And a saucer of salt may always be found on the sacred table during mourning rituals. Red fabric, pencils and scissors are used to ward off evil spirits.

With the right knowledge, therefore, one can control even the spirit world. The *obeahman* is invested with this knowledge, which he uses mainly for harm, but which anyone may use to personal advantage: charms and amulets for protection; oils and powders to achieve certain goals.[2]

But perhaps the benefit of nature is its healing properties. A general belief is that there is no illness for which nature provides no remedy. The healing process may take place at not one but several levels, from the straightforward application until relief comes to treatment which combines nature with magic and ritual. The religious healer practises in a 'balm yard'. A good practitioner is able not only to heal but to divine and read the future.

Hence, the general attitude toward nature is one of respect and harmony. The individual is regarded as a sinful creature, but also as a vital part of nature and subject to its laws. As in the case of the children of Israel of old, enslavement and oppression are consequences of sin, a condition which will be remedied only in the next world, following a life of righteousness in this. Black skin colour is a sign of debasement. Not only are there common expressions which assume this – for example, blaming race for the failure of Blacks as an ethnic group to advance – but there are also folk-tales which tell, not without humour, how Blacks came to be black. They all tell of some aberration or weakness of character.[3] When the great Revival preacher and healer, Alexander Bedward, told ethnographer Martha Beckwith that in heaven his hand will become as lily white as her own, he was expressing commonly held views about black skin colour, sin and oppression (Beckwith 1929:169-70). Holding such views, however, did not prevent him from calling for the overthrow of White rule (Chevannes 1971).

Humanity as a whole is sinful, but in the Revival worldview woman represents a particularly serious danger to man, even as she also represents a particularly delightful pleasure. The Adam and Eve myth tells the tale of what lies in store for man if woman is allowed to control him. Woman is therefore not to be trusted, even when she is loved. Eve and Delilah are prototypes of the female. Man is vulnerable during woman's menstrual flow, and to avoid all possibilities of contamination female underwear is strictly segregated from the laundry. Indeed, only a woman herself may wash her own underwear. Menstruating and pregnant women are also thought to have a malignant effect on certain crops.

At the same time, women are a source of male delight and comfort. Feelings about sex are not as guilt-ridden as would appear from the attitudes preached by the Christian and the Evangelical churches, though the situation could be changing, given the dramatic growth of the latter. Women are believed to be always satisfied in sexual intercourse. But it is in their role as mothers that women elicit the greatest respect from men. A woman's pride in motherhood is strong. The bond between mother and son is the strongest of all domestic relationships, and the greatest insult possible to any man is to berate his mother. Motherhood is so highly valued that the title *Mada* is given to women who gain the wide respect of their communities, and those who become Revival leaders.

Ethical and Social Values

The worldview fashioned by Myal in its interaction with Christianity holds to a sense of moral and cultural equality for all Blacks, as Robotham (1988) points out. It has also imbued the people with a strong sense of community. For instance, it values individualism and respects achieved status, but only if communal values are also upheld. People who achieve but by their actions and attitudes reject their community are sanctioned. 'The higher monkey climb, the more him expose'.

The world, God, spirits, nature, and humanity are all governed by order and interdependence. It is really one world. Nowhere is this more deeply manifested than in the concept of 'helping out', whereby voluntary and spontaneous acts of responsibility and sharing are undertaken, often on behalf of strangers, out of a sense of mutual interdependence and reciprocity. The good one does today will redound to one tomorrow; the good that is done one today is the result of the good one did yesterday. The concept is akin to the Christian teaching about storing up treasures in heaven, except that the reward is expected in this life rather than the next.

For this reason, the belief in retribution and fate is equally strong. The evil which one does will be repaid sooner or later. 'What is fiyu kyaan be anfiyu' (one cannot escape one's fate).

This summary of the worldview of the Jamaicans is neither exhaustive nor intended to imply that these beliefs are shared fully by everyone. I do argue, though, that they are generalized throughout the population, which is why the Revival religion could be found anywhere in the island without ever having had a centrally organized structure of the type possessed by most churches. The closest it came to this was under the great prophet Alexander Bedward, and even then not all Revival groups entered into formal affiliation with him; those that did seemed in any case to have been allowed to retain their autonomy. This process of a generalized worldview giving rise to non-centralized religious expression is replicated in identical fashion in the rise of the Rastafari.

Rastafari Beliefs

The most important belief of the Rastafari is that Haile Selassie, the late Emperor of Ethiopia is God. This alone was enough for the general public to identify them by (Ras, the Ethiopian for Prince, and Tafari, the Emperor's personal name), although they originally called themselves the 'King of Kings people'. But underlying the belief in the Emperor's divinity is the conclusion that Black people were destined to return to their native Africa, after centuries of injustice at the hands of the Whites. Repatriation, as the return to Africa is known, thus became the first important departure from Revival, and remained until recently a source of inspiration for the faithful as a whole and for Rastafari artistes in particular.

> Babylon is a wicked one
> Babylon is a wicked one
> Babylon is a wicked one
> O, Jah Rastafari O, Selah!

Our forefathers were taken away
Our forefathers were taken away
Our forefathers were taken away
O, Jah Rastafari O, Selah!

Open up da gate mek I repatriate
Open up da gate mek I repatriate
Open up da gate mek I repatriate
O, Jah Rastafari O, Selah!

The motif in this plaintive song, which may be heard at Rastafari celebrations, is quite common among Blacks with a Christian tradition, namely, their likeness to the ancient children of Israel who were rescued from captivity by the intervention of God. Here, the image is used not as metaphor, but as reality itself. We are the true Israelites; what is written in the Bible is only a foreshadowing of real events now unfolding. The Babylon of old is none other than the White colonial and neo-colonial world. These themes are not confined to ceremonies, but may be found in popular songs as well. *By the rivers of Babylon* is perhaps one of the best known Rastafari songs, made internationally popular by the European group, Boney M.

In Jamaica one of the most popular songs of all times evokes images of the promised land:

There is a land, far, far away,
Where there's no night, there's only day.
Look into the Book of Life and you will see
That there's a land, far, far away.

The King of Kings and the Lord of Lords
Sits upon his throne and he rules us all.
Look into the Book of Life and you will see
That there's a land, far, far away.

Originally sung by the Abyssinians in the 1960s, by 1980 there were over seventy different versions. The far-away land was Ethiopia, where the 'King of Kings', Haile Selassie, ruled. Its title is *Sata Amas Agaana*, the Amharic for 'Give Thanks and Praises'. *Babylon Burning*, with musical motifs of the round *London Burning*, sung by the Wailers, *I Want to go Back Home*, by Alton Ellis, *Seven Miles of Black Star Liners* by Burning

Spear and numerous others express the same theme of exile and repatriation.

By contrast, one is hard put to find a single Revival song which expresses the wish to return to Africa. There is the following:

> I want to go home to that land,
> I want to go home to that land,
> I want to go home to that land where I am from;
> For there is joy in my soul,
> Peace and happiness in my mind –
> I want to go home to that land where I am from.

The 'land where I am from' could be interpreted as Africa, but the feelings of present joy, peace and happiness are not congruent with yearnings of return. Rather, the song expresses the readiness of the faithful, the saved, to go 'home' to heaven. This is particularly clear in another very popular Revival song, which was adopted with a change of words by the Rastafari.

> Fly away home to Zion, fly away home:
> One bright morning when my life is over,
> I will fly away home.

The Rastafari change of the word 'life' to 'work' reflects the main difference between the two religions: salvation in the here and now of this life as against postponement into the next. 'Zion' is no longer the heaven in the skies but Ethiopia, or Africa, where God is.

A second major tenet of the Rastafari, which also marks an important divergence from Revival, is the conclusion that God is Black. It derives from the racial characteristic of Haile Selassie himself, and gives to Black people a sense of being one with, of sharing in an attribute of God. Black man is thereby elevated in status.

Two things follow. First is the rejection of the hegemonic system of values whereby 'if you are White, that's right; if you are Black, you stay back'. Second, the alienation between God and Man need no longer exist, because there is a profound way in which God shares a part of his being with those who were once poor. Man, that is Black Man, is also divine. Rastafari resist speaking of becoming converted. One does not become converted, one begins to *manifest* Rastafari, thereby implying the evolution or unfolding of something already within.

Where does this leave White people? Rastafari, instead of going the way of the Black Nationalists of the United States with a mythology that makes Whiteness an attribute of the Devil, allow the possibility of salvation for Whites, based on inward acknowledgement and rejection of the evil of White society.

Second, the elevation of Man to the status of shared identity with God is at the same time an elevation over the world of Spirits. Rastafari do not recognize the existence of, let alone communicate with, those beings which are so central to Revival. They have no need of them. If there are no spirits but only God and Man, and if Man is also part God, then God himself no longer is the distant 'Big Maasa', without a real role in the affairs of Man, but a loving Father. When Rastafari speak of 'the Father', they do so with great reverence and with an awareness of His central place in their lives. To some extent the identity with the Father gives coherence to the strong patriarchal orientation for which the movement is noted. This alteration in how the spirit world is conceived marks a radical departure from the African tradition, so far as the retention of a particular form is concerned. But, as we shall see later, there is strong retention of belief in the immanence of God.

The two tenets of Rastafari discussed above are the most fundamental, and they characterize the main divergence from Revival. They were made possible by a most important development in the history of Blacks in the Western hemisphere, the rise of Marcus Garvey as a great visionary and teacher. Although his back-to-Africa scheme failed,[4] his Shipping Line and other economic enterprises foundered and his years of involvement in Jamaican politics came to naught, Garvey positively and permanently laid the foundation for a transformation in the thinking of Blacks through his tireless teachings on their past achievements and future possibilities and through the respect he won by the magnitude and daring of his schemes. He identified 'race' as the defining characteristic of a Black nationality, thereby giving a sense of common identity to millions in the new and old worlds, and a new sense of power. The early Rastafari, leaders and followers alike, all considered themselves Garveyites. To them he was John the Baptist, leading them to the one to come who would be greater than himself.

So great was Garvey's impact on popular consciousness, that the Bedwardites paired him with Bedward in the roles of Moses and Aaron, respectively. But other people also influenced by Garvey had other ideas: if Garvey was Moses (his middle name was Mosiah), the land of Jamaica must be Egypt and there must be a real promised land, not a metaphorical one.

Rastafari, then, started off as a radical departure from all that had gone before it. The image was shaped as much by the two central doctrines as by the adoption of certain symbols, notably the beard and, by the 1950s, the use of ganja and the dreadlocks, and by millenarian and non-millenarian activities to effect repatriation.

However, despite the centrality of and insistence on this belief in Repatriation, Rastafari is essentially not a Repatriation movement. Orlando Patterson (1964) made a similar point years ago, supporting it with socio-psychological arguments backed by Peter Worsley and other scholars. In my view, the issue is how one interprets the past sixty years of the movement.

For one, repatriation initiatives have not been many in the six decades. In 1934 Leonard Howell, one of the founders of Rastafari, was believed to have preached that repatriation would take place on August 1. Following the failure of that prophecy, the main focus of attention fell on the theological concepts of God, and it was not until the mid- to late-1940s that we begin hearing about back-to-Africa marches. These were sponsored by Garveyites like Z. Munroe Scarlett, but joined by the Rastas. Rasta-organized marches began with the appearance of the Dreadlocks, but were not explicitly Repatriation marches. In 1958 Prince Emmanuel Edwards called an all-Rasta convention and some Rastafari reportedly sold out their belongings and gathered in expectancy of the ships to take them 'home'. In 1959, Claudius Henry distributed blue cards to be used in lieu of passports for a 'miraculous repatriation' to take place on 25 October, and in the following year his church was associated with attempts to force its way back to Africa.[5] These last episodes (one by Prince Emmanuel and two by Claudius Henry) were related to the mass migration to Britain at the time and therefore cannot be seen in isolation. Moreover, Henry's initiatives were not supported by most of the young Dreadlocks. They viewed him with suspicion, because he wore neither dreadlocks nor beard. Subsequent to the Henry affair, Repatriation activities were confined to the occasional individual such as the Rastafarian who tried to board an outgoing plane, and attempts by some leaders to pressure the Jamaican government and the United Nations. The Repatriation picture then roughly looks like this: the first twenty years, one episode at the beginning; the next ten years three episodes within a three-year time span; thereafter none.

Furthermore, Repatriation is a theological, not a political, concept. There are three aspects to it. First, Repatriation is a divine not a human act. It is different from migration, Rastafari insist. Many Rastafari even dissociated themselves from activities like the 1961 Mission, holding that while governments could bring about migration, only Jah could bring about Repatriation. This explains why other opportunities are not taken. In gratitude for their generous support of Ethiopia in the anti-fascist war, Emperor Haile Selassie made available through the Ethiopian World Federation several hundred acres of land for Blacks who wish to settle there. It is instructive that very few have seen Sheshamane and even fewer have stayed for good, including members of the Twelve Tribes of Israel, which adopts the position that since God helps those who help themselves, there is nothing wrong in trying to get its members one by one to Ethiopia. Second, Repatriation means the return of Africans not to any country of Africa, nor even to West Africa, but specifically to Ethiopia. When Rastafari sing and speak of Zion, Ethiopia is meant. Zion is where God dwells. Third, Repatriation also includes the concept of justice, by which Europeans would give up the lands they have seized from the Amerindians and return to Europe. As a theological concept Repatriation serves as a critique of White racism against Africans and other 'coloured races' and a call for a new order of justice in the world. It functions for the Rastafari in the same way that the Second Coming of Christ functions for the Christian without Christianity as a whole being called a millenarian movement – a theological and practical criticism of evil in this world to be followed by justice in the next.

Finally, none of the Repatriation initiatives referred to above at any time had the full support of Rastafarians, for the movement is highly fragmented and unorganized, a characteristic which works against united action. This point being of some relevance to the present discussion, I think some explanation is needed.

Leadership and Organization

Rastafari is an acephalous movement. There are groups, quasi-groups and individuals, who while sharing the core beliefs, nevertheless remain separate and independent. Consequently, the fortune of the movement as a whole is not tied to the fate of any particular leader or group, and it has been able not merely to survive the ups and downs of its relations with the society over the years, but also to influence it.

Leonard Howell is generally thought to have been the very first to reach the conclusion that Haile Selassie was God. But Joseph Hibbert claimed to have done the same independently. Whether or not the initial Rastafarians influenced one another, the point is that from the very inception there were several men all preaching the same thing but doing so *independently* of one another. There was one exception: Robert Hinds first began preaching with Howell but soon went his separate way. Thus Howell, Hinds, Hibbert, Archibald Dunkley, Brother Napier, Brother Powell and a few others were preaching Rastafari on the highways and byways of the city and countryside, and organizing the converted into churches which they gave the name 'King of Kings', all at the same time, and without reference to any one as leader, even *primus inter pares*.

A second feature was, thus, its resistance to centralized organization. Except among three very specific sects – the influential Twelve Tribes of Israel, the Bobo led by Prince Emmanuel Edwards and the remnants of Claudius Henry's church – the Rastafarian refuses to surrender his freedom and autonomy by joining any organization, Rastafari or not. A common explanation of the brethren is, 'wa jain kyan brok!' (what is joined together can be broken). But in truth it is their ethical value of complete freedom from the force of unnatural rules which informs this resistance. If one acts, it should be out of inner conviction, rather than out of the need for outward conformity. 'Man free' is another common expression, which means 'Do as you feel justified to do'. There have been repeated attempts in the past to forge a united body, to no avail. The Ethiopian International Unification Committee led by Attorney Michael Lorne is only the most recent of a series which has included the Rasta Movement Association and other initiatives.

Third, this value of freedom from outward constraint finds expression for the majority of Rastafari in the quasi-organization they refer to as the 'House', that is the House of Nyabinghi. The House is run by an 'Assembly of Elders', theoretically numbering 72, but in reality far fewer. Dr Homiak (1985:490-1) summarizes Eldership as combining cunning and resourcefulness with initiative and trust, but avoiding selfishness, arbitrariness or conceit. One does not become an Elder by appointment or election. The Elders oversee the affairs of the House, such as planning liturgical events, settling disputes, or appointing delegations as the need arises. But beyond the Assembly of Elders, there is no membership, as such. All are free to come or stay away, to participate or remain silent, to contribute or withhold financial dues. Yet one retains one's qualification as a member of the House simply by being a Rastafari. The openness of this sort of structure permits a great measure of democracy, in which all are equal, regardless of age, ability or function. But at the same time it makes a united, organized structure difficult if not impossible.

These characteristics of the Rastafari have a remarkable similarity to Revival, whose origin is traced to the incorporation by Myal of Christianity. The first Baptist to convert slaves, George Lisle, was himself a Black slave who was brought to Jamaica by his Loyalist master fleeing the American Revolution. But the more slaves Lisle converted, the less control he had, as converts went on their own, preaching their own understanding of Christianity, which in effect was Myal. Thomas Gibb, George Lewis and Moses Baker were three such preachers. They had no central organization, no mutual cooperation. Their movement reproduced itself in a cellular way.

Yet, it was clear by what the missionaries referred to as 'Myal outbreaks', beginning not long after the turn of the century and appearing as late as 1860, that there was a fairly uniform system of beliefs widely distributed across the length and breadth of the island. This allowed Revivalists everywhere to distinguish between two broad trends (or 'houses' in fact), the 'sixty' and the 'sixty-one'. As already mentioned in Chapter 1, the former worship only the sky-bound spirits, Jesus, the prophets, etc.; the latter worship these as well as the earth-bound spirits. Anywhere they go across the island, Revivalists are able to identify 'sixty' and 'sixty-one' and to associate with the one or the other.

No attempt was ever made to organize Revival into a united body, though as I said in the preceding chapter, scores of groups throughout the island were affiliated to Bedward.

I do not intend to stretch the comparison by saying that Revivalism, like Rasta, was impervious to organization, but the similarities in their spontaneous and acephalous nature are indeed striking.

There are similarities of a different kind, which in the context of the discussion deserve mention. I refer to the many examples where it is evident that certain crucial aspects of the Revival world outlook are very much alive in Rastafari. I distinguish two kinds: first, direct traces, where the forms are the same; and second, indirect traces, where Revival traditions provide the basis for what appear to be new Rastafari traditions. Direct traces are far more numerous than generally recognized, and may be summarized as follows:

Ritual Structure

Revival meetings, as pointed out before, are basically divided into two parts: an initial period of drumming, singing, dancing and spirit possession, followed by the specific rituals which define the purpose of the meeting. Thus, the healing ritual, testimony service, and table all begin more or less the same way. The Rastafari meetings retain this element: an initial period of considerable duration in which the drumming-sing-ing-dancing triad reigns, but without spirit possession. At the time of my fieldwork in 1975 this initial period gave way, just as in Revival, to a different element, namely Bible reading and preaching. At one ceremony I attended in Westmoreland, the Table from which the Elder spoke hosted a glass of water – another Revival trace.[6]

Ritual Instruments

It is very interesting that in Professor Simpson's description of the anniversary celebration by one group of Haile Selassie's coronation in 1953 the musical instruments included rhumba boxes, saxophones, guitars, violin, banjo, tambourines and rattles (Simpson 1955:143). All this changed within ten years, as uniformly throughout the movement, a bank of drums had replaced all other instruments and a rhythm, called nyabinghi, peculiar only to the Rastafari. The drums are of three types: a huge bass, larger than Revival's but struck the same way with the padded end of a stick; the funde, which establishes the rhythm; and the repeater, which pronounces the variations. The latter two are played with the hands and fingers. These drums are central to all Rastafari gatherings. Bilby and Leib (1986:23) trace the origins of this music to a complex inter-penetration of Buru, Kumina and Revival styles of drumming in West Kingston, and thus establish the accuracy of 'Rastafari insistence on the "African roots" of Nyabing[h]i' (Bilby and Leib 1986:27). Most of the ceremonial songs of the Rastafari with adjustments in certain key words, as observed above, are legacies of Revival.

Magic

To 'dance nyabinghi' against an identified oppressor was, Rastafari believed, to invoke in a sure and compelling way the power of God to destroy him. According to one informant, fire was made to consume an effigy of the person. Although the practice may have ceased, I have heard Rastafari threaten to dance nyabinghi for public personalities they considered oppressive to Rastafari. The dreadlocks are also believed to have magical properties, not to be used to harm the owner, but to be able to wreak destruction on Babylon. Such beliefs in magic are not surprising, since, according to Robert Hill (1983:38) 'popular belief in the power of the occult played a formative role in the early stages of Rastafari consciousness'.

Divination

Rastafari believe in the power of the Bible to expose evil. In one incident concerning the loss of money belonging to the House, the Holy Book was used to distinguish the guilty from the innocent.

Herbal Lore

Rastafari place heavy stress on nature as a gift of the Father 'for the healing of the nation'. This attitude applies not only to ganja but to all of nature. Thus, with almost the force of doctrine, they reject artificial things pertaining to life, preferring the natural: herbal medicinal cures, herbal teas, natural spices and flavouring such as pepper and coconut milk.[7]

Visions

The same worldview which Rastafari share with other Jamaicans distinguishes dreams from visions. Dreams are the images and fantasies which appear in sleep. Visions are dreams of particular significance, usually rich in symbolic meaning, and regarded as encoded messages from the world of the spirits. Although not believing in spirits other than the Father, the Rastafari nevertheless believe in His communication through visions.

Indirect traces may be found in many new traditions which seem uniquely Rastafari but which in fact owe much to the earlier world outlook. I now present some of the more obvious.

Word Power

The creation of a new mode of speech by the Rastafari has been noted by linguists (Pollard 1985; Alleyne 1988). Underlying it is a belief in the magical power of the word. Alleyne, while being too uncertain 'about the earlier stages of language development in Jamaica to be able to reconstruct a continuous process through the seventeenth, eighteenth and nineteenth centuries', does not doubt that Rastafari ideas about language are 'an expression of African culture' (Alleyne 1988:150). What he obviously implies is that more research is needed to establish the link, more research in fact on the worldview I have been calling Revival and its belief in the magical power of the word. To begin with, ethnographers have noted the predilection of the Jamaican peasant for the spoken word (Beckwith 1929), a tendency not adequately explained by the absence of a tradition of literacy, since even literate people have the feeling that to address one in person is more effective than in writing. And a predilection, one might add, not just for the spoken word but for 'big words', as if their use transforms the speaker's ability to be more effective. These traditions persist. Contemporary Jamaican culture, observes Brathwaite (1986), is essentially oral.

Names were viewed as somewhat like extensions of one's person, and therefore as the possible object of imitative magic. Hence, at night, one never answered to one's name being called, unless it was uttered three times, the number three thought to be outside the range of duppies. Similarly, one should not call out another's name in public. One attracts the other's attention either by a clapping of hands or the hissing of teeth. This custom considered it bad etiquette to do otherwise, but it was also believed that it exposed one to possible evil being conspired by strangers. The tradition still persists of giving children, especially girls, 'pet names', that is names by which they were known by family and community, and official or 'real names', sometimes known not even to the owner until read in adulthood on a birth certificate.

Nowhere is the power of the word more manifest today in non-Rastafari contexts than among the Pentecostal sects, where spirit possession takes place through the power of the preacher's words. But even in other conventional denominations the measure of satisfaction with the worship is directly a function not of the singing or the ritual but of the sermon. If good, it is described as 'sweet'.

These examples indicate that Rastafari predilection for the spoken word did not originate with them. I see no difference between the Dreadlock's preference for 'performing' over writing his complaint or petition and the peasant's. His attribution of power to the word, so beautifully expressed as 'Word, Sounds and Power!', is but a refinement of a tradition.

Contamination of Death

I noted the elaborate rituals which traditionally follow death, and the fear of contamination of the world of the living by the spirits of the dead which inspires them. Rastafari carries this fear of contamination to its extreme. The brethren do not believe the true Rasta will die. I am not now in a position to say whether this belief was institutionalized from the 1930s, though it is not unlikely. None of my 'ancient' Rastafari ever mentioned death or burial. At any rate, up to the very recent past the belief that Rastafari cannot die was very strong. A change became noticeable in the 1980s, following first the report of the death of His Imperial Majesty in 1974 and that of Bob Marley in 1981. Today, some brethren admit that man is put on earth only for a time, not to live forever. This, however, is not the majority view.

As a result of not believing he will die, the Rastafari will have nothing to do with death: he attends no funerals, takes no part in their arrangement, no matter how close the deceased, does not mourn or even discuss the event. Thus, in an ironic way, his ideological distancing has the same source as the ritualized distancing of the traditional believer: belief in the contaminating power of death.

Woman as a Source of Evil

Much is made of the Rastafari belief in male supremacy (Kitzinger 1971; Nettleford 1970; Rowe 1980; Yawney 1983), buttressed by beliefs in woman's natural inferiority and power to contaminate. Rastafari believe that a woman is of such wayward nature that only through her male spouse, her 'king-man', may she attain the enlightenment of Jah. Relationships are therefore marked by female submissiveness and obedience to the male, and ritual avoidance and even confinement during the menstrual flow. While this strong patriarchal tradition is indeed a direct contrast to traditional household patterns in Jamaica, its ideological root within the traditional worldview is often missed.

Man as God

I have already drawn attention to the rejection of the spirit world by the Rastafari and its replacement with a belief in the nearness of God and oneness of being between Him and Man. Yet it may be argued that the new doctrine is but an elevation of the most essential feature of the Revival beliefs about the relationship between the human and spiritual world, namely the fusion of identity which is possible in the form of ritual possession. Just as Revival possession is the means by which the spirit performs, so is Rastafari identity with God the means whereby God's works are manifest. Father Owens, to date the only presenter of a comprehensive view of Rasta theology, explains:

> Simple man is not completely divine, in the Rastafarian view, because he is still partly under the sway of Satan, the embodiment of all that is in opposition to God in man. Just as the God of the Rastas is not allowed to be an other-worldly, intangible being estranged from the ways of man, so also Satan is conceived by the brethren as being immediately present to the working of history: 'Satan is the people who live upon earth who manifest themself in Satan way. In other words, Satan is the man who trying to keep you down. Yes, that is the devil!' (Owens 1976:132)

Thus, to do good means to allow the God in you to perform his work, just as to do evil means allowing Satan to perform his. But, as Owens (1976:130) carefully notes, the brethren do not allow their identity with God to gloss over 'the real distance that they know exists between man in his present state and man in his divine state to which he is summoned'.

General Implications

The view of the Rastafari I have so far presented is one which, when silhouetted against the historical backdrop of the worldview of which Revival was the religious expression, appears as a new departure but also as a continuity. The question now is: what does it all mean? This is what I think it means.

(1) Rastafari must be included when considering Africa-derived religion in Jamaica and the Caribbean. It is more authentic an expression of that tradition than generally thought. Alleyne is hard put to find anything of African continuity in Rastafari beliefs and behaviour. 'Rastafarianism', he surmises, 'is probably an excellent example of a cultural form being generated virtually *ab initio* out of the social circumstances' (Alleyne 1988:103). But evidently conscious of the implications of such a statement,[8] he later on observes that the religion, by integrating language, music and religion at a higher level than before, merely continues an African and African-Jamaican tradition (Alleyne 1988:149). It is in this latter context that he regrets the paucity of knowledge that might have allowed linguistic, and obviously other, links to be proved.

(2) Owing so much to the Revival past, yet being so remarkably different, Rastafari may be regarded as its fulfillment. For it is clear, particularly after Marcus Garvey, that the Revival worldview was inadequate in pan-African terms, since it had no really viable answer to the problem posed by White racism. After Garvey, a return to a worldview that accommodated black skin as an ontological deficiency to be rectified only by transmogrification was out of the question.

(3) Thus, Rasta is itself essentially a worldview movement, 'a system of beliefs and a state of consciousness', as Post (1978:165) correctly put it. This accounts for its acephalous and somewhat spontaneous nature, very much in the same vein as Myal and Revival. Its greatest impact lies here, and it would be quite wrong to judge it by the failure of its prophecies of repatriation.

(4) While Rastafari has manifested millennial tendencies, which give the movement a political character, it is much more fruitful to conceive of it as a cultural movement. What has accounted for its growth is not the dream of the millennium but the appropriation of a new and more coherent reality. There is the real revolution. As I have already said, Rastafari search for the millennium occurred four times. Yet it is a fact that its periods of greatest growth occurred *after* them: in the decade of the 1930s and first half decade of the 1940s, when the focus was on spreading the message that Selassie was God; and in the 1960s and 1970s, with the rise of the Dreadlocks and their symbolic announcement of a new and separate identity.

This is not to deny the impulse to action inherent in the appropriation of any new ideas about the cosmos, which is obviously present in the Rastafari movement. It was present, too, in Myal and Revival, which did as much in the struggle against slavery and colonialism as Vodun did in Haiti, yet no scholar, as far as I know, would regard any of them as essentially activist in the broad political sense. It is one thing to recognize these impulses, it is another to make them the essence.

No other scholar has treated the subject matter in quite the same way or has been able to document the living continuity within the Rastafari of Jamaica of a unifying worldview honed out of a variegated tribal melange. The thrust of the Nettleford essays (1970), for example, was on the issue of a Black identity. He perceived, notwithstanding the millennial dream of the movement, that the centre stage was Jamaica itself and its Black majority. But Katrin Norris (1962) had sounded a similar note almost a decade before, when she observed that the Rastafari were facing the issue of a Black identity, which the Black middle classes were avoiding. Among more recent scholars Ernest Cashmore and Laennec Hurbon adopt a similar position. Cashmore (1983) bluntly dismisses the Rastafari's potential as a revolutionary force but argues that in fact previous scholars underestimated its importance in creating a culture. Hurbon (1986:164) sees the movement as building a new identity for Jamaica and all the Caribbean islands, but he too lapses into seeing it as a sort of nativist 'revival of the basic core of the slave and nineteenth-century cultures', again, I think, because of the failure of scholarship to uncover its living continuity with the past. And precisely this constitutes the insight of Mervyn Alleyne, whose central thesis it is that the culture of West Africa lives on in the Jamaican worldview. For example, he says:

> The reluctance of Jamaican peasants to accept modern scientific agricultural techniques, including the use of chemical fertilisers and other agents that artificially quicken growth must be seen within the philosophical framework of this oneness with nature. The Rastafarians, whose complex eating taboos reflect a belief that body, mind, and nature form an integrated whole, have developed and enriched this philosophical tradition. (Alleyne 1988:157)

It is easy to miss this because 'worldview . . . cannot be observed directly like artifacts' (Alleyne 1988:157), and in the study of religion, where it could have been gleaned, the focus has been on ritual and organization to the neglect of the 'underlying philosophies'.

Alleyne's observations are well founded. Nevertheless, the approach taken in this chapter to the Rastafari phenomenon raises a number of issues which need airing. Is the existence of a worldview enough of an explanation for the lack of centralized leadership in religious movements? After all, ideas do not spread *sua sponte*. They need human agents. And is it not often the case that what makes some people leaders is their quicker grasp of ideas and better ability to communicate them more lucidly? What, therefore, is the place of charismatic leadership in religions of this sort? Among the Rastafari all four of the most mentioned early leaders, Howell, Hinds, Hibbert and Dunkley, were invested with heroic, if not divine, abilities. De Albuquerque tells of one Rastafari who would come every morning and reverently kiss the locks of Mortimo Planno. Henry up to the time of his death was thought to be part of the triune deity, as is Prince Emmanuel presently. The lack of central leadership should not allow us to gloss over the presence and role of leaders.

Inasmuch as changes in worldviews imply changes in the conception of Man and Man's place in the world, are Africa-derived religions in the Caribbean any different from religious movements generally described as messianic, nativist and millenarian? Burridge, for example, reduces all religions to concern 'with the discovery, identification, moral relevance and ordering of different kinds of power whether these manifest themselves as thunder, or lightning, atomic fission, untrammelled desire, arrogance, impulse, apparitions, visions, or persuasive words' (Burridge 1969:5). The logic of his argument would lead us to answer no, for although each situation may be specific, what he calls the 'logic of social relations' may allow a generalized explanation. This needs to be examined.

Notes

1. This chapter has since appeared in *New West Indian Guide*, Volume 64, Numbers 3 & 4, 1990.

2. According to Elkins (1986:215) oils and powders are early twentieth century additions from the influence of DeLaurence, which 'significantly influenced the development of the new type of obeah in Jamaica' known as 'Science'. DeLaurence was a publisher of books about magic and necromancy.

3. Daryl Dance (1985:5-8) collected no fewer than six, as late as the 1970s. In one, God had not made anyone Black, only straight haired people. As a set of them laughed at monkey because his tail was on fire, he thrashed his tail around in the air. 'The fire burned the hair [and made them] black'. Similar stories may be found in the United States. They are taken with only half-serious intent. At the same time, like all jokes which are based on real people, they have a serious side.

4. It was also grossly misunderstood. Garvey did not campaign for all Blacks to return to Africa, but for Blacks to resettle, develop and unify the continent. With united Africa a major power in the world, Blacks could command the respect denied them by Whites. Were he leading an exodus, the Black Star Shipping Line, linking Africa,

North America and the Caribbean and Central America in a triangular trade, would have made no sense.

5. Significantly, sometime after he returned from serving a ten-year prison sentence, Henry told his congregation that the Emperor had told him on a visit to Africa that there was no need for Black people to leave Jamaica, because Africa was already in Jamaica (Chevannes 1976).

6. That experience was very formative. It first alerted me to the existence among the Rastafari of links of continuity with the historically earlier Revival religion. The insight gained was to become my central thesis. See my *Social and Ideological Origins of the Rastafari Movement in Jamaica*, from which most of the examples of direct and indirect traces of Revivalism discussed in this chapter are drawn.

7. Even the taboo against salt may derive from this prejudice against artificial things, since as a commodity bought in shops, salt is not 'natural'. Another possibility is the re-emergence of a retention from slavery. I am grateful to Roland Littlewood for bringing this to my attention. Alleyne (1988:104) also mentions that avoidance of salt recurs among the Maroons of Jamaica and among Kumina cultists.

8. The burden of proof must be to show how it is possible for people to be bereft of culture. Even in rejecting the past they would have to do so in culturally meaningful ways, such as through language and other symbols.

3 Religion as Resistance in Jamaican Peasant Life: The Baptist Church, Revival Worldview and Rastafari Movement

Jean Besson

Chapters 2, 4 and 5 of this volume by Barry Chevannes provide a new understanding of the much studied Rastafari movement of Jamaica. This chapter explores complementary themes from a Jamaican case study, namely, the free villages of Trelawny parish, at the heart of the Caribbean plantation-peasant interface, where I have conducted long-term fieldwork during the period 1968-91. As such, it is also a continuation of earlier work on the Trelawny peasantry and African-Caribbean peasant life (Besson 1974, 1979, 1984a, 1984b, 1987a, 1987b, 1988a, 1988b, 1992, 1993).[1] The first part of the chapter presents a brief evaluation of Chevannes' perspectives on Rastafari, while the main body explores related themes from the Trelawny villages.

The New Approach to Rastafari

Each of the three chapters by Chevannes presents a new perspective on Rastafari, while together the three provide a fresh approach. In Chapter 2 Chevannes argues that Rastafari must be seen as both a new departure from, and a continuity with, the traditional African-Jamaican peasant worldview, Revival, and draws four related conclusions from this argument. Firstly, Rastafari is an African-derived religion with direct continuity with Myal, Native Baptism and Revival. Here Chevannes goes beyond Alleyne who, in the search for African continuities in Jamaican religion, finds such continuities in Myal, Native Baptism and Revival, but argues that 'whereas Africa remains very high among Rastafarians

43

at the level of ideological consciousness, there isn't very much of African continuity in the system of religious belief and religious behaviour' (Alleyne 1988:103). Secondly, Rastafari may be regarded as the fulfilment of Revival – though from Chevannes' analysis it is clear that this is seen as fulfilment through rejection, Rastafari being anti-Revival and patriarchal. Thirdly, Rastafari represents a worldview movement rooted in Myal and Revival. Fourthly, Rastafari is a cultural movement constructing a new reality rather than a political millenarian movement.

Chapter 4 establishes, through new evidence based on oral sources, that the Rastafari matted hair complex was the innovation of the Youth Black Faith in the 1950s; rather than originating earlier in Howell's Rastafarian camp at Pinnacle (Smith *et al.* 1961). Chevannes further concludes that the Youth Black Faith, founded by young activists in 1949, 'represented a reform trend of younger converts bent on purging the movement of Revivalist practices'. In addition, the adoption of the dreadlocks by the Youth Black Faith symbolized both the construction of a greater social distance from Jamaican colonial society and the perception of Rastafari by that society as derelicts and outcasts.

Chapter 5 takes this perspective further, showing 'that the dreadlocks phenomenon symbolized both a rejection of social control as well as a triumph of male power over the female'. In this process, '[t]he Dreadlocks sought to overthrow the religion of the peasant, Revival' and 'attempted to ... isolate the negative ideas about women which were abroad in the culture, ritualize them and by so doing establish ritual distance from the contaminating source of their confinement in Jamaican society, in Babylon'.

While providing a new approach, aspects of Chevannes' perspective find support in other analyses of Rastafari and related African-Jamaican religions. For example Barrett (1977), while advancing the view of Rastafari as a messianic-millenarian movement, sees its roots in the ideology of Ethiopianism in Jamaican slave religion. Campbell (1980) in contrast to Chevannes highlights the political aspect of Rastafari, but like Chevannes questions the centrality of millenarianism to Rastafari and also sees Rastafari as a culture of resistance. Robotham (1988) interprets Myal and Native Baptism as bases for forging a Black ethnicity in Jamaican slave society, a point that strengthens Chevannes' case; as does Schuler's (1979a) analysis of Myal as a basis for pan-African slave resistance (cf. Besson 1981; Schuler 1979b, 1980).

Support for Chevannes' new approach to Rastafari can also be found in the historical anthropology of the free villages of Trelawny, a parish that was the centre of the Myal movement in Jamaica and an important area of Baptist proselytizing and Native Baptist development, and where the Baptist Church, Revival worldview and Rastafari movement co-exist today (Besson 1987b:124-5, 1988b:7, 1993). For here, at the very heart of Jamaican plantation society, the continuity between these religious forms can be clearly seen.

The Trelawny study also, however, suggests a revaluation of Revival within the context of Revival-Rastafari continuity, one that highlights Revival itself as cultural resistance and points to the role that women play in such resistance. This analysis develops the thesis of an earlier essay (Besson 1993), which challenges Peter Wilson's (1969, 1973) contention that African-Caribbean women are passive imitators of colonial culture in contrast to African-Caribbean men, who are seen by Wilson as the creators of an indigenous counter-culture. Within this context, Wilson argues that the primarily male value system of 'Reputation' includes African-Christian cults, citing Jamaican Rastafari as an extreme example of the general case. Women, by contrast, are seen by Wilson as upholding Eurocentric 'Respectability', which includes a commitment to the White churches with their concern for European marriage and the propriety of domestic life.

However, as I have shown elsewhere (Besson 1993), women are central to African-Caribbean peasant cultures of resistance – a resistance that includes religious life. African-Caribbean peasant women participate in indigenous cults, such as Revival, established in the face of the dominant colonial culture and the plantation system; and the so-called White churches that women (as well as men) support are the Nonconformist churches, such as the Baptist Church, that opposed colonial orthodox Christianity and fought for the abolition of slavery. Paradoxically, this critique strengthens Chevannes' argument for Revival-Rastafari continuity, as the Trelawny case study shows.

The contention of this chapter, that the Baptist Church, Revival worldview and the Rastafari movement co-exist as variants of cultural resistance in Trelawny villages, is further strengthened by Cross' analysis of Caribbean religious forms (1979:96-100). He argues that Nonconformist sects, African-Christian cults and Rastafari are points on a continuum of rejection – more or less powerful – of colonial orthodoxy. Cross contends that while the Nonconformist sects, such as the Baptists in Jamaica, are 'hardly a very radical rejection of orthodox Christianity', they were nevertheless 'of great importance' in challenging the orthodox churches in the colonial context (p. 97). Accordingly, the Nonconformists represent the opening point of Cross' continuum. At mid-point on the continuum lie the African-Christian cults, such as Revival; while Rastafari is seen as the most radical rejection of colonial Christianity.

Cross' thesis on African-Caribbean religious forms is set within an analysis of urbanization, and he further argues that the Nonconformist sects are found in both rural and urban areas; with African-Christian cults typifying rural communities, and Rastafari existing 'on the rim of a major Caribbean city' (1979:100). However, Alleyne contends that Revival is largely urban (1988:96) and Barrett notes that, while Rastafari's early incubation period was in the slums of Kingston, the first Rastafari settlement was the rural community of Pinnacle, with the movement subsequently spreading to both the urban and rural areas of Jamaica (1977:84-9, 146, 160-1). The Trelawny case study not only reveals the co-existence of all three religious variants as modes of cultural resistance in Jamaican villages, suggesting a model of greater complexity than Cross' continuum, but also resolves the contradictions regarding rural-urban contexts of African-Jamaican religions and develops, as well as modifies, Chevannes' analysis of the link between Rastafari and Revival.

The Trelawny case study also reinforces Chevannes' argument regarding the significance of oral history for interpreting Caribbean cultural resistance, for the Trelawny data were collected through a combination of social anthropological, historical and oral history research (cf. Besson 1984b, 1987b, 1989a:29-30). In addition, the Trelawny case reveals the relationship between religious resistance and the economic and symbolic significance of land in Caribbean society (cf. Besson 1979, 1984a, 1987a); for all three variants of religious resistance in the villages are interwoven with the theme of land. The case study also highlights the dynamic process of Caribbean culture-building as the context for African continuities in Caribbean culture (cf. Besson 1987b:124-5), a perspective that resolves the 'creativity-continuity' debate (Alleyne 1988:11-27) and advances Chevannes' new approach to Rastafari.

In turning to explore the co-existence of religious variants as cultural resistance in Trelawny peasant villages, this chapter will focus first on the significance of the Baptist Church in Jamaican and Trelawny plantation slave society, and the related role of the Baptist Church as a formal symbol of resistance to colonial orthodoxy and the plantation system in the island's and parish's post-slavery peasant communities.

The Baptist Church as a Formal Symbol of Resistance

Following the capture of Jamaica from the Spanish by the British in 1655, the island was rapidly transformed into a sugar and slave plantation society under British rule (Patterson 1973:15-27). By 1700 Jamaica was the world's leading sugar producer and, in the eighteenth century, the very centre of New World plantation slavery and the most important colony in the British Empire (Walvin 1983:35; Williams 1970:152, 154).

In eighteenth-century Jamaica, the Anglican or 'Established' Church was the only church allowed by law to function in the island, and as the official religion of the slave masters, the Established Church supported the status quo of slavery and was as inefficient and corrupt as the plantation society that it served. At this time the planters' church also completely neglected the spiritual welfare of the slaves. Near the end of the eighteenth century, however, the abolition movement and the religious revival in England led to Nonconformist missionaries being sent to Jamaica, and this missionary activity had a greater impact on the slave population. The Established Church was violently opposed to the preaching of these missionaries, which they regarded as a threat to the slave system (Patterson 1973:40-1, 207-9).

The Moravians were the first English Nonconformist missionaries to arrive in Jamaica, in 1754, followed by the Methodists in 1789 and the Baptists in 1813. The Moravians had the least impact on the non-White population, while the Methodists became the stronghold of the free coloured and Negro group. The Baptists were the most successful in converting the slaves, one of the main reasons being that the Baptist faith had previously been introduced to the slaves by Negro preachers in the late eighteenth century. The most important of these Black preachers were George Lisle (or Liele), an ex-slave from Virginia and Georgia, who came to Jamaica in 1784, and Moses Baker, also an American ex-slave, who was baptized by Lisle in 1787. In 1788 Baker began preaching in St James parish (Alleyne 1988:89; Patterson 1973:209-15), which bordered the new parish of Trelawny that had been created from eastern St James in 1771. Trelawny would become the very centre of Jamaican plantation slave society, with more plantations and slaves than any other parish in Jamaica (Besson 1984b:6, 1987b:112).

In 1813 the Baptist Missionary Society in England sent out its first missionary to Jamaica, the Reverend John Rowe, who took up residence in Falmouth, Trelawny's capital, in 1814. Following Rowe's death two years later from yellow fever, Falmouth was without a Baptist missionary until 1827. In that year the Reverend Thomas Burchell, stationed in St James, established the Falmouth Baptist Church, whose first pastor was Burchell's assistant, the Reverend James Mann. In 1830 Mann died of malaria, having established two other Baptist churches in Trelawny at Rio Bueno and Stewart Town. Mann was replaced in Falmouth, in 1830, by the Reverend William Knibb, an outspoken opponent of the Established Church and slavery. Knibb's congregation consisted largely of Trelawny's plantation slaves (Knibb Sibley 1965; Patterson 1973:211; Wright 1973).

Following the so-called 'Baptist War' slave rebellion in Jamaica's western parishes in 1831, Knibb, regarded by the plantocracy as one of the ringleaders of the rebellion, was arrested and briefly imprisoned. In 1832, as a deputy for the Baptist Church in Jamaica, Knibb contributed to the anti-slavery campaign in Britain, and in the Falmouth Baptist Church on 1 August 1838, Knibb celebrated the full emancipation of the slaves. Following emancipation, Knibb negotiated the first wage settlement in Jamaica with the Trelawny plantocracy on behalf of the former slaves. With another Baptist minister, the Reverend James Phillippo, Knibb also initiated the island's church-founded Free Village System within a context of acute plantation-peasant land and labour conflict. Trelawny was the vanguard of this village movement, under the sponsorship of Knibb (Besson 1984b; Knibb Sibley 1965; Mintz 1974:160; Wright 1973).

A crucial role of the Nonconformist post-slavery village system was the provision of freehold land to the ex-slaves, through the purchase and subdivision of properties by the churches. This was especially significant as many planters refused to sell land to the former slaves (Besson 1984a:64-5). Thus, in conceiving of the free village scheme, Knibb wrote to Dr Hoby, a member of the Baptist Committee in England, in September 1838:

> I believe that I could now, if I had the means, purchase from 500 to 1,000 acres, ... for about £2 or £3 sterling per acre. This I would purchase at once. I could soon re-sell to families, in lots of from two to four acres each, which would enable the worthy members of my church, with others who are fearfully oppressed, to settle, and form a village of their own. (Quoted in Wright 1973:167)

In November of that year Knibb was able to tell Hoby and the Birmingham abolitionist, Joseph Sturge, of the purchase of 500 acres in his 'cousin Dexter's' district for the founding of Trelawny's first free village. This property was the coffee plantation of Alps in the Stewart Town area in the south-east of the parish, where the Baptist missionary, the Reverend Benjamin Dexter, was stationed. This village, now renamed Alps but originally called New Birmingham after Joseph Sturge's hometown, was laid out around a Baptist chapel, providing accommodation for 550 persons, and a school. Founded with the assistance of Dexter, under the sponsorship of Knibb, it was settled by ex-slaves from the former Alps estate. By January 1839 over seventy families had purchased land and were erecting homes in this new village. Along with Sligoville, Jamaica's first free village, founded by Phillippo in the St Catherine hills, Alps provided a model for the Jamaican free village system. As my research in 1983 confirmed, the Baptist Church still provides the formal focus of Alps village (Besson 1984b:7, 17-18).

By 1845 Trelawny had twenty-three free village communities (Paget 1964:51). These included Refuge (originally named Wilberforce), Kettering and Granville, founded in 1838, 1841 and 1845 respectively by Knibb and studied by me in 1983 (Besson 1984b). These three villages were established through the subdivision of properties purchased through the Baptist Church, on marginal mountainous land bordering or surrounded by sugar plantations, to absorb ex-slaves from these estates.

Refuge, situated six miles east of Falmouth where Knibb's church was located, was founded, like Alps, in the year of full emancipation (1838). The records note the founding of the village, on some ninety acres of mountainous land purchased and subdivided by Knibb, around a Baptist chapel, accommodating 1,500 persons, and a school. The Baptist Church continues to provide the formal framework of Refuge village today. As in the case of Alps, originally called New Birmingham, Refuge's original name of Wilberforce – after the abolitionist William Wilberforce – reflects the Nonconformist anti-slavery stance and the emancipation theme (Besson 1984b:10, 13-15).

The free village of Kettering, named after William Knibb's hometown, was founded by Knibb in 1841 on a former pimento estate bordering Duncans town three miles east of Refuge. The village was laid out in 400 building lots, which were sold to ex-slaves, around a Baptist Church and school. On Kettering Hill, in the centre of the village, the freed slaves of the Baptist Church built Knibb a large stone house in gratitude for his efforts on their behalf in the abolitionist cause. Here

Knibb made his home until his death in 1845. Today, nearly one hundred and fifty years after Knibb's death, the Baptist Church persists as an active force in contemporary Kettering village (Besson 1984b:15-16).

Granville village, named after the abolitionist Granville Sharpe, was founded by Knibb two and half miles inland from Falmouth in 1845. It was established on some ninety acres of mountainous land (a former livestock pen), purchased and subdivided by Knibb, and resold to ex-slaves. The settlement was founded around a Baptist prayer house, which also served as a school. The Granville prayer house has since been replaced by a Baptist Church, which is the formal focus of village life and is presently being enlarged. This church is part of the Falmouth Baptist Circuit and the church services in Granville are conducted by the Falmouth Baptist Minister (Besson 1984b:10-13).

The free village of Martha Brae, the main context of my long-term research in Trelawny, was established by ex-slaves on the ruined site of the former planter town of Martha Brae, which had been the first capital of Trelawny but was eclipsed around 1800 by the new town and port of Falmouth (Besson 1984b:8-10). Unlike the other four villages studied, there is no record of the Baptist Church having founded Martha Brae. However, my research reveals several clues that suggest that Martha Brae is a variant on the Baptist Church-founded village theme (Besson 1987b:114-15). Both documentary evidence and oral history strongly suggest that the village was founded in the early post-emancipation era, probably in the 1840s. In addition, names of Martha Brae residents appear in the membership book of the Falmouth Baptist Church kept by William Knibb himself. The location of Martha Brae, just one mile south of Falmouth in the heartlands of the Trelawny plantations from which Knibb drew his congregation, would also have made its post-emancipation settlement of direct concern to Knibb.

The presence of a Baptist prayer house in Martha Brae, 'Class 5' of the Falmouth Baptist Circuit, which the oldest villagers remember as always being there, is also a central clue. In addition, the villagers are strongly Baptist in formal faith and regularly attend the William Knibb Memorial Baptist Church in Falmouth. Moreover the Baptist prayer house in Martha Brae, in disrepair in the 1970s, was renovated in 1986 under the supervision of the Falmouth Baptist Church; and in November of that year the prayer house was reopened at a large village function attended by members of the William Knibb Memorial Baptist Church and the Vice-President of the Jamaica Baptist Union (Besson 1987b:123).

In the five Trelawny villages studied, then, the Baptist Church is the formal symbol of the free village established and perpetuated in the face of colonial orthodox Christianity and the plantation system, a system that still encompasses Trelawny's fertile land today.

The Paradox of Baptist Religious Resistance

The Baptist missionaries in Jamaica were reformers, however, not revolutionaries. The slaves were their potential converts and the free villages were both captive congregations and reservoirs of labour for the plantations. Thus, as seen above, Trelawny free villages such as Alps, Kettering and Refuge were laid out around a Baptist church; Granville was founded around a Baptist prayer house, later replaced by a Baptist church; while Martha Brae village also developed around a Baptist prayer house linked to the Falmouth Baptist Church. Moreover, an explicit rationale for the establishment of Granville, two and a half miles from Falmouth, was 'in order that a portion of the people might be near enough to ensure a good congregation at the parent chapel' in Falmouth (Underhill 1861:370). While absorbing dispossessed ex-slaves from surrounding plantations such as Green Park, Carrickfoyle, Merrywood and Maxfield, Granville also provided a labour supply for these estates. Martha Brae was even closer to Falmouth than Granville, and was situated on the borders of Holland and Irving Tower plantations, while Refuge adjoined Oxford plantation (Besson 1984b).

The role of the Baptist free villages as reservoirs of plantation labour was made explicit by Knibb himself, in response to a question by the Select Committee of the House of Commons in 1842, using the example of Kettering village (adjoining the town of Duncans) in Trelawny founded by Knibb the previous year:

> Q.: Has it (the settlement of free villages) not a tendency to diminish the supply of labour to the estates?
>
> Knibb: During the time they are building their house, but not afterwards; but perhaps the Committee will understand it better when I inform them that whenever I had to do with buying a place for a free village, I have tried to select a spot surrounded by a number of estates. For instance, I purchased a Pimento Walk at Duncans in Trelawny which was surrounded with sugar estates. I sold the

land in lots; seldom any person bought more than two lots;
each lot was 52 feet by 108 feet. The persons from the
neighbouring estates bought up this land very fast, and
during the time they were building there was a diminution
upon the property; but after the houses were built the
planters and overseers said, 'Now we can get labour by
task work whenever we want it; there is no quarrel about
rent. They go and take a job to build a wall at so much a
yard, or to clear a pasture at so much an acre'. (Quoted in
Robotham 1977:49)

In Trelawny's contemporary free villages, which persist today hemmed
in on marginal land by two vast corporate sugar plantation 'centrals' and
several 'properties' or large farms that have replaced the former slave
plantations, many villagers still work as labourers on these surrounding
estates.

In addition to providing captive congregations and reservoirs of labour, the post-emancipation communities may also have been subject to
social control by the Baptist Church through the regulation of access to
village land. Mintz cites a case, recorded in 1952 in the Baptist village of
Sturge Town in St Ann parish neighbouring Trelawny, which suggests
such social control. The case concerns a Sturge Towner who:

walked twenty-two miles each time he went to his fields,
which he rented. He was anxious to acquire the right to
work a piece of church property in Sturge Town. But he
was not a faithful member of the local church and did not
get the use of the land. This is by no means to claim that
church membership was a condition for economic or social assistance; but it seems likely that churchgoing im-
proves one's community standing and, accordingly, one's
local economic opportunities. (Mintz 1974:175)

Mintz is unable to establish the extent of such incidents in the earlier
history of Sturge Town, but oral history in contemporary Granville suggests that membership and status in the Baptist Church was, indeed, a
relevant factor in the internal differentiation of the post-emancipation
villages. According to Granville villagers, the subdivision of the Granville lands was delegated by Knibb to a Baptist Class Leader, a position
that the villagers also refer to in explaining why Knibb's 'land butcher'
had access to the largest and best portion of land in the new village of

Granville. This oral tradition is supported by the fact that the contemporary descendants of Knibb's surveyor hold inherited rights to the best portion of the Granville lands (Besson 1984b:11-12).

In his summation of the features of Jamaican church-founded villages, Mintz concludes, citing Cumper, that to some extent, in the context of constituted authority, the 'minister became a substitute – an altogether preferable substitute – for the estate owner, the overseer, the slave driver, the judge, and the custos' (Mintz 1974:179).

This paradox of the Baptist missionaries in Jamaica, as both challengers and perpetuators of the status quo, is paralleled by the Methodist missionaries of eighteenth and nineteenth century Nevis, where, on the one hand, Olwig (1990:94, 99) argues, 'the Methodist notion of brotherhood . . . had quite revolutionary [*sic*] implications when applied to British West Indian plantation society'; while on the other hand the missionaries, in providing the slaves with 'a more divine purpose to live for', were 'instituters of social order in colonial society'.

In Jamaica, this paradox in the role of the Baptist missionaries was fully perceived by the slaves and their descendants, who responded with a paradox of their own: supporting the Baptist Church in a formal context, while remaining committed to their African-Caribbean traditions. In the contemporary Trelawny villages, this paradox can be clearly seen. For within the formal framework of Baptist free village life, the villagers have evolved an African-Caribbean peasant culture in response and resistance to imposed colonial culture and the plantation system (cf. Mintz 1974:132-3). This peasant life-style is rooted in the tradition of slave resistance, which was very pronounced in Trelawny at the heart of Caribbean plantation slave society and manifested itself through slave rebellion, marronage and proto-peasant culture-building (Besson 1984b, 1987b, 1992; cf. Mintz 1971, 1974:131-250). The following section briefly delineates this peasant culture of resistance, by way of background to elucidating the co-existence of Revival and Rastafari with Baptist Christianity in Trelawny's post-slavery peasant communities.

The Peasant Culture of Resistance

At the heart of the peasant culture of resistance in Trelawny's Baptist villages is a customary form of land use, tenure and transmission known as 'family land' (Besson 1984b, 1987b, 1988a). The roots of this institution, which is widely found in Caribbean post-slavery peasant communities, lie in proto-peasant culture-building on the slave plantations

(Besson 1989b, 1992). There, wherever possible, the slaves established customary rights of use, tenure and transmission in relation to slave village yards and plantation backland provision grounds, as the basis of proto-peasant economies and communities. This customary tenurial system, which included both male and female slaves and their descendants, drew on the symbolic as well as economic significance of land in Caribbean plantation slave society, and transformed the principles of colonial legal freehold within the formal framework of the plantation.

After emancipation, this proto-peasant kin-based tenurial system mushroomed into the customary institution of family land in those Caribbean peasant communities, including Jamaica's Baptist land settlements, established by ex-slaves purchasing small landholdings. The creation of family land from these small plots of purchased land was effected through the transformation of the principles of colonial legal freehold, which was the basis of both the Caribbean plantation system and the Baptist founded villages (Besson 1979, 1984a, 1984b, 1987a, 1987b, 1988a, 1988b; cf. Momsen 1987:65-6).

Thus, rather than being perceived as alienable and a market commodity, as in legal freehold, family land is considered the inalienable corporate estate of a family line. Land rights to this joint estate are generally validated through oral tradition, rather than legal documents, and transmitted through intestacy. Moreover, all children and their descendants in perpetuity are regarded as co-heirs of the land, regardless of sex, birth order, residence or legitimacy, with marriage not being regarded as a basis for inheritance. In Jamaica, and elsewhere in the British West Indies, this system of unrestricted cognatic descent was in direct contrast to the system of primogeniture associated with colonial legal freehold. Houses are distinguished from the family land estate and considered moveable property, and may be either individually or jointly owned. In addition, the use of family land is not governed by the values of capitalist monoculture, but by a complex of economic and symbolic values forged within the proto-peasant and post-slavery peasant communities. Family land is the spatial dimension of the family line, reflecting its continuity and identity and providing inalienable freehold rights, house-sites, a spot for a kitchen garden, a place for absentees to return in time of need, and a family burial ground.

While the concept of the landholding kin group associated with the family land system may be seen as an African continuity, this continuity exists within the context of Caribbean culture-building. The unrestricted cognatic descent principle at the heart of family land contrasts with the unilineal systems predominant in Africa, and was created in resistance to the Caribbean plantation system. For in contrast to unilineal descent, unrestricted descent systems generate ever-increasing and overlapping family lines. In the Caribbean context this maximized not only the kinship lines that were legally denied to the plantation slaves, but also the transmission of post-emancipation freehold land rights among the ex-slaves' descendants in a context of plantation engendered land scarcity. This was especially significant to the descendants of former chattel slaves, who were not only denied access to freehold land but were also themselves considered property.

These family land estates and their unrestricted descent lines, which were more significant in Caribbean peasant communities than the colonial nuclear family upheld by both Established and Nonconformist Christianity, form the basis of identity and continuity in Trelawny's Baptist villages today. For example, the two Baptist deacons in Refuge are members of the village's two most central family lines. One of these Old Families traces its ancestry four ascending generations from the oldest living members to an African slave woman, one of three sisters brought from Africa into slavery, who worked on Oxford estate bordering the village, and who was subsequently one of the original ex-slave settlers of Refuge who purchased land from Knibb. The other central family line traces its ancestry four ascending generations from the oldest living members to an African-born slave couple and their son, a Creole slave on nearby Hyde Hall estate, who was also one of the original ex-slave settlers of Refuge who purchased land from Knibb. Both of these Old Families have transformed this purchased land to family land, with family burial grounds (Besson 1984b:13-15). Similar themes of family land and family lines, embedded in oral tradition, can be identified in Granville, Kettering, Alps and Martha Brae. Moreover, the creation of family land from purchased land continues wherever possible in Trelawny's contemporary Baptist villages, in the face of persisting land monopoly not only by plantations but also by the mining and tourist industries (Besson 1984b, 1987b, 1988a).

Around the institution of family land and its unrestricted descent lines in Trelawny's Baptist villages, are woven other themes of African-Caribbean cultural resistance to imposed colonial culture and the plantation system. These include Creole language and oral tradition, transforming the standard English of colonial society and its Eurocentric history; the house-yard complex, providing the nucleus of the peasant culture and community; provision grounds and peasant market, transforming the export-oriented monocrop plantation economy; a multiple tenurial complex for yard and ground, maximizing land resources within the constraints of land scarcity; bilateral kinship networks, maximizing ego-focused kinship ties and bases of mutual support and exchange; complex marriage systems of multiple conjugal forms and serial monogamy, transforming colonial legal marriage and maximizing ties of alliance and affinity; and occupational multiplicity, migration and mutual aid, expanding and reinforcing the peasant economy (Besson 1984b, 1987b).

Women as well as men are central to this peasant culture of resistance: as transmitters and trustees of family land, and as crucial agents in socialization, cultivation, marketing, kinship networks, marriage systems and mutual aid. Women also play a central role in the Revival cult, which is an important dimension of the peasant culture of resistance (Besson 1993). Like family land and other aspects of the peasant economy and community, the Revival worldview – which co-exists with the Baptist Church in Trelawny's villages – is rooted in African-Caribbean proto-peasant cultural resistance. Emerging from the Myalist traditions evolved in slavery, Revival, like family land with which it is closely interrelated, can also be seen as reflecting African continuities within the context of a dynamic process of Caribbean culture-building (Besson 1987b, 1988b, 1993), as the following section shows.

The Revival Worldview: African-Caribbean Cultural Resistance

On the Jamaican slave plantations, where the slaves were untouched by Christianity until the arrival of the Nonconformist missionaries in the late eighteenth century, the slaves forged a new African-Caribbean cosmology following the shattering of their African religions. This creative process of Caribbean culture-building and cultural resistance drew on the African baseline beliefs in witchcraft, medicine, ancestral cults, and a pantheon of gods and spirits, remoulding them within the slave plantation system. At the heart of this recreated worldview were the magico-religious cults of Obeah and Myalism (Patterson 1973:182-207; cf. Mintz 1970).

Obeah was 'essentially a type of sorcery' using 'charms, poisons, and shadow catching' (Patterson 1973:188). Involving clients and an Obeahman, it was practised at an individual level for protection, punishment, or revenge. Obeah was also instrumental in slave rebellions, and in this and other respects, such as the manipulation of spirits, over-lapped with Myalism (Alleyne 1988:84; Patterson 1973:186-95).

Myalism was centred around community rituals including spirit pos-session and the Myal dance, which honoured the African-derived minor spirit deities of the Myal pantheon (rather than the distant Supreme Deity) and the departed ancestors who, it was believed, could possess the living. Integral also to Myalism was the belief in a dual spirit or soul. One spirit, the *duppy*, was believed to leave the body at death and, after remaining for a few days at the place of death or burial, to journey to join the ancestors. Elaborate funeral ritual was practised to effect and mark this transition. Another spirit was believed to be the shadow of the living person, which could be caught and harmed through Obeah and restored by Myalmen. Myalism, which was both a belief system and a re-ligious organization, was modelled on West African secret cult societies, and initiation ceremonies symbolizing death and the restoration to life were also performed. The Myal cult united the slaves in resistant re-sponse to slavery and European values, and was thought to protect their communities from external and internal harm (Alleyne 1988:85-8, 102-3; Patterson 1973:190-5; Schuler 1980:32-3).

Schuler argues that Myalism, which appeared in Jamaica around the middle of the eighteenth century (Robotham 1988:35), 'appears to have been the first religious movement in Jamaica which addressed itself to the entire slave society, rather than to the microcosms of separate Afri-can groups' (Schuler 1979a:129). As such, it may be seen as either the basis of a pan-African solidarity (Schuler 1979a:129) or, perhaps more accurately, of an African-Jamaican identity (cf. Robotham 1988:35). Consistent with both of these perspectives, Alleyne (1988:88-9) con-tends that 'Myalism was the broadest reference' of slave religion in Jamaica, 'and serves as a cover term for all religious observances that developed from African religions'; and that 'Myalism must be viewed along a diachronic continuum of change beginning in Africa, and along a continuum of synchronic variation within the population at any one particular time'.

From the late eighteenth century these African-derived beliefs merged with Christianity, as Nonconformist proselytizing replaced the neglect of the slaves by the planters' Established Anglican Church (Pat-terson 1973:207-15). As noted previously, of particular significance was the teaching of the Black Baptists George Lisle and Moses Baker, American ex-slaves, and the subsequent arrival of British Baptist missionaries. As seen above, the slaves embraced the Baptist faith at a formal level and attended the Baptist Church, which provided an added dimension to plantation life. However, the slaves also remained committed to their Myalist traditions. As a result, two variants of Baptist faith emerged: the 'Orthodox' form, taught by the missionaries and practised by the slave congregations in the churches; and the 'Native' or 'Black' Baptist variant, incorporating and controlled by Myalism, taught by Negro Class Leaders in the proto-peasant context on the slave plantations. This latter variant played a central role in the 1831 slave rebellion, the so-called 'Baptist War', led by the Native Baptist Class Leader, 'Daddy' Sam Sharpe, a domestic slave in Montego Bay, St James (neighbouring Trelawny), which hastened the abolition of slavery (Alleyne 1988:90-1; Patterson 1973:211-12, 273; Schuler 1980:34-7; Turner 1982:94).

After emancipation, this parallel commitment continued among the former slaves. Orthodox Baptist faith provided the formal framework of free village life (Mintz 1974:157-79); while the Native Baptist variant, rooted in Myalism, formed 'the core of a strong, self-confident counterculture' against the persisting plantation system (Schuler 1980:44), and the basis of a Black ethnicity (Robotham 1988:35-6). In the 1860s, Native Baptist beliefs, reinforced by the Myalist Revival of the 1840s and 1850s, and by the religion of post-emancipation African indentured immigrants, contributed to and controlled the Great Evangelical Revival (Alleyne 1988:99-100; Patterson 1973:187-8, 214-15; Schuler 1980:40-1, 104-5). This produced a new African-Christian variant, 'Revival', which is the basis of Jamaica's Revival cults, Revival Zion and Pukumina (or Pocomania), today. Alleyne (1988) describes these contemporary religious forms as 'important points in the continuum of religious differentiation created by the meeting of Myalism and Christianity' (p. 96); with Pukumina being the closer of the two to Myalism, and Revival Zion being nearer to Baptist Christianity (p. 101).

The parallel themes of Orthodox Baptist Christianity and Myalism were very pronounced among Trelawny's proto-peasants and post-emancipation peasantry who, as seen above, were at the heart of Baptist proselytizing in Jamaica and who were also at the centre of the island's Myal movement (Schuler 1980:35, 40-1, 43). These parallel themes form the basis of the dual commitment to the Baptist Church and Revival worldview in Trelawny's contemporary peasant communities. The increasing 'creolization' of Baptist beliefs through Myalism, which occurred within the slavery and post-slavery contexts and generated the Native Baptist variant and the Great Revival, provides the roots of the Revival worldview in Trelawny villages today.

Evidence of the existence of African-Jamaican religion within the context of Baptist free villages dates back to the post-emancipation era (Mintz 1974:157-79). From the perspective of the Baptist Church, this was regarded as 'backsliding':

> 'backsliding' sometimes took the form of religious innova-
> tion, innovation that involved in some ways the restoration
> of the more traditional (or 'African') religious forms that
> had been supplanted by Christianity. (Mintz 1974:177-8)

For example, in the case of Sturge Town founded by the Baptist missionary John Clark in the parish of St Ann (neighbouring Trelawny), Underhill's observations include the following in 1861, around the time of the Great Revival:

> STURGE TOWN TABERNACLE. Rev. John Clark, pas-
> tor ... (It is necessary to mention that this church is a se-
> cession from the church under the native minister, Mr
> McLaggan, and arose out of certain occurrences con-
> nected with Obeahism, in which the minister and some of
> the members were involved) ... There are about 700 per-
> sons in Sturge Town; all attend either the Tabernacle or
> Mr McLaggan's ... Very few backsliders ... People are
> not getting rid of religion, though it is not as it was twenty
> years ago. A little before and after freedom there was
> more piety, everybody 'was going to chapel' ... (Underhill
> 1861:312-13, cited in Mintz 1974:168)

Mintz notes that Underhill's description suggests 'that, while the Baptist Church still wielded considerable influence in the village, new forces had arisen which were causing change in various ways', including the provision of 'competing faiths' (Mintz 1974:168).

In my comparative study of land, kinship and identity in five Trelawny villages in 1983 (Besson 1984b), Revival cults were observed as co-existing with the Baptist Church in at least three of these free village communities: Refuge, Granville and Martha Brae. In the case of Refuge, the Revival leader was the daughter of an elderly woman whose membership of the Baptist Church was the longest in the village, and the daughter had built her Revival cult house in their yard. In Martha Brae, where a study based on participant-observation in the Revival Zion cult was conducted by me in 1983 and followed up thereafter (Besson 1993), it was found that individuals who attended the Baptist Church also participated in Revival Zion. For, as I have argued previously:

> rather than providing competing faiths [from the perspective of the villagers], church and cult in Martha Brae share the same adherents to a large extent and have complementary roles. The Baptist Church provides a formal faith and moral guidelines for daily Christian life, while Revival Zion cosmology orders the villagers' entire world, including relations between the living and the dead, and promotes inter-community solidarity. Furthermore, both have complementary functions in village funerary ritual and mutual aid. (Besson 1987b:123)

In 1983 there were two Revival 'Bands' in Martha Brae, both led by women, and fieldwork focused on the oldest and most active of these groups, led by Mrs K. (Besson 1993). Her leading role as prophetess and healer was supported by her husband's role as chaplain, pastor or preacher, and by a secretary who is female. The cult house is beside the Ks' house in their yard, which is marked by a tall flag-pole believed to be instrumental in attracting the Revival spirit pantheon. Made of corrugated iron sheets, the cult house is furnished with wooden benches, a holy altar, and several goat-skinned drums – symbols of resistance from the slavery past (Campbell 1985:25). Other ritual symbols include bottles of holy water, believed to aid mediation with the spirits; vases of crotons representing the spirit world; and doves, kept outside the cult house in the yard. Revival meetings, attended by both men and women, but especially women, are held three nights a week, each lasting for several hours.

Revival cosmology in Martha Brae closely parallels that outlined by Chevannes in the preceding chapter for the traditional Revival worldview. Revival in Martha Brae is essentially a spirit possession cult related to a cosmology of an integrated world of living beings, God, the spirits and the dead. While the unseen portion of this world includes the Christian Trinity, the total spirit pantheon is Africa-derived (cf. Patterson 1973:182-207; Schuler 1979a:133). Likewise, spirit possession and baptism through immersion (the latter taking place on trips to a Revival 'Bands' at Lethe on the Great River in St James), stem, as Schuler notes of Myal, 'from an African and not a Christian or European tradition' (1979a:133). The spirits, including the spirits of the dead, are thought to cause good fortune and misfortune and to be open to influence for good or evil. The latter is believed to be effected through an Obeahman, while the former is the true role of Revival.

Spirit possession in Revival – believed to be induced through drumming, dancing, the singing of Revival hymns and 'trouping' around a basin of holy water, and culminating in trance and sometimes glossolalia – is seen as enabling communication with the spirits for protection, prophesy and healing. Individual members of the congregation experience different stages of possession, the most intense being manifested by the 'Leadress', Mrs K. It is believed that the spirit world may also be revealed to individuals through visions in dreams (Besson 1988a:51, 1993; cf. Chevannes, Chapter 2, this volume). Contact with the Revival spirit pantheon is perceived as a source of both power and of danger, and this is reflected in the symbolic colours of red and white associated with the cult: white symbolizing the sacred spirit world; red standing for the power and the danger involved in spirit contact. Revival turbans (cf. Chevannes, Chapter 5, this volume) therefore tend to be red or white; and women especially also dress, when possible, in red and white for Revival meetings.

The Revival Zion worldview in Martha Brae may also be seen as African-Caribbean cultural resistance, rooted in the slavery and post-emancipation past. As seen above, Myalism united the slaves against slavery and European values and was thought to protect the slave communities from harm; while the Native Baptist variant was the basis of a Black ethnicity and significant in the 'Baptist War' slave rebellion, which included Trelawny slaves. In the post-emancipation period, Myal and the Great Revival were central to the counter-cultures of resistance that emerged against the persisting plantation system, which retained its stranglehold in Trelawny (Besson 1981, 1987b:113, 124; Robotham 1988:35-6; Schuler 1980). Revival Zion continues this role in contemporary Martha Brae, integrating the peasant community, and is perceived as protecting it against misfortune from neo-colonial society, the spirits and the dead.

Revival Zion in Martha Brae also promotes inter-community solidarity, as did Myal, Native Baptism and the Great Revival in the past. Historically, the 'Baptist War' and the emergence of a Black ethnicity are obvious examples of this theme, another being the way in which this shared body of ritual and belief 'drew semi-autonomous plantation slave villages or free villages together' (Schuler 1979a:128). In Martha Brae, Revival Zion links the village with Revival 'Bands' in other village communities – both elsewhere in Trelawny and in other parishes, especially neighbouring St Ann and St James. Visits are made by Martha Brae Revivalists to 'Bands' in these other communities and are reciprocated by visits to Martha Brae. In the summer of 1983, four such visits to Martha Brae took place (Besson 1993).

The Revival worldview is also reflected in the elaborate rituals surrounding death in Martha Brae (cf. Chevannes, Chapter 2, this volume) and here continuity may be seen with African-derived death rituals on the slave plantations (Besson 1987b:124; Patterson 1973:195-8). The contemporary rituals, consisting especially of the 'lyke-wake' and 'Nine Night' wake, mark and are believed to effect the transition of the *duppy* of the deceased to join the spirits of the dead; while the tombing is thought to complete this process of transition (cf. Hertz 1960). Should these 'rites of passage' (van Gennep 1960) be incomplete, it is believed that the restless, unplaced *duppy* will wander among the living causing harm. One such reputed case is well known in Granville and Martha Brae.

In Martha Brae, Revival mortuary ritual also comforts the bereaved and symbolizes community solidarity. Grave-digging is also a community responsibility, the only payment being rum to keep the *duppy* at bay (cf. Chevannes, Chapter 2, this volume). Despite this communal service, mortuary ritual entails large expenditures by the bereaved and this is generally organized through the village Friendly Society, which regulates ritual mutual aid. The Society also officiates at funerals and holds annual fund-raising 'Anniversaries'.

The Baptist Church plays a complementary role to the Revival cult in such mortuary ritual and mutual aid in Martha Brae. Funeral services are often held in the William Knibb Memorial Baptist Church in Falmouth, following village wakes and before proceeding back to Martha Brae for the burial – where the Falmouth Baptist minister may also officiate. The fund-raising Anniversaries may also be held at the Baptist Church or William Knibb Memorial School, situated between Falmouth and Martha Brae.

Burial also reflects the interrelationship of the Revival cult and Baptist Church in Trelawny's post-slavery villages; for the graves that are the focus of Revival ritual are located on Baptist free village land. Such land has also often been transformed into family land estates, with family burial grounds linking the living and the dead of the Revival worldview. In contemporary Martha Brae burial is in the village cemetery rather than in family land yards, but oral history indicates that in the post-emancipation past interment was in the yard, the change being due to health regulations regarding proximity to the urban settlement of Falmouth. In Granville, one mile further inland from Falmouth than Martha Brae, the traditional pattern of yard burial continues undisturbed. The same is true of Refuge, six miles east of Falmouth and three miles west of Duncans. In Kettering, adjoining Duncans, the transformation of the traditional burial pattern that occurred over time in Martha Brae is reflected here spatially, for family land burial persists in those parts of Kettering furthest from Duncans town, while other Kettering burials now take place in the Duncans cemetery. In Alps, the most remote of the five communities studied and Trelawny's first free village, the family burial grounds are the most extensive (Besson 1984b:18-19).

These family burial grounds, which symbolize the family lines at the heart of Trelawny's post-slavery peasant communities, have been a central feature in the transformation of Baptist freehold land to family land. The family burial grounds also reflect the embedding of the Revival worldview and the peasant culture of resistance in the formal framework of the Baptist free village land settlements – where the Rastafari movement is also now emerging.

Rastafari in the Peasant Culture of Resistance

Like the Revival worldview, the roots of Rastafari can be traced in part to eighteenth century Jamaican slave religion, with the emergence of the ideology of Ethiopianism among the plantation slaves (Barrett 1977:68), a link that Barrett observes is seldom made (p. 70). Barrett argues that 'By the time of the emergence of the Black churches' in ante-bellum America:

> Africa (as a geographical entity) was just about obliterated from [the slaves'] minds. Their only vision of a homeland was the biblical Ethiopia. It was the vision of a golden past – and the promise that Ethiopia should once more stretch forth its hands to God – that revitalized the hope of an oppressed people. Ethiopia to the Blacks in America was like Zion or Jerusalem to the Jews. (Barrett 1977:75)

Barrett notes that Ethiopianism developed even earlier in Jamaica and highlights its link with the Baptist Church and the subsequent development of the Native Baptist variant:

Long before Ethiopianism came to America, the term had
been adopted in Jamaica by George Liele, the American
Baptist slave preacher who founded the first Baptist
Church in the island in 1784 – which he named the
Ethiopian Baptist Church. This church ... grafted itself
onto the African religion of Jamaican slaves and developed outside of the Christian missions, exhibiting a
pure native flavour .... From it came the grass-roots resistance to oppression. (Barrett 1977:76)

The ideology of Ethiopianism would flower in the twentieth century into
the Rastafari movement, nurtured by the teachings of Marcus Garvey,
the crowning of Ras Tafari as Haile Selassie, the preaching of the Howellites, and the innovations of the Youth Black Faith (Barrett 1977;
Chevannes, Chapter 4, this volume).

Barrett also sees a link between the first Rastafarian community of
Pinnacle, established by Howell around 1940 'deep in the hills of St Catherine', and 'the Maroon communities of Jamaica' (Barrett 1977:86).
However, a closer parallel would be with Sligoville, Jamaica's first free
village, founded in the St Catherine hills (Paget 1964:46). From these
perspectives, too, Rastafari can be seen as a variation on the African-
Jamaican tradition of slave and post-slavery resistance.

The link between the ideology of Ethiopianism and the Baptist
Church during slavery can be clearly seen for the parish of Trelawny.
For in the Falmouth Baptist Church, whose congregation during slavery
consisted mainly of slaves from Trelawny plantations, a plaque com-
memorating emancipation was erected by 'The Sons of Africa' – namely, the Trelawny slaves. This plaque can still be seen in the William
Knibb Memorial Baptist Church, with the following inscription:

Deo Gloria! Erected by emancipated Sons of Africa. To
commemorate the birth-day of their freedom, August The
First 1838. Hope hails the abolition of slavery throughout
the British colonies as the day-spring of universal liberty.
To 'All nations of men, whom God hath made of one
blood'. – 'ETHIOPIA shall soon stretch out her hands
unto GOD' LXVIII Psalm, 31 verse.

Below the inscription is carved the profile of the Baptist missionary,
William Knibb, who championed the emancipation cause. As seen
above, Knibb would also lead Jamaica's post-slavery village movement,

especially in Trelawny, with the establishment of villages such as Alps, Refuge, Kettering, and Granville. Within these communities would flower the rich complex of interrelated religious forms – the Baptist Church, Revival and the Rastafari movement – which co-exist in their contemporary peasant cultures of resistance; and which are rooted in the interweaving of Myalism, Baptist Christianity, Ethiopianism and the Native Baptist faith that were variants of religious resistance among the Trelawny slaves.

However, while co-existing with the Baptist Church and Revival in contemporary Trelawny villages, Rastafari is less prominent in these communities than either. Historical, geographical and cultural factors account for this, as well as the age structure of these communities.

For example, while the roots of Rastafari go back to the ideology of Ethiopianism in Jamaican slave religion (Barrett 1977), and while Baptist Christianity, the Native Baptist variant and the Ethiopian theme co-existed in Trelawny at emancipation, the Rastafari movement itself has a shorter history than either the Baptist Church or the Revival worldview as variants of resistance among the Jamaican slaves and their descendants. Emerging in the 1930s, following the teachings of Marcus Garvey and the coronation of Ras Tafari, the movement only gelled with the Howellites at Pinnacle in the St Catherine hills in the 1940s and the Youth Black Faith in the 1950s (Barrett 1977:80-9; Chevannes, Chapter 4, this volume).

The destruction of Pinnacle by the police in 1954 dispersed the Howellites to Kingston and other parts of Jamaica, and only since then has the Rastafari movement grown in the rural parishes. Within this context Rastafari has spread to the parish of Trelawny and taken root within the peasant cultures of resistance in free villages such as Granville, Kettering, Alps and Martha Brae. Rastafari arts and crafts also now play a significant role in the tourist industry, and are displayed in stalls along the Falmouth-Montego Bay North Coast Road in Trelawny and St James.

However, cultural factors contain the growth of Rastafari in Trelawny's villages. For, as noted previously, the parish was the centre of Myalism and Baptist missionary work in Jamaica, and continues as a stronghold of both the Baptist Church and the Revival worldview. The age structure of the Trelawny village communities also inhibits the rapid spread of Rastafari. For the core of these villages are the 'Older Heads' (cf. Chevannes, Chapter 5, this volume), the older representatives of the Old Families and trustees of their family land. These are the stalwarts of the Baptist Church and the Revival religion, while Rastafari tends to be found among young men. Heavy rural-urban and overseas migration

have been major factors in determining the age structure of these communities, while migration in turn is closely interrelated with the poverty
of the peasant economies and the rationale of family land. For the latter
is a symbolic as well as an economic resource, ensuring freehold rights
to all descendants in perpetuity and a place to go in time of need. As
such it encourages migration by those with other options, especially
among the young (Besson 1979, 1984a, 1984b, 1987a, 1987b, 1988a; cf.
Mintz 1984).

Within the context of these constraints, Rastafari co-exists with the
Baptist Church and Revival worldview in Trelawny's villages. Moreover,
this co-existence sometimes occurs within the same household or village
yard. For example, in Granville the male Revival leader has a Rastafari
son who shares his household; while in Martha Brae a woman who is
committed to both the Baptist Church and Revival cult has a Rastafari
'son-in-law' living in her yard. The central figure of contemporary Alps,
Mr B., a stalwart of the Baptist Church and member of several of the
village's overlapping Old Families including the central family line (Besson 1984b:17-18), also has a Rastafari son living in his yard. This 'Dread'
is well versed in the Rastafari faith and has links with Prince Edward
Emmanuel, 'one of the oldest Rastafarian leaders since the days of Leonard Howell', whose 'leadership is still the strongest and his group the
most organized on the island' (Barrett 1977:94). Originally situated in
Back-o-Wall in the slums of Kingston destroyed by the Jamaican government in 1966, Prince Edwards' 'camp' is now located in Bull Bay in
St Thomas (Barrett 1977:156-8, 181-185), on 'seven or eight acres of
"captured lands"' (p. 182). Mr B's Rastafari son is part of this organization and regards his name, including his Old Family's surname, as his
'slave name in Babylon'.

This emergence of the Rastafari movement within Trelawny's peasant cultures of resistance, and its co-existence within this context with
the Baptist Church and the Revival worldview, raises many questions
for research into the intra-community dynamics of these religious variants, including the attitudes and relationship of Rastafarians to land, the
basis of these free communities. It was shown above how both the Baptist Church and Revival worldview interrelate with Trelawny free village
land, and an example from Granville village will serve to suggest how
Rastafarians in these communities are a variant on this theme.

A Rastafarian 'crew' (cf. Peter Wilson 1973) often meets under a
shady tree in a Granville yard, where two members of the group live on
family land in this free village community. The focus of the crew is a
dice-and-board game reflecting the Rastafari faith. The board is bright-

ly painted in Rastafarian colours: red, green, gold and black – a combination (as the Dread in Alps explained) of the red, gold and green of the Ethiopian and Israel Covenant, and the red, black and green of the Marcus Garvey Covenant. The route pursued around the board – 'Jamaica, Ethiopia, Adis Ababba, Home' – reflects the Rastafari repatriation theme. Three different styles of dreadlocks adorn the Rastafarians' heads and, on one occasion, a member of the crew had just prepared some *I-tal* (natural, salt-free) food. The crew – four young men and an 'Older Dread' – explained that there are not many Rastafarians in Granville, but that they are part of a wider Rastafari network spreading from the village to other parts of the parish, Montego Bay, Kingston and Prince Edward Emmanuel in St Thomas:

> We are not individually, we are universally. When we get together for meetings, we go to Kingston. We have certain dates in every month, such as the date for the King [Haile Selassie's] birthday, when we celebrate. We meet any part that they choose. The other day we ask for Hague show ground [in Trelawny], but up to the time they don't give the key to us.
>
> [We are] not in Granville alone. We scatter all round over the whole district [in Trelawny]. Plenty Rastas. . . . [We go] different, different places. Sometimes it keep at Bogue, in St James; keep in Kingston at Nine Miles, after you pass Harbour View. They have direct time, they have a time they keep it. They have meetings there regular. At Prince Edward's we keep regular. [I go there] whenever I find it possible.

Despite this island-wide Rastafari network and Ethiopian ideology, the Granville 'Dreads' are firmly rooted in the Trelawny peasant culture of resistance, for the Older Dread and his adult son, who hosts the crew, live on family land in a free village yard. The trustee for the family land is the Older Dread's maternal aunt, Miss E. who in 1983 was nearly 70 years old. She was born in Granville in 1914, grew up in this yard, has lived here all her life, and has never been abroad. The land, about one acre, was purchased by her parents and transformed to family land through customary transmission to their seven children and their descendants, and by burial in the yard:

> [The land was passed on] just by word of mouth, for all the
> children and we are to live on the land, and the land is not
> to be sold. Every family come and live on the land, and
> pass it on to the generations .... Graves on the land ...
> my mother and father, and also a son.

Miss E. herself also plans to be buried in the yard.

There are four houses on the land, one empty and in disrepair. Miss
E. lives in a second house with her adult daughter, who was 24 years old
in 1983. In a third house lives the Older Dread ('I and my father Jah'),
who in 1983 was 58 years old. Born in Hammersmith, a nearby village in
Trelawny, he came to Granville as a child to live here in this yard, and
inherited his chattel house from his mother, sister to Miss E. He is a
peasant farmer who, in addition to a little cultivation in the yard, farms a
provision ground wherever he can find access to such land:

> I do my own work, like farming, anywhere I can get. I farm
> at other else place on free land [on the properties around],
> but farming just now in the Deeside area [near another
> Trelawny village], farming about a acre, and plant every-
> thing that can plant. I don't pay rent. The owner of that
> place give it to farmers to work free.

His adult Rastafarian son lives in the fourth chattel house, 'a board
house with two rooms' built by the Older Dread, who used to live there
himself, and which is embellished with Rastafari graffiti on the door:
'Jah lives within. Do not disterb [sic]'. A male friend of the younger Rastafarian shares this house with him. The friend is related to another
Rastafarian – the son of Granville's male Revival leader – who lives in
another Granville yard. The Older Dread's Rastafarian son was born in
Kingston, 'came to Granville long ago' and is now a mechanic by trade.

Miss E., the trustee for this family land, has had eleven children, one
of whom died and was buried in the yard. The father of the first seven of
these children is a member of one of Granville's central family lines,
which also has family land in this free village community. Miss E.'s
children, now all adults, are scattered throughout Granville, Kingston
and overseas. But 'all of them could use the land', as can her 'plenty'
grandchildren who 'could come in and use the land'. Her siblings, who
retain inalienable rights to the land have all gone abroad, but 'if they
want they could come and pick [from the fruit trees on the land]. Don't
have to get permission to pick. [And] they could build on the land'. In-

deed, all the 'generations' descended from Miss E.'s parents have these same inalienable rights to this family yard. As noted previously, this principle of unrestricted cognatic descent lies at the heart of family land as an institution of cultural resistance, and contrasts with the traditional principle of primogeniture in colonial legal freehold. Thus, in this family land yard the Rastafarian culture of resistance is embedded in the Caribbean peasant culture of resistance, with its central themes of family lines and family land.

The Significance of Land in the Rastafari Movement

The theme of land, so significant in the above case study of the Granville Dreads and so central to both the Baptist land settlements and the Trelawny peasant culture of resistance, is a crucial theme for understanding symbols, continuity and change in the Caribbean Rastafari movement. For attitudes and relationships to Caribbean land are central to gauging the true orientation of Rastafari, generally regarded as a 'Back to Africa' or Repatriation movement. Yet as Chevannes points out (chapter 2, this volume), the Rastafari search for the millennium occurred only once in the first two decades, three times between 1958 and 1960 and thereafter not once. Against this in the balance is the growth, establishment and spread of the Rastafari movement as a Caribbean culture of resistance, and its development as a vehicle of pan-Caribbean identity (Barrett 1977; Campbell 1980; de Albuquerque 1980). Within this context the centrality of Caribbean land to Rastafari has not received the full attention it deserves. However, some authors do provide brief insight into the relationship between Rastafari and Caribbean land, and this penultimate section of the essay draws together material on this theme reinforcing the Trelawny case study.

As seen above, Barrett (1977:182) notes the re-establishment of Prince Emmanuel's Rastafari camp on captured lands in St Thomas, and his account of the Rastafarians of Jamaica briefly returns time and again to the theme of land. For example, he interprets the Rastafari movement as 'a reaction to the grinding poverty experienced by the peasant class' (Barrett 1977:110) and notes that, as the Rastafarians:

> prefer to eat foods from their own plantations [*sic*] . . . one
> of the most coveted items among the cultists is land on

which they can live and cultivate their own foods. A Montego Bay 'dread' put it this way: 'We need lands on which we can pitch the tents of Jacob'. (Barrett 1977:142)

Elsewhere Barrett (1977:225) observes that '[t]he constant cry of Rastafarians is for land on which to live and work'. He also quotes an extract from *The Rastafarian Voice* of July 1975, which reflects this theme:

> The people of Jamaica are near to starvation. Everywhere there is a hue and cry for food. Government claims it is interested in I and I planting the land. Yet still when I and I plant food to feed I fellow African, I and I are harassed and driven off the land. When will this wickedness stop? (Quoted in Barrett 1977:144)

Ras Samuel E. Brown's article, given by its author to Barrett in 1965, had also focused on the significance of land: 'Without ownership of lands one cannot amount to much' (Barrett 1977:164, 248 n. 11).

Land was also crucial to the process of 'routinization' identified by Barrett, whereby the Rastafarian movement became institutionalized in Jamaican society from around the 1970s, and during which 'the government began to turn its eye the other way to the Rastafarian capture of "crown lands" where communal communities began to develop' and on which 'the cultists built their homes where they lived and worked tax free' (p. 161). Barrett also regards access to land as crucial for the future of the movement, and recommends that there should be 'a conscious effort to place the Rastafarians on land on which to build permanent communes' in Jamaica (p. 227).

De Albuquerque (1980), writing three years later on the spread of the Rastafari movement through the English-speaking Caribbean and its significance as a vehicle of Caribbean cultural identity, also touches on the significance of the theme of 'captured lands'. He notes that in Dominica, the capturing of land by 'Dreads', 'on which to raise fruits and vegetables', was seen by the Establishment as 'setting a dangerous example for the landless poor and challenging the proprietary members of society' (p. 238). He notes further that 'squatting on land or "land capture" [by Rastafarians] has become increasingly popular, particularly in Jamaica and Trinidad'; and that 'in Jamaica, it had the tacit sanction, now since withdrawn, of the Manley government' (p. 238).

In examining factors influencing the spread of the Rastafari movement through the Caribbean region, de Albuquerque also refers to the significance of access to land:

> The availability of land, preferably in the hills, for squatting, growing herbs, and ground provisions, is an important variable contributing to the growth of the Rastafari community in the E-sC [English-speaking Caribbean]. The movement in Jamaica had its roots among the urban unemployed [*sic*], but the persecution of Rasta in Jamaica resulted in a rural exodus in the early 1950s – thus establishing an alternative to urban shanty town living. In a similar fashion the persecution of Rasta in Trinidad, Dominica and St Croix has resulted in a rural exodus – a latter-day marronage – or to use the metaphor of Rasta youth – slaves running away from the urban plantation, fleeing the pernicious influence of Babylon and the harassment by its agents.
>
> In smaller islands where tenure rights to every piece of land are widely known and recognized, the Rastafari movement has remained quite small . . . . (de Albuquerque 1980:241)

As noted previously, Jamaica's first Rastafari community was the rural settlement of Pinnacle in the St Catherine hills (rather than the urban shanty towns), established in the 1940s and disbanded and dispersed to Kingston and elsewhere in 1954. However, de Albuquerque's account may be interpreted as pointing to 'the incubation period of the movement . . . in the slums of Kingston between 1930 and 1933' (Barrett 1977:84), and the post 1954 spread of Rastafari from Kingston to the Jamaican countryside and the establishment of rural settlements elsewhere in the region.

In examining the historical background to the Rastafarian movement, Campbell (1985) also notes the significance of land and of the Jamaican free village movement as bases of resistance to the plantation system among the former slaves:

> The planters were vehement in their opposition to free villages such as Sligoville which had been set up by the Baptists, for these villages reduced the number of workers available and enhanced the industrial strength of those

who remained. The movement of the slaves to the hills to form free villages was a clear example of the quest of the Black man to have some control over his labour .... (Campbell 1985:33-4)

And in the years immediately before the Morant Bay Rebellion, when 'strikes broke out on many sugar estates in 1863 and 1864 ... the free village communities became the centres of protest' (Campbell 1985:34). Moreover, the leader of the Morant Bay Rebellion in 1865, which focused on land rights, was 'the spiritual leader of a free village community', for Paul Bogle was a Black lay preacher from the village of Stony Gut, St Thomas (Campbell 1985:35).

Campbell also notes the continuity of land scarcity for the Jamaican masses in the transition from colonialism to neo-colonialism in the 1960s, which formed the context for the growth of Rastafari:

The acute land shortage of the society was further aggravated by the expansion of the bauxite multi-nationals; for as the companies bought up the land of the small farmers the foreign capitalists became owners of over 191,000 acres of land, or 7 per cent of the land area of Jamaica, in 1976. Most of the land was purchased from small farmers, to the point where the activities of the transnationals displaced *560,000* rural Jamaicans from the countryside between 1943 and 1970. (Campbell 1985:86)

Chevannes also touches on the theme of land with reference to the Rastafari movement. For example, commenting on the rural-urban migration of the 1940s generating the slums of Kingston, he notes that 'Up Trench Town also the poor settled on all available pieces of land'; that each such slum 'was a network of yards'; and that it was one of these Trench Town yards that became the camp of Arthur and Panhandle of the Youth Black Faith (Chevannes, Chapter 4, this volume). He also notes that in April 1953 members of the Youth Black Faith staged a demonstration from their Trench Town yard in support of Kenyatta, sentenced to imprisonment for leading the Mau-Mau movement:

To both [the Jamaican] state and society, the Mau-Mau were 'terrorists', but to the Rastafari they were freedom fighters. A group of Rastafari defied the Central Housing Authority and began to rebuild the day after being evicted from Government lands. Their slogan as they set about their work was 'Mau-Mau'!

Significantly 'Mau-Mau', which provided a symbol for Rastafari, was the designation for the Kenyan 'Land and Freedom Army' (Campbell 1985:95).

Conclusion

Though much remains to be researched, the theme of land is clearly central to an understanding of the Caribbean Rastafari movement, for land not only represents crucial threads of continuity and change in Caribbean society from slavery to the present time, but also provides a barometer for assessing the orientation of the Rastafari. The evidence reviewed above on the relationship of Rastafarians to Caribbean land, suggests that Africa is the symbol rather than the reality of Rastafarian resistance. For this resistance is rooted in the Caribbean slave and post-emancipation past, and is interrelated with other aspects of African-Caribbean cultural resistance. These include the Baptist Church and Revival worldview, and the peasant cultures of resistance in which all three religious variants are interwoven. This provides support for Chevannes' thesis that Rastafari is essentially a cultural movement which should not be considered in isolation, and that the Revival-Rastafari link should be explored.

However the Trelawny data highlight more fully than Chevannes' perspective the role of the Revival worldview as a mode of cultural resistance. For while the Rastafari movement has only made an impact in Trelawny since the 1950s, Revival and its precursors – Myalism, Native Baptism and the Great Revival – have been central themes of African-Caribbean cultural resistance in Trelawny, at the heart of Caribbean plantation society, for three centuries of African-Caribbean life (cf. Besson 1987b:125). This underlines the strength of the Revival cult as a vehicle of resistance, rather than as simply a traditional worldview reaching fulfilment only through Rastafari (Chevannes, Chapter 2, this volume).

The alternative perspective on Revival presented in this chapter also highlights the role of women in African-Caribbean cultural resistance, from the days of slavery to the present time (cf. Besson 1992, 1993). During slavery this included the creation of proto-peasant adaptations and the embedding of African-Caribbean culture in plantation slave communities. It was at the heart of these communities that Myalism evolved, a movement which has culminated in the Revival worldview of today; and in Revival, so integral to the peasant culture of resistance, women play a central role as in other aspects of the peasant economy and community. African-Caribbean peasant women are therefore not, as Wilson argues, perpetuators of Eurocentric values in either their daily or religious life; nor are men the sole creators of African-Caribbean cultural resistance, as Wilson's analysis suggests (Wilson 1969, 1973; cf. Wright 1984).

These perspectives on Rastafari and Revival reveal a further link between the two which paradoxically strengthens Chevannes' case. In Revival the symbol of resistance is other-worldly – the Africa-derived spirit pantheon; while in Rastafari it is Africa itself – another country. But in both these religious variants the reality of resistance, as well as their African continuities, are firmly rooted in the dynamic and creative process of Caribbean culture-building, embarked on in resistance to colonialism, neo-colonialism and the plantation system (cf. Mintz 1974:132-3).

From all of these perspectives Chevannes' thesis of Rastafari as Caribbean cultural resistance is more fully underlined. For the Revival-Rastafari link may now be seen as a transformation on a wider theme of African-Caribbean resistance through the complementary modes of accommodation and escape, much of which has been played out in relation to Caribbean land – which was the central focus of plantation slave society (Besson 1984a, 1984b, 1987a, 1987b, 1992; Mintz 1974:75-6, 131-250). For example, during slavery the proto-peasants resisted slavery through accommodation: building new African-Caribbean religions, communities and economies on the slave plantations, where they established customary systems of land use, tenure and transmission in relation to plantation slave yards and provision grounds; while the maroons resisted slavery through escape and the establishment of autonomous agrarian communities. After emancipation some ex-slaves resisted planter power through emigration (Thomas-Hope 1978), while others resisted through establishing free village communities. At the heart of these land settlements evolved the unrestricted descent system of family land, ensuring that migrants and their descendants retained inalienable rights to Caribbean landholdings. Likewise, while Rastafari has resisted through a symbolic escape to Africa, Revival resists within the context of Caribbean free village life. Moreover, it may be, as the Trelawny case study has suggested, that the future reality of Rastafarian resistance may lie, at least partly, in the context of Caribbean free villages and peasant cultures of resistance, where Revival has long had a central place.

Note

1. A first draft of this chapter, entitled 'Religion as Resistance in Jamaican Peasant Life', was presented to the Religious Studies Departmental Seminar at the University of Aberdeen in 1985. That paper was concerned to develop and modify, in the light of data from Trelawny parish, Jamaica, Cross' thesis of a continuum of distinct African-Caribbean forms of religious resistance to colonial orthodoxy in different rural and urban contexts (Cross 1979:96-100). The co-existence of various religious forms as modes of cultural resistance in Trelawny's villages suggests a greater complexity than Cross' thesis, as this chapter – greatly stimulated by Chevannes' perspective on the Revival-Rastafari link – demonstrates.

   The fuller analysis advanced in this chapter was presented, in a previous draft, at the Workshop on 'The Rastafari Movement: Symbols, Continuity and Change in the Caribbean', convened by Barry Chevannes at the Institute of Social Studies, The Hague, in September 1989; and to the Anthropology Department Seminar, National Museum of Natural History, Smithsonian Institution, Washington, D.C., in December 1989 at the invitation of John Homiak. My thanks to Barry Chevannes, John Homiak and all those who commented on these presentations, including the Jamaican Rastafari Elder, Brother Maurice, at the Smithsonian seminar, who supported the analysis of the complex co-existence of religious variants in Jamaican rural communities.

   In this chapter I use the concept 'peasant' as defined by Dalton (1967:265-7; 1971), to denote a broad middle socio-economic category between the two extremes of 'tribal' and 'post-peasant modern farmer', typified by subsistence production combined with production for sale; incomplete land and labour markets; the virtual absence of machine technology; and the retention of traditional social organization and culture to a significant degree. Dalton's definition encompasses various sub-types, including the 'hybrid/composite peasantries' of contemporary Latin America and the Caribbean; and within this sub-type the 'reconstituted peasantries' of the Caribbean may be further distinguished (Mintz 1974:132). The socio-economic organization of the post-slavery villages of Trelawny fits these definitions (Besson 1984a:75-6; 1984b; 1987a:13; 1987b; 1988a; 1992).

   The fieldwork in Trelawny on which this chapter is based was funded in part by the Social Science Research Council, the Carnegie

Trust for the Universities of Scotland, and the University of Aberdeen Travel Fund.

4   The Origin of the Dreadlocks[1]

Barry Chevannes

It is the commonly held view that the long matted hair called dreadlocks
first originated among the Howellites at a place called Pinnacle where
they had settled between 1942 and 1954 (Smith *et al.* 1961). More recent
attempts have been made to trace it to East Indian indentured workers
in Jamaica (Mansingh and Mansingh 1985) and to the Kenyan Mau
Mau warriors (Campbell 1985). This chapter presents fresh oral evidence which establishes that the matted hair complex, which has now
come to characterize the Rastafari, was the innovation of a group of
Rastas known as the Youth Black Faith. Youth Black Faith represented
a reform trend of younger converts bent on purging the movement of
Revivalist beliefs and practices. The evidence is evaluated for its significance in providing the key to unlock the symbolism of dreadlocks. The
reform was prompted by what I believe to have been the failure of the
earlier generation of Rastas to attain any advance on Rastafari goals,
due, so the rebels believed, to a collaborationist attitude to the society.
They substituted instead a defiant rejection of society and an equally
defiant assumption of society's rejection of them as outcasts. This they
symbolized in their dreadlocks. Hair cultivation and treatment are so
paramount in the presentation of self that the dreadlocks phenomenon
merits further contextualizing. This is given in the succeeding chapter
where the specifics of hair symbolism in Jamaica is analysed.

The Youth Black Faith Reform

Hair culture among the Rastafari began in about 1934 with the growth
of beards by certain members. As the practice spread, the name Rastafari became synonymous with *bearded men*, or simply *beards* despite the
fact that many were clean-shaven and the fact that the cult included
women. The dreadlocks trend, on the other hand, had its beginnings

77

late in the 1940s, and was the work of a small band of young converts led by Wato, a migrant worker from the rural parish of St Mary, but including Kurukang, Panhandle and Arthur.[2]

Like the older Rastafari leaders of the 1930s, Howell, Hinds and Hibbert, Wato and his colleagues used to walk the highways and byways preaching the still novel doctrine to the ready ears of migrating peasants, who like themselves had exchanged rustic for urban poverty. Kingston, even in the 1940s, was already bulging with large slums, concentrated in the west where the main markets were to be found. Back-o-Wall had already grown into Ackee Walk, adjacent to the large May Pen cemetery, and stretched a kilometre south all the way to the sea, but for an intervening portion occupied by the Water Commission. Between the Redemption Ground and Coronation Markets was located the Dungle. In Trench Town as well, the poor settled on every available piece of land. Each slum was a network of yards fenced off for privacy with discarded galvanized roofing material, tin sheets and cardboard, and connected by footpaths and alleyways. It was in one of the yards in Trench Town that Arthur and Panhandle lived when Wato met them and they decided to pool resources. Their preaching encompassed parishes as far away as St Ann and Clarendon, but their Trench Town yard served as their base and eventually became a 'camp'. Many brethren simply came there and stayed to listen to or take part in the religious reasoning and discussion.

Theirs was not the only 'camp'. According to informants, there were several around. A 'camp' was any yard where ganja was retailed *and* smoked. Indeed, the idea seemed to have been part of the 'ganja complex'. A very old informant remembered taking part in ganja-smoking contests in the yard of an East Indian who used to peddle it, around the time of the First World War. The East Indians, he said, would take offence if the 'Creoles' (his word) smoked more than they, and once he himself barely managed to escape without injury. From this it may be inferred that as much as eighty years ago ganja smoking, still very much an East Indian activity, used to take place in yards. Judging by present practice among urban-based East Indians, ganja smoking was only a part of a more generalized form of recreation. Conducting research in the Cockburn Gardens community in Kingston in 1971, I was surprised to find that the East Indian Rastas who gathered after work in Bongo Lu's yard conducted no 'divine reasoning' when they smoked the 'herbs'. To them ganja-smoking was, usually, the last of a series of other activities, such as racing 'horses' in the gutter,[3] playing Indian music, or drinking alcohol, after which they retired to their homes. These practices were in striking contrast to those of the African-Jamaican Rastas, among whom the smoking of ganja became an act of serious import. Thus, while the idea of the herbs camp may have had antecedents in the East Indian herbs yard, new elements seemed to have been introduced by the African population, of which the idea of the *camp* was one. What the word was intended to portray was a place open to others to come and remain for as long as they wished, rather than the bivouac of an army. But there were other important innovations as well. Traditionally, ganja smoking was done by male East Indians, using a chillum pipe with a dampened rag, called a *saapi*, wrapped around the mouth. Females smoked only tobacco, but they used the huka, or water pipe. In the camps, however, the huka became the preferred vessel and passed from left to right in the circle of partakers.[4] Other codes in the camps were: emptying the cup only when all the herbs was burnt and not before; constraint against leaving the camp before all the herbs was consumed; and good behaviour while in the camp.

By the time he joined up with Panhandle and the others, Wato would have already been familiar with all this, for he had spent several years in another camp run by a Rastafarian named Gorgon. He would have been familiar also with the strict enforcement of the codes, violation of which could fetch fines and other sentences, such as suspension. Wato's camp was different, in that they made it into an organization, which they called Youth Black Faith.

Anti-Revivalism

Youth Black Faith was founded in 1949 by what we may call activists.[5] They were young and on fire with the doctrine. They were, for the most part, men who entered adolescence in the late 1930s, who left the countryside for Kingston and embraced the faith, or as the Rastafari would say, *manifested* Rastafari, in the following decade. As one of the most influential members, Wato describes the leadership of the new group as being born out of their disgust at the waywardness of the older leaders:

> I remember I and Breda Arthur used to go among Downer and those brethren and hear how they administrate. We walk among them many days and see their movements. And it always impress my spirit so much, that I say of a truth those men who carry the doctrine of Rasta-

fari they really preach and teach. But there was something in the midst. For I know one named Downer who had some other scientific ways to deal with, such as burning candles, and we condemned those things. Men like Hibbert, they have other powers that they use. Yet the prophecy preach against those things. For those men used to burn candles. I wouldn't say directly about the drug store oils; but I know that if you go to the drug store to buy candles to burn for a purpose, peradventure you would want to buy oil too. And seeing that they do these things over and over in our presence, we say that these things are not necessary.[6]

Hibbert, of course, was one of the founders of the Rastafari. Downer had broken from Hinds to form his own group early in the 1940s. This was clearly a revolt against the traditional religious outlook of the Jamaican peasant. Candles of various colours are used extensively in Revival ceremonies. At the same time they are also used by obeahmen. To threaten to 'bu'n candle for' someone implies being willing to contract the evil services of an obeahman, whose range of fetishes, charms and manipulable material includes the 'drug store oils', to which are attributed special powers: oil o' forget me not, oil o' look-but-don't-see, oil o' prempeh, and so on.

Belief in these powers remains strong, as is the general practice of obeah. However, the young radicals couched their repudiation of them in Christian terms, reasoning that burning candles contravened the revelations of the Apostle John, who had declared Christ as 'de only golden candle stick'. Said Brother Wato:

An' we always verse up these things to the elders: 'If you have any candle, let your own self, you' temple be the candle. We will look at you, we will listen to you when you talking to you' administration. We will life you up, for your good organization and your good principle that you have to all the faith. But to any other supernatural thing or auspicious thing you would bring in that is not corresponding to the spirit of truth, we will condemn that'.

They made it clear that they did not reject the old leaders outright. Theirs was not a naked power struggle. Paying them their dues as teachers of the faith, they offered to strengthen what they had already achieved, but in so doing laid down a condition: that they reformed the movement by getting rid of the Revivalisms.

Institutionalization of the Beard

But that was not all they wanted reformed. Up to the period of the Youth Black Faith, the public image of the Rastafari was not a happy one. Most people saw them as a benighted, lunatic fringe. Anyone who could believe that the Emperor of Ethiopia was God, the returned Messiah, Jesus, whom Christians worship, had to be deranged. Their leaders were from time to time interned in the Bellevue mental asylum. Marcus Garvey, while apparently not thinking them harmful, thought they were of no credit to the race. In a letter to the press in 1937, the late Vivian Durham, an attorney, sought cooperation against

> a sudden plague which has besieged this beautiful island.
> ... I refer to a new cult that has taken hold of the unfortu-
> nate and inarticulate masses known as the '*Ras Tafarian
> Cult*' with its headquarters in the parish of Saint Thomas.
> (*The Daily Gleaner*, 6 January 1937)

He proposed banning them from the 'Metropolitan Parish of the Island if not the entire island, at least'. This was followed two weeks later in the same medium by a letter from an ex-soldier in the West India Regiment, who declared that the cult should not be allowed to function, and instead its members be educated to know that they would not be accepted in Ethiopia except as slaves (*The Daily Gleaner*, 21 January 1937).

Not all were entirely against the Rastas, as the contribution of one Mrs Kirton (*The Daily Gleaner*, 6 February 1937) makes clear. Defending race consciousness, she called the 'threatened suppression' of the Ras Tafari movement 'one of the most iniquitous crimes planned against the Black people of Jamaica'. Durham's view, however, and not Mrs Kirton's, prevailed. According to some Rastafari informants, on their way to ceremonial occasions during the 1930s they sometimes had to travel with their ceremonial garb wrapped up in a bag to prevent it being soiled with mud thrown at them. Hostility could be so great at times that at Hinds' Mission a system of guards had to be set up against intruders.

This was the climate of opinion in which the Rastafari bore witness to their faith, some more than others because there was, as yet, no visible distinguishing mark as to who was and who was not a Rastafari. Facial hair culture was not yet a universal feature of the movement. Members of Hinds' King of Kings Mission or of Howell's Pinnacle settlement were apparently quite free to wear beards or not. However, those that did not were quite indistinguishable from the Revival groups or from the increasing number of wayside Pentecostal churches, except when they wore ceremonial dress, at Baptism, for example. Being clean-shaven, they blended easily into the wider background, and in this way escaped public contempt. Bearded men, on the other hand, could be, and indeed were, immediately singled out by the public for what they were perceived as being: a lunatic, anti-social, criminal fringe which thought the Emperor of Ethiopia was God and life in Africa better than in Jamaica. To the members of the Youth Black Faith, these were the truer and more authentic witnesses, not the clean-shaven, who in effect compromised their faith by hiding behind the anonymity of a clean face. Wato again:

> And Downer. Brother Downer now, used to lick out against a man who carry beard, for him don't carry beard – him shave clean. So in fi him House, him never like fi see much of the beard man come in. Him call we ram goat. So it always fiery to I how you teaching about His Majesty Haile Selassie, and is a man who carry beard, yet among the brethren, you just on the brethren about his beard.

Downer's attitude to the bearded men reflected that of the general public. Unlike the earlier generation of leaders, he was not content with being indifferent to beards but, according to Wato, he campaigned against them. His only reason was that the beard, not being accepted by society, was a symbol of the anti-social and sinister. Downer refused to allow the movement to be branded thus. He was clearly the kind of person we would call 'moderate' today. But in light of what was soon to come, even the beard was to seem moderate, as, according to Wato, the reformers began

> to step more deeper in the whole security than the principles and the actions that we see many other brethren, even man who was older than us, administrate. And when we step within the prophecy, we find that most of those action is condemned by the prophecy.

The Youth Black Faith was probably not the only group to insist on the beard, for, as already noted, beards were in vogue among the Rastafari early in the 1930s. Wato's testimony implies that the rationalization at the time was the Emperor himself. Undoubtedly, the sacred Scriptures also contributed their fair share, for to 'step within the prophecy' meant bringing daily practice in line with the word of God. The book of *Numbers* set out clearly the hair taboo to be adopted by those who take the sacred Nazarite vow to set themselves apart. At any rate, by the early 1950s *Bearded men*, or *Beardman* or simply the *Beards*, became the designations by which the Rastafari were referred to by the press.

The Warriors or Dreadfuls

As the Youth Black Faith grew, a new structure evolved. Offices such as leader, chaplain and even the 'secretary', the leftovers of Revivalism, were discarded. A simpler structure took their place: chairman and tableman. The function of the former was that of chief spokesman, to 'make statement as to whatsoever aim and office we have, to administrate to the congregation'. In other words, the convener and guide of all meetings of the organization. The tableman was necessary, since literacy was not high, but he derived his name because his place was at the table where the Bible and all the books to be read were kept. At first, membership was open to all those whose names appeared on the register, but soon the practice was discontinued, because 'we say everyman have free access to the tree of life'. Thus was institutionalized among the Rastas the concept of being *free* – free to come and go, solely on the basis of one's conviction, free from constraint, free to be responsible for one's actions. This concept is now so very much a part of the Rastas that the expression 'the man free' is often used to replace 'Yes', as when one requests something from, or requests permission of, another. Rastas do not coerce or indoctrinate, because 'man free'.

Replacement of registered membership by the concept of conviction had the effect of turning Youth Black Faith into a kind of quasi-organization, which they simply called the 'House,' thereby emphasizing the natural and spiritual bonding which united all therein, rather than the artificial links implicit in membership by registration. But at the same time it had the effect of becoming the single criterion by which control was exercised over the membership, as the more convicted were soon upholding Youth Black Faith principles against their violation by the less convicted. It was in this way that the designation *Warrior* or *Dread-*

ful came to be applied to the more ascetic and disciplined. According to Wato:

> They used to say I was very 'dreadful'. I was very strict to my duties, to see that a man don't come anytime him want to come. Him come whenever the time is appointed. If we say the House is to meet tomorrow morning to discuss something, I always stand up to see that him don't come ten o'clock or twelve o'clock, and all that time. I am always strict to them things.

A duty was an obligation. The group had only one duty as a regular weekly feature, and that was the prayer-meeting which they held every Wednesday night. Other duties were such as the House decided should be convened at other times. These were the formal meetings of the Youth Black Faith, and Wato and Panhandle demanded of other members strict discipline in both punctuality and conduct. The terms *Dreadful* and *Warrior* reflected the manner in which the ascetics behaved: constantly 'at war' with the neglectful, in whom they inspired dread. They were clearly not hated by the others so much as respected and feared with the holy fear of God. In time, then, was added a more appropriate Biblical designation: *Bonogee* (Boanerges), or 'Sons of Thunder', the appellation Jesus gave to the brothers James and John. Those who earned the name were known for the forthrightness and frankness of their critical remarks and defence of the principles on which Youth Black Faith rose up.

Sacralization of Ganja

Outside of formal duties, the Youth Black Faith met in a continuous stream of reasoning, for, as already mentioned, their headquarters was also a camp. This meant that ganja was smoked. Ganja smoking and drinking had become so common throughout Jamaica, that, in adopting the Hague Convention against narcotics in 1913, the Jamaican Government added ganja. Effective measures to suppress both the trafficking and use of it began to be applied only after the Second World War, in part, due to pressure from the United States. Up until the 1950s ganja smoking was not an identifying mark of the Rastas. True, Howell made such a living from it that the police valued the amount seized after their raid on Pinnacle in 1954 at £5,000 at street value. But if news items in the press are anything to go by, many offenders were non-Rastafari. For example, the Salvation Army handed back to the City Council their overnight hostel, 'declaring themselves unable to control the gamblers, thieves, ganja smokers and debauchees who infest' the place (*The Star*, 10 March 1953). People who smoked ganja were not particularly Rastas, but whoever they were, one thing was certain: their activity placed them among the dregs of society.

Pushed underground, ganja was no longer purchased in the open market along with other herbs and plants, but became confined to the camps and individual retailers operating out of their homes. Among the other code names it came to be known by was *the herbs*, or *the weed*.

As ganja trading and smoking came in for increased suppression by the police, some Rastafari groups tried to restrict its use. Hinds, for example, had strict rules, which forbade bringing it into his Mission, let alone using it there, while allowing members the private use of it. Youth Black Faith, however, decided on a different course. Seizing on the name *herbs*, and reasoning that it had divine sanction, so that Government's attempt to suppress it was tantamount to an attempt to suppress the people, the Warriors and Dreadfuls led the House into adopting ganja as an integral part of their movement. Wato explains:

> We don't count ganja as a criminal offence. We show the policemen at all times that we rather if you destroy us. For God says, 'The evil things 'pon this earth is the hand-made things'. These are the things that brought up falsehood 'pon the people, those is the things that destroy the people. So this is not the things that hand-made, this is God's natural creation, and it always virtuous to show the man the Bible and Revelation 22: 'The herbs that bear the various fruits, the leaf of it shall be the healing of the nation'. And in Psalm 104 him says: 'All the herbs that bearing seeds upon the land is made for man'. So this is the chief argument we always confront them whenever we have an attack by the police.

And to make sure that their use of ganja was explicitly religious, Wato said that the Youth Black Faith instructed members of the House not to carry it on their person, so that police action could be targeted not at the individual but at the whole assembly of the faithful:

If the policeman intervene in our congregation, him couldn't find no other charge. The Father say: 'When they persecute you fi other things it is not; but when them persecute you fi the word, I Jehovah God is with you'.

Thus, they did not try to hide ganja or to hide their use of it. But by giving it ritual sanction they were in effect expressing their contempt for the state and society. Ritualization of ganja was not the only form their contempt took.

Early one evening in September 1954, according to Wato, a police constable arrested three members of the Youth Black Faith for indecent language and refusing to give their names. In solidarity many members of the camp were on hand to hear the case tried.

We never go there to make no upsturbance. Each and every one of us who left that habitation, left with this conversation that each man's meditation today is that them free the brethren.

So we was there from court call till court adjourn in the afternoon. Go back to court again after lunch time, then court call around 2 o'clock. And when these brethren was called upon before the court, the Judge remand them until such time. One breda in the lot, called Derminite, he have a spirit that say 'Hoooop! Back them up!' Him never do any other much talking; that was just him sound: 'Hoooop! Back them up!' And him make the sound. A little after, you find that we were surrounded with a lot of police. And while breda Derminite give a hoot, I really gave a sound, 'Fire!' because them time I was a hot 'fire' man. While him say, 'Hoooop! Back them up!' I say, 'Bu'n them! Fire! Bu'n!' That give the Government them strong words, and them was on us.

From there now, we were hold up by the police and beaten, and locked down and charged three months for contempt of court before the final case try. That show the Judge was ignorant and illiterate. For him say, 'What is your name?' 'Ras Tafari!' Him say, 'Thirty days for contempt of court; take him away!' And in the same time, you have fi try the same man with the same name and sentence him to twelve months in prison.

According to the account given in *The Star* (Wednesday, 15 September 1954), the Beards, 'eighteen of them, were arrested in an attempt to free their three colleagues' as the latter were being led from the Half-Way-Tree Court house to the lockup in back. A riot squad had to be called out to quell the disturbance. When called on by the Court, the eighteen refused to give any other name but 'Ras Rasses,' whereupon they were detained for medical examination, which must have found them all sane, for they appeared before the Court the following week. This time they gave their name as 'Ras Tafari,' and were again remanded in custody. The third week, however, his patience no doubt exhausted, the Magistrate cited them for contempt of court and imposed on each a £10-fine or thirty-day prison sentence. The group, which included two women, 'went cheerfully off to the lockup when the sentence was pronounced' (*The Star*, Wednesday, 6 October 1954). According to Wato's oral testimony above, the Judge must have given up, for when they had served their sentence and reappeared in Court, they were sentenced to twelve months on the original charge, under the same name, Ras Tafari.

One might compare this defiant attitude towards the system of justice with the conduct of Leonard Howell before the Court. On the very last day of May 1937, Howell and fourteen others were involved in a riot, sparked by the attempt of outsiders to obstruct their meeting. They received a fine of forty shillings or a prison sentence of thirty days 'despite their defence and their calling in tongues unknown' (*Plain Talk*, 3 April 1937). *The Daily Gleaner* was more specific, reporting that Howell wept, 'calling out in an 'unknown tongue' to the 'King of Kings' to avenge his cause' (2 April 1937).

According to Robert Hill, the 'unknown tongue' was a Hindu prayer, for Howell was fascinated by Hindu mysticism (Hill 1983).[7] The point is, if *The Daily Gleaner* is accurate, that Howell broke down in Court when his defence failed. After all, he had been imprisoned for two years earlier for sedition. The Youth Black Faith, on the other hand, accepted their sentence 'cheerfully'. There was something new here; a new quality had appeared among the Rastafari, a new attitude towards the society. Spearheaded by the Dreadfuls, it needed some symbol to announce both its difference from the earlier compromising trends as well as from the faint-hearted members of the House. This they found in the matted locks.

The Dreadlocks

It should be evident to the reader by now that both head and facial hair were sacred to the many Rastafari who from 1934 wore beards. They neither trimmed nor shaved. Still, they were not locksmen. Their hair was not matted, because, although they did not trim, they combed. Any hair, regardless of texture, will grow into knots if left uncombed, more so if it had been exposed to water. To acquire matted locks one must refrain from combing or brushing it; soon, the strands curl into tufts, which become heavier and heavier the longer they are left to grow uncultured. When such hair is the tough curly hair of Africans, the knots tend to begin almost from the very root.

It is not quite accurate to say that prior to the Youth Black Faith no one wore matted locks. Derelicts did. These were people who, because they had lost touch with reality, had no reason to conform to the acceptable human standards of behaviour. They lived in the open on sidewalks or under trees, foraged among the refuse, talked only to themselves or not at all, were unwashed and foul-smelling. They were outcasts. The prototype was Bag-a-wire. Bag-a-wire was well known because it was said that he had been a close follower of Marcus Garvey on whom Garvey had set a curse for his treachery. The name Bag-a-wire seems to be an elision of 'Bag and wire', from the clothes he wore: burlap or crocus bags held together by wire threads. Society treated him as an outcast: people shunned and children used to stone him. The Dreadfuls and Sons of Thunder knew this was precisely the model society would have of them when they chose the matted hair. Wato explains:

> It appears to I many times that things that the man comb would go out and do, the man with the locks wouldn't think of doing. The appearance to the people when you step out of the form is a outcast. When you are dreadlocks you come like a outcast.

They elected to wear their hair matted, like the outcasts from society, because not only were they treated thus, but they did not consider themselves part of it. As Ethiopians, they wanted out. Some even went as far as adopt the burlap dress of the derelicts, so much so that for many years Rastas were thought to be dirty people. *Dutty* [dirty] *Rasta!* became a curse word. It was even alleged that they matted their hair with grime and dung.

Debate inside the Youth Black Faith became heated. The issue was not whether hair was sacred or not, but whether combing was profane or not. To the Dreadfuls it was. If being clean shaven was one way of conforming to society, so that one's actions could be indistinguishable from those around, so too was combing. In other words, those who combed had the same in common with those who were beardless: they conformed. Thus the beard really did not separate the children of Israel from the children of Babylon, but the outcast did.

Had there been any new developments to suggest that beards, though equated with the Rastafari, had become socially more acceptable? An interesting column in *The Star* of 30 April 1954 had the following to say:

> The popularity of 'Beards' is increasing rapidly in the city. Even members of the higher social stratum have now gone in for hirsute rearing. This new fad has both ideological and economic backgrounds, namely: the suggested visit of the Emperor, Haile Selassie, and a recent increase in the price of razor blades.

The 'suggested visit' alluded to by 'The Feature' column was clearly being mooted publicly, because it was picked up by the People's National Party in a motion moved by Noel Nethersole, destined in the following year to become Finance Minister under the new Norman Manley Government, calling on the Governor to extend to the Emperor an invitation to visit Jamaica after he had completed his state visit to the United States. Haile Selassie had been held in high esteem in Jamaica ever since the Italian invasion. This was the 'ideological' background. But there was more to it than that, which on examination ought to help to clarify even more why the Dreadfuls found it necessary to symbolize their separation even further.

The mooted visit of His Imperial Majesty came against the background of a sustained heightening of the Back-to-Africa movement in Jamaica. From as early as 1945 a march was staged under the slogan, 'Give us work or send us back to Africa', thus linking external migration with the bad internal economic situation, which would have been felt all the more bitterly given the high hopes the year before with the first elected government under universal adult suffrage. Many, having no intention of waiting on the government, actually left for Liberia in 1948, in what was seen as the start of a minor trek (*Daily Gleaner*, 21 August 1948).

Indeed, the Back-to-Africa movement was quite respectable, receiving wide support from the elected politicians. Isaac Barrant, who rose from the lowly status of a labourer to become a popular representative in the Jamaica Labour Party (JLP) Government in the 1940s and 1950s, was a consistent supporter. In 1948, B.B. Coke, another Black member in the JLP Government, moved the following motion in the House:

> Whereas there is great desire on the part of many Jamaicans today to migrate to Liberia for economic and other reasons;
>
> Whereas great difficulties are being experienced by these Jamaicans in obtaining the necessary funds so that they may travel and establish themselves in that Country;
>
> Be it resolved that the Government of Jamaica favourably consider the removal of all hindrances in the way, and the proffering of full aid to those would-be migrants.

The text of the resolution, unanimously passed, makes it quite clear that the movement was not confined to a fringe. The Rastafarians were not the only ones seeking to leave for Africa. Late in 1949 a delegation led by the Liberian Assistant Secretary of State paid a visit to Jamaica and raised further hopes for 'the permanent settlement in Liberia of people of African descent from the West Indies' (*Jamaica Daily Express*, 31 December 1949). Relations with Liberia were to reach an all-time high with the state visit, four years later, of President Tubman.

In such a climate, Back-to-Africa marches, such as the one led by the Garveyite Z. Munroe Scarlett in August 1950, which included one of the founders of Rastafari, Archibald Dunkley and his King of Kings Ethiopian Mission, were a common enough event around Kingston. Thus, when the People's National Party tried to get the Governor to invite His Imperial Majesty to Jamaica in May of 1954, the Party had widespread support behind it. The Governor took the request to his Executive Council, his Cabinet, which issued the following rather significant reply:

> The Council has decided that you should be informed that while all the members of the Council hold the Emperor in highest esteem and would welcome any opportunity to pay respect to him, there are reasons which, in the opinion of the Council, make it undesirable to pursue the suggestion which you have put forward.

> In particular, the Council have in mind that there are
> small numbers of people in Jamaica who might cause em-
> barrassment to the Emperor if he visited Jamaica, and that
> the actions of these people might be offensive to the Em-
> peror and be harmful to the reputation of Jamaica. (*The
> Star*, 24 April 1954)

The Executive Council turned down the request to invite the Negus of
Africa to visit Jamaica on grounds that there are 'small numbers' of
Jamaicans who would be a source of embarrassment to him and Jamaica. There can be no doubt that the Rastafari were meant. But at the
same time, the Council was at pains to point out that the Emperor was
held by its members 'in highest esteem'.

What seemed to have been taking place was a co-optation by the society of some of the main symbols of separatist identity. It had quite
suddenly become respectable to have relations with the two independent African nations, Ethiopia and Liberia, and to talk of migration
there. The word 'Africa' no longer stood completely for savagery and
darkness. This was the full import of the 'ideological background' suggested by the *Star* columnist. No doubt, 'decent' people could now be
counted among those who hold African heads of state and their countries in esteem.

This co-optation created the need for new symbols of resistance and
identity among the people, where interest in Africa was at no time confined solely to the question of migration. Jamaicans have always felt a
genuine affinity with the peoples of the continent, a feeling which today
finds expression in the many and frequent acts of solidarity with the
people of South Africa. But back in the mid-1950s, the feelings of solidarity were with Kenya. In January 1953 a large public meeting in Jones
Town passed a resolution calling on Britain to withdraw her troops from
Kenya and instead seek alternate ways of dealing with the Mau-Mau.
The word 'Mau-Mau' soon became a catch-word used to express defiance. By 1954 there was a well-entrenched criminal gang calling itself
the Mau-Mau, strong enough to battle with the police for 'several
hours,' before their leaders were captured.

And so, while identification with certain leaders and peoples of Africa was no longer the source of shame it once was before Marcus Garvey, identification with the Mau-Mau now became, for an important
segment of the urban masses, one way of expressing exactly how they
felt about the society. This was at the same time that the banana-boat
trek to England was gaining momentum, and with it the idea that, with

Jamaica hardly being the place where one can make a livelihood, one's future lay across the sea. That vast, blue expanse of water became a powerful symbol of hope and at least earthly salvation for the large numbers of workers and peasants, who, many of them beholding the sea for the first time, braved the unknown in search of a better life. It was a symbol of hope, too, for the many who could not muster the £75 for the voyage, or who, convinced that it was the duty of those who brought them against their will to these shores to return them whence they came, waited for the seven miles of Black Star liners to arrive to take them to Africa.

The members of the Youth Black Faith were adamant that they did not belong in Jamaica, and so they developed a more aggressive stance against the state and the society. From their Trench Town headquarters they staged a protest demonstration in support of Kenyatta in April 1953, when it was announced that he had been sentenced to seven years in prison for organizing and directing the Mau-Mau. To both state and society, the Mau-Mau were 'terrorists', but to the Rastafari they were freedom fighters. A group of Rastafari defied the Central Housing Authority and began to rebuild the day after being evicted from government lands. Their slogan as they set about their work was 'Mau-Mau!' And one 'Bearded man' was actually fined £20 for 'preaching the Mau-Mau doctrine', for saying, that is, that 'the people of Kingston should organize themselves "so we can chase the White man out of this country"' (*The Star*, 18 August 1953). In April 1954 when the Youth Black Faith members were arrested for marching through the city without a permit, they had no particular objective in mind other than that Brother Arthur had received a vision that they should. It was exactly one year since Kenyatta was imprisoned. They not only refused to give their names, but created such a disturbance in court with biblical quotations and unknown tongues that the judge had them gagged, strait-jacketed and examined by Monsignor Gladstone Wilson, a psychologist. It was several weeks before they could reappear in court, whereupon Mr Justice Duffus simply admonished and dismissed them. Said Brother Arthur,

> Same time we here 'pon the work, same time Kenyatta
> there 'pon the work in Kenya. So this Youth Black Faith is
> the first throughout the whole world march for freedom!

To identify with the Mau-Mau was to identify with people regarded as criminals and anti-social elements. The Youth Black Faith conceived of themselves as a people struggling to leave a society to which they felt they did not belong. They took on a more aggressive, non-compromising stance. This they symbolized in adopting a new approach, a new way of presenting themselves: the dreadlocks. The Dreadfuls or Warriors were the first to start the trend, and as their hair grew they became even more 'dreadful'. According to Kurukang, who credited himself with introducing the nyabinghi dance into the Youth Black Faith, the debates were heated. The Dreadfuls were very vociferous and quarrelsome. They were so uncompromising that they brought about a split, as those who could not take the new order 'shif up', that is, departed their various ways. By 1960 there were two Houses, the House of Dreadlocks and the House of Combsomes. In 1961 when an official mission was being sent to Africa to examine the possibilities for migration there, the three Rastafari members of the delegation included one young Dread. By the middle of the 1960s the Combsomes had all but vanished, as would appear even from Leonard Barrett's fieldwork (1968).

An Assessment

It is entirely possible that the account presented here failed to overcome the distortions inherent in oral testimonies (see, for example, Henige 1982; Mercer 1979; Vansina 1973). I do not deny this. For example, there is no doubt that in relying on Brother Barnes, an eighty year-old tailor who turned out to be one of my most important brokers, I was led down a path trod mainly by Hinds' group and therefore missed more of those who belonged to groups led by other founders, with their own alternative experiences, views and insights. Indeed, given the dissatisfaction of the Youth Black Faith founders with the earlier leaders, one cannot rule out the theory that in the interest of their own self-promotion they could have suppressed the Howellite angle of the origin of the Dreadlocks. However, what gives the Youth Black Faith explanation the decisive edge, in my opinion, is the corroboration with other oral sources. First, three Howellites residing in Tredeager Park, a few miles from Pinnacle, where they moved following their 1954 dispersal, denied that there had been Dreadlocks there. Corroborative evidence also came from Kurukang. I came to know him only because a broker-contact in the Tower Hill community of Kingston thought he might have been a Rasta 'ancient' from the 1930s. He was not, but during the several weeks he spent tracking down Brother Barnes, he happened to recount many things, including the Youth Black Faith story, the war between the Dreadlocks and the Combsomes and the role of Wato, whose testimony

he later corroborated. What gave Kurukang's testimony special value
was that throughout his years in the Youth Black Faith he was, and had
remained up to the time of the interview, a Combsome. I judged him as
having little personal interest in promoting Youth Black Faith as the
originator of the Dreadlocks knowing that this was not so.

Mansingh and Mansingh (1985) do not venture to say why, if as they
claim there were locksmen from as early as the late 1930s, it took over
two decades for dreadlocks to become popular, or why the practice was
adopted from the Hindu workers. The question is highly relevant because while among the Hindus matted locks were a sign of a holy man,
among the African-Jamaicans it was a sign of the insane and derelict.
While it is true that both prophet and derelict have one thing in common, namely their marginality from society, it is by no means insignificant that the holy man is a revered intercessionary, whereas the derelict
is a despised vagrant outside society altogether. It seems odd that Rastafari would have emulated the matted hair practice of the Hindu sadhus but discard its symbolic meaning. And why imitate sadhus, when
there are derelicts? Was the intention that they be taken as Black sadhus rather than outcasts? And why would the Howellite guards adopt
the symbol of holy men, when their function was not to be revered but to
guard?

In bringing this chapter to an end, I need to point out that the position I have presented does support that of Horace Campbell, except in
one respect. While we concur that dreadlocks was a phenomenon of the
1950s, not prior, he nevertheless maintains that it was adopted in keeping with the warrior image of the Mau-Mau, whereas I have argued that
it was adopted in keeping with the lunatic image of the outcast. One is
active, the other passive. Furthermore, the Youth Black Faith evidence
contains elements of both the warrior and derelict origins of dreadlocks.
The truth is that the contradiction is not one of logic but of real life. As I
have shown, to the non-Rastafari Jamaican public matted hair was the
sign of lunacy, dereliction and withdrawal from society.[8] Jamaicans had
no reason to believe that the people who started wearing locks were
warriors rather than derelicts. We must not forget that the Courts regularly remanded Rastas in custody for medical examination. Public attitude would have been shaped by stories like that of the 'bearded Rastafarian who went to King's House grounds yesterday gesticulating and
shouting "justice and mercy"'. By the time the radio car arrived, he had
vanished only to turn up at the Half-Way-Tree police station later in the
day 'repeating his calls for "justice and mercy!"' He was arrested and
charged for lunacy (*The Star*, 16 April 1955). All Rastafari who stepped

out of line with the society were first thought of as mad and *then* dealt with harshly when found not to be: Howell, Hinds, and Dunkley were at the head of an illustrious list that later included Claudius Henry and unnamed others. Resistance to the University *Report*, when it first appeared, was in part motivated by a feeling that it defended lunatics. Monsignor Gladstone Wilson, who argued that line, was the very person called on to examine the Youth Black Faith members who were arrested for marching without a permit. One of Wilson's doctorates was in psychology.

In short, the derelict image of the Dreadlocks was the public's perception of them. The only doubt now concerns whether the dreadlocks originated first inside the Youth Black Faith, as the evidence presented above leads me to claim, or among the I-gelic House as the evidence in Chapter 6 leads Jake Homiak to claim. Both versions agree that the innovation was intentionally symbolic. To the Dreadlocks and the cause for which they stood, they were warriors, dreadful; to the society lunatics and outcasts. Public image was soon to change, first with the Claudius Henry affair in 1960 and the Coral Gardens incident in 1963, when violence erupted, lives were lost, and the image of an aggressive fanatical sect took root. By then, as I have said, most Rastafari were already Dreadlocks.

Conclusion

The new evidence presented here indicates that the dreadlocks phenomenon was the innovation of a younger group of Rastafari adherents who, disillusioned with the relationships of their elders to the society, sought greater symbolic distance from it, which they found in the matted locks. As such it is at variance with earlier suppositions that the practice emanated from the Howellites. While the evidence is consistent with the more recent view of a Mau-Mau origin, it is argued that the Youth Black Faith Rastafari who adopted the practice were also very much aware that to the Jamaican public they were adopting the role of derelicts and outcasts.

Notes

1. This chapter is based on doctoral research carried out between 1974 and 1975, while I was a Research Fellow at the Institute of Social and Economic Research, UWI, Jamaica. An earlier version was presented at the 13th Conference of the Society for Caribbean Studies, Hoddesdon, UK, 4-6 July 1989.

2. All but Panhandle were interviewed. Kurukang was living at the time in the working class suburb of Tower Hill, while Brother Arthur had returned to live on family land in the parish of Manchester.

3. 'Horses' were small pieces of floatable material – hard plastic or cardboard, which the owners put to race in the gutter. This activity always took place after heavy rain.

4. The explanation that in being passed the cup comes from the heart seems more like a rationalization for a cultural practice common to Revival and Kumina, in which the circle of dancers move from left to right.

5. E.S.P. McPherson and L.T. Semaj (1985), however, put the date of the founding of YSB as 'early 1940'.

6. This and subsequent quotes from Brother Arthur and Brother Wato are taken from interviews conducted with them between May and July 1974.

7. Without disputing that Howell's unknown tongue might have been Hindi, I think it hardly likely that the Rastafari who on several instances up to the 1950s were reported as speaking in unknown tongues were speaking in Hindi. These were not Howellites. In my view the practice was a vestige of Revivalism.

8. This point is dealt with more fully in Chapter 5.

5   The Phallus and the Outcast: The Symbolism of the Dreadlocks in Jamaica

Barry Chevannes

The use of head, facial and body hair, or the lack of it, to convey meaning is a fairly universal phenomenon. Matted hair in particular, may be found in widely different parts of the world – Africa, India, North America and Western Europe. Leach (1958), in his well-known essay, finds the 'link between hair as a symbol and the phallus as a symbol' persistent in ethnography. He argues that while anthropology may not accept psychoanalytic methodology, psychoanalytic theory may nevertheless be quite useful in illuminating that link. Obeyesekere (1981), giving psychoanalytic method a higher rating than Leach, uses life history data to argue that the matted hair of some Sri Lankan female ascetics is a sublimation of the penis. Unhappy that such theories of the subconscious origin of symbols are not subject to empirical verification, Hallpike (1969:261) advances the view that 'Long hair is . . . a symbol of being in some way outside society, of having less to do with it, or of being less amenable to social control than the average citizen'. Synnott (1987:406), in a recent article updating hair symbolism in Britain and North America, warns that such an issue is much more complex than the straight 'one-on-one equations of symbols and meanings' put forward by Leach (1958) and Hallpike (1969). Hair may have, he says, many symbolic functions.

The aim of this paper is to explore further the symbolism of the matted hair among the Rastafari of Jamaica. With Synnott's caution in mind, I nevertheless argue that the dreadlocks phenomenon symbolized both a rejection of social control as well as a triumph of male power over the female. Further, analysis of the hair symbolism leads to the suggestion of an identity between the two.

Hair symbolism among the Rastafari went through two phases, which also coincided with the social development of the movement. The first was from 1934, a couple of years after the founding of the movement to the late 1940s, the second from about 1949 to the present.

Hair Symbolism Among the Rastafari, 1934-49

In the first phase, and indeed for some years into the second, the Rastafari were known as *bearded men, the beards,* or *beardmen*. According to Ken Post (1978:189), Rastafarians had decided a month before the August 1934 Convention of Marcus Garvey's Universal Negro Improvement Association (UNIA) 'that male believers should allow their beards to grow', a decision which was connected to a belief that their beards would be instrumental in parting the sea to allow them passage to Abyssinia. The image here was that of the children of Israel, with whom Blacks had identified from their earliest adoption of Christianity late in the eighteenth century, crossing the Red Sea on their long sojourn to the Promised Land. Then, it was a strike from the rod of Moses which had caused the waters to part; now it was the beard which was to accomplish a similar feat. The decision was Howell's, for it was he who had projected 1 August 1934 for the exodus, a day that was itself symbolic, since this was the centenary anniversary of the declared abolition of British slavery. While the temptation to treat both rod and beard as symbolic of the same thing is great, the critical aspect at this juncture is the separatist identity which the beard gave to those who wore it. It set them apart from other people. Pictures and sketches of Blacks appearing in the daily and weekly newspapers of the thirties show cleanly cut and shaven men, whether the rising Black middle class (*The Daily Gleaner*, 10 January 1936, p. 19) or the Black working class. *The Daily Gleaner*'s photographs of the demonstrating workers in the week of 23 May 1938, for example, reveal clean shaven faces. Not only were beards not fashionable, they were regarded by society as something sinister and inspiring dread. This attitude prevailed well into the 1950s, up to which time male Rastafari (there were occasional references to females) continued to be known as *beardmen*. The bards Slim and Sam captured the essence of social attitudes towards Blacks wearing beards in the chorus of one of their songs:

> Run, man without beard,
> Beard man back o' you!

It should be noted that what society found reprehensible was facial rather than head hair. This was, I believe, because head hair, if groomed, not only remains 'manageable', but does not alter one's appearance as dramatically as does facial hair, all the more so if prevailing customs also dictate some form of headgear. Norman Manley and Alexander Bustamante, the two 'founding fathers' of the modern political system of Jamaica, both wore heavy shocks of soft wavy hair (they were coloured men), but these were combed and brushed backwards. Even so, a heavy head of hair was not the style worn by Black men, and neither was the beard.

Given the prevailing attitude, it is not surprising that not all Rastas wore beards or untonsured hair. The early recruits to the new religion were drawn mainly from among the migrant population swarming into the city of Kingston in the 1930s and 1940s in search of a better way of life. They were integrated into the formal and informal sectors of the economy, whether as port workers loading bananas onto the boats, as employees in the baking industry, as domestic or service workers, or as peddlars, trading in ganja or pushing handcarts in and around the west-end markets. For the workers among them, not to shave and trim would have been tantamount to an invitation to be fired from their jobs. Kuru-kang, one of my informants cited in the previous chapter, reported that he was fired for wearing a new-style expensive shirt to work, and that he thought the reason was because he dared to dress like his White boss. Wearing a beard would have incurred a similar fate. For the self-employed Rastafari, there might have been more flexibility and freedom, depending on the type of occupation or on the level of demand for their service or skill.

The main leaders as well did not wear beards. Robert Hinds did not, nor did his secretary, Mr Brandford. Many of his members did, however. In Hinds' King of Kings Mission, one was free to wear or not to wear the beard. The same apparently also among the Howellites. Notwithstanding the strong probability that the practice of beards originated with him, Howell himself apparently did not have a beard. *Plain Talk* referred to him as the '*dapper* leader of the cult' (3 April 1937; my emphasis), a period description for a fashionably dressed man, hardly one, I think, for anyone who also wore a beard. In 1975 when I was shown 'the Gong,' as Leonard Howell was called by his followers (Hill 1983; Mansingh and Mansingh 1985), he was beardless, as were the three of his followers whom I interviewed. And according to a Rastafari informant, who attended three or four conventions called by Howell at his settlement at Pinnacle, 'If one or two in there had beard they had to prune it. They were ashamed of a beard' (Chevannes 1989a). This would have been in the 1940s. But, if *The Star* (an evening daily) is to be believed, the bearded men who raided land belonging to the Jamaica Public Service Company at Rockfort were 'from Pinnacle' (6 July 1953). These two accounts are not necessarily contradictory, since they relate to slightly different time frames, and, as I have said, Howellites were free to wear or not.

Oral and newspaper evidence, however, establish that certainly by the mid-1950s, beards were associated with the Rastafari, in fact synonymous with them. Some typical *Star* headlines of the period were:

> BEARDS RISE UP (23 January 1953)
> BEARDS BACK JO. KENYATTA (9 April 1953)
> HOWLING 'BEARDS' JAILED (14 April 1954)
> BEARDS BESIEGE COURT (15 September 1954)
> BEARDS CHEER MILK-AND-HONEY TALK (23 September 1955)

It would take another few years for the word *Locksmen* to supplant the word *Beards* as meaning male Rastafari.

As the practice of beards became commonplace among the Rastafari brethren, rationalizations other than the parting of the sea were found. First, the Emperor himself wore one. In the first decade and a half, Rastafari placed much emphasis on visual images. *National Geographic* gave extensive pictorial coverage of the 1930 coronation, and this was circulated widely. But it was not the picture of His Majesty alone which was popular. Many of the early preachers had acquired pictures of the Black Christ, which they circulated among their street corner audiences, and which was instrumental in converting many to the new faith. The second rationale derived from the Nazarite vow, which enjoins on the devotee a number of private and public symbols. These have found their way into the Rastafari movement. Among them is letting 'the locks of the hair of his head grow' (*Numbers* 6:5). As a part of Mosaic law, the vow established a temporary, not a permanent, order of consecration. In the case of Samson, however, the vow was defined by the angel of God as a permanent feature of his identity, from conception (*Judges* 13:5). Destined to free Israel, Samson allowed his weakness for Philistinian women to gain the better of him and so reveal the secret of his strength.

If I be shaven, then my strength will go from me and I shall become weak and be like any other man. (*Judges* 16:17)

Although the Nazarite vow enjoins other symbolic prohibitions, it is the hair taboo which locked the secret of Samson's strength. In adopting this rationalization many of the early Rastafari laid the basis on which a later generation was to uphold and cherish its dreadlocks.

And so facial hair became identified with the Rastafari movement in the first phase of its development, although the membership diverged in the actual practice.

Hair Symbolism among the Rastafari, 1949-Present

Sometime in the 1950s a change took place in the physical appearance of the 'beards'. As already described in Chapter 4, this was largely the work of a group of young militants grouped together in the Youth Black Faith, a name which captured their youthfulness, Black nationalism and idealism. A quasi-group, they undertook to enforce a fresh image of Rastafari as a force opposed to the entire Jamaican society, and this, as I have shown, they symbolized in their adoption of the illicit ganja as a sacred herb, their illegal marches, and, to be sure, in the dreadlocks.

Given the traditional meaning of matted locks in the society, their dreadlocks appearance linked them to derelict and insane people, outcasts. They were noticeable because they did not cover their locks. The 'tam', or tricoloured woollen cap, was a later introduction of the 1960s. Early photographs, for example in *Ian Fleming Introduces Jamaica* (Cargill 1965:33), showed the Rastafari in the glory of their locks. Rastafari became synonymous with locksmen, an indication that the hair was displayed, not hidden, and the derelict image gave way to one of fear. According to one anecdote, a lady turned a sharp street corner in downtown Kingston only to find a Dreadlocks doing the same but going in the opposite direction. In her fright she exclaimed: 'Jesus!' Calmly penetrating her with his red, dilated eyes, he said: 'Shh! Tell no one thou hast seen I!'

There were other acts of symbolic separation. One which deserves some mention here is their cultivation of a new argot. According to Youth Black Faith founder, Brother Wato,

It just arises in conversation, describing many things. Or several times you have several different types of reasoning and you step up with the words. Now that you have seen that the Chinamen in this country, if him want to destroy you, and you can stand in his presence and he speaking something to destroy you and you can't know. You can stand in the presence of the Indian man and him speaking something to destroy you and you don't know. And you have other people here who speak different language and you can be in the midst of them and them speaking something to destroy you and you don't know. So we, the Rasses, supposed to speak, that here, there and anywhere we find ourselves, we suppose to speak and no one know what we speak beside ourself. That's how we get to start.

The process was collectively self-conscious and stemmed from what they perceived as a particular deficiency in the nationalism of the Black man, namely the lack of a language unintelligible to the English ear.[1] And they were reminded of this deficiency daily. For Chinese shopkeepers could be found in every major town and district of the island, and as most were in the 1950s no more than second generation immigrants, they still conversed in Chinese in the presence of their Black Jamaican customers. Wato is quite right that a Black man could be oblivious to the evil being plotted against him in foreign conversation in his very presence, but his point is not that there was anything to fear from the Chinese, or the Indian, but that they were distinct nationalities with their own language. Language was itself a symbol of their separate identity. Where was Black people's language?

Jamaican language has been described as a continuum, one end of which is Standard English, the other a Creole dialect comprised of English- and African-derived words within an African linguistic structure (Cassidy 1961). Most Jamaicans not only understand but are able to and do communicate at all points of the continuum, in what is generally referred to as code switching. For what determines the particular speech pattern and vocabulary is the class and social situations the speakers find themselves in. Standard English is the official and public way of speaking. It is used by public officials, in the schools and churches, court, etc. Dialect is the informal way of speaking, used at home, work, play, etc. But the point is that the difference between any two points along the continuum is one of degree not one of kind, though taken at the two extremes what we have are two different languages.

Thus, talking in the dialect, in the opinion of the young militants who used to reason in the Youth Black Faith camp, did not give the speakers sufficient difference from English to warrant the appropriation of an identity parallel to that of the Chinese or the Indian. This they set about creating.

But speech patterns in Jamaica are not a matter simply of a continuum between Creole and English, which, as far as languages go, are equal. They are also about class, status and legitimacy. By changing that continuum from a horizontal to a vertical plane, with English at the top, one could visualize the social positions of Jamaicans by the way they speak.

Exactly which linguistic innovations among the Dreadlocks appeared when, has not yet been established, though Homiak's work in the next chapter sheds much needed light on the process, but by the late 1960s and early 1970s Rasta or Dread talk was sufficiently popular for an incumbent Prime Minister to use it as a symbol of his identity with the masses. Linguist Velma Pollard (1982) identifies three categories of Dread Talk. In the first, known words from Jamaican Creole and Standard English are given new meanings, such as *chant* ('discuss; talk about religious matters'); *sait* (see); *sounz* ('words; not necessarily their intention'); *Babylon* (Babylon; policeman). In the second category are 'words that bear the weight of their phonological implications,' (Pollard 1982:36) by their reconstruction. Thus *blainjaret*, in which *blind* replaces *ci* (see) of cigarette; *ovastan*, in which *over* replaces *under* in *understand* ('for *if* you are in control of an idea, you must stand *over* it'.); or *downpress*, in which *down* replaces *op* (up) in oppression; and so on. The third category comprises the '*I* words'. Here, 'the pronoun "*I*" of [Standard Jamaican English] gives place to "mi" in [Jamaican Creole] and is glossed as "I, my, mine, me", according to the context' (p. 36). *I* retains the pronominal function of Standard Jamaican English and replaces certain initial consonants, such that researched becomes *Isercht*, elected becomes *Ilektid*, declaration *Iklerieshan*, hour *Iowa*, and so on. Commenting on the entire process, Dr Pollard (1982:32) remarks:

> Jamaica Creole has traditionally been the speech form of the Jamaican poor. Education and exposure to the middle class with its Standard English aspirations has accounted for the JC/SJE (Standard Jamaican English) continuum which has become a commonplace in describing the Jamaican language situation. But the socio-political image which the poor Black man, in this case the Rastaman, has

had of himself in a society where lightness of skin-tone, economic competence and certain social privileges have traditionally gone together must be included in any consideration of Rastafarian words. For the man who is making the words is a man looking up from under; is a man pressed down economically and socially by the establishment. His speech form represents an attempt to bend the lexicon of Jamaica Creole to reflect his social situation and his religious views.

'Looking up from under', and rejecting the perspective, the Rastafari propounded an ideological view of the world and the relationships of those within it based on Garveyite concepts of a proud, achieving Black nation. The attempt to fashion a new language was clearly a part of that conception. In intent at least (whether they succeeded or could have is another matter), they rejected the axis/continuum, on which each point was already contaminated and compromised by the necessity of its being: it was a part of the whole. Just as without points there can be no line, so also without the varied flow of Creole speech there could be no continuum of *Jamaican*. And so Dread Talk rejects not only Standard English but Creole patois as well. For though it is the speech of Black people, it is not the speech of those who are *conscious*, who by appropriating themselves have achieved true identity as Black man, or, to use the preferred phrasing of the Rastafari, *conscious Ethiopians*. Until some Rastafari extracted the word *Jah-mek-ya* (Jah made here) from *Jamaica*, sometime in the late 1970s I believe, it was insulting to call a Rastafari Jamaican.

The Dreadlocks sought to overthrow the religion of the peasant, Revival. They sought to overthrow his speech as well.

To summarize thus far, hair culture among the Rastafari went initially through a beard phase and subsequently to a dreadlocks phase. By way of contextualizing both of these developments, I would like to present a brief sketch of traditional attitudes, beliefs and practices of the Jamaican people concerning hair.

Hair, Race, Gender and Magic

Given the dominating issue of 'race' in Jamaican society, the first relevant fact is that Negroid hair is quite unique in its woolly texture combined with the spirals and crinkles in which it grows. Caucasoid hair is also unique: fine in texture and straight in growth (or gently curling). But for the fact that they are obviously and essentially hair, these two species types have nothing in common.[2] Mating between these two racial types produces hair quality that is neither fully Negroid nor fully Caucasoid: the more Negroid the progeny, the less fine and straight the hair; the more Caucasoid, the less woolly and crinkly. Mating between people of various admixtures of Negroid and Caucasoid genes have produced a wide range of hair types over the centuries of contact between Europeans and Africans. Thus, hair quality, exactly like skin colour, became for the Jamaicans (as also for other Caribbean people) a way of classifying people.

As Norman Girvan (1988) argues, the failure to integrate Blacks into the emerging societies of the new world was due to the status to which European racism rose as an ideology. As we know, this ideology presents Europeans and Africans as polar types along a value continuum, along the vertical axis in fact, the former belonging to the heavenly world of all that was good about humanity: civilization, purity, honesty, justice, refinement, Christianity, even the concept of God; the latter belonging to the netherworld of all that was possibly the worst about humanity: savagery, heathenism, bestiality, laziness, debasement of spirit, the forces of evil. The ideology of racism, Girvan explains, is what accounts for the fact that non-Black immigrant groups, economically as deprived and oppressed as Blacks, have been able to move ahead of them.

Ideologically speaking, to this day, hair in Jamaica is either *good* or *bad*. *Good* hair is also described as *pretty*, not soft or fine, but *pretty*, or sometimes *nice and straight*. *Bad* hair is *nati-nati* (knotty). These ideologically laden terms are often used purely descriptively, and do not necessarily reflect the outlook of the user. I may detest someone but describe his/her hair as *pretty*, or, conversely, love someone but describe his/her hair as *bad*. When deriding someone, however, *bad* hair may become *Black pepper grain*, or *coir*, as in the folk song, *Shine Yaiy Gyal*. A 'shine yaiy gyal' is a woman who wants everything she lays eyes on. She is 'a trouble to a man'. The song ridicules every aspect of her anatomy: fins for ears that want earrings; stick for finger that wants gold ring; wire for waist that wants crinoline; jackfruit for heels that want backless shoes, and so on. When it comes to her hair and her lips, the derision is decidedly racist:

'ier fieba kaya – bout she want 'air net!
lip fieba liba – bout she want lipstick!

(Hair like coir, yet she says she wants hair net;
Lips like liver, yet she says she wants lipstick)

From an objective point of view, the coconut fibre does provide an apt description of Negroid hair, as also the heaviness of liver for thick, extrovert lips. But using them to poke fun betrayed the negative value they were culturally assigned.

The matter did not end at the level of values. Society produced for the grooming not of 'bad' hair but of 'good' hair. The purveyors of hair pomades and oils assumed that everybody either had or wanted to have 'good' hair, and the combs manufactured or imported into Jamaica were designed for grooming only 'good' hair. Up to the Black Power era, that is up to 1968, combs were of basically two types, the one of coarse teeth used by women (Figure 1, A1 and A2), the other of fine teeth used by men (B1 and B2). A1 and B1 were the ideal types, so to speak, whereas A2 and B2 were mixed, having both fine and coarse teeth, the difference being both quality and size: the coarse part of B2 was not as coarse as the coarse part of A2, and the fine part of A2 not as fine as the fine part of B2. Besides, B2 was always smaller. These two basic types and variations of them may still be found in any cosmetic store in Jamaica.

Figure 5.1   Types of Combs

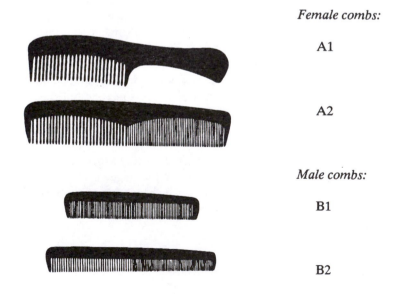

Female combs:

A1

A2

Male combs:

B1

B2

Both Black men and women had some difficulty combing, given the texture of their hair, but because female combs were coarser they more easily penetrated the hair. Even so, the patience with which women sat to have their hair combed was also a matter of socialization, for as girls they too used to encounter the pain associated with combing. In order to minimize the pain, when females comb they do so with the assistance of a firm brush, alternating between brush and comb until the latter is able to pass through the tangle of hair smoothly. The comb was also necessary for parting the plaits. Men faced the following dilemma: either use female coarse combs or keep the hair length short enough for the coarse part of men's combs to penetrate.[3] Up until the late 1960s, judging from hair styles, most seemed to have chosen the latter.

Thus, the ideologically rooted ideas which upheld the racial superiority, almost divinity, of Whites, and the racial inferiority of Blacks in Jamaica's racially stratified and prejudiced society had implications for the kind of grooming implements available and, possibly also, for the length of the head hair of Blacks.

Gramsci makes the point that the ideological hegemony of the ruling class at no time commands the universal following of the working class, among which may be found tendencies running counter to the dominant ideology. There is evidence in surviving folk traditions in Jamaica of norms of beauty which ran, if not counter to, certainly away from, those determined by the race/class structure. This should not surprise us when, during slavery, there was so much interracial sexual contact and love.[4] Jamaican males, for example, value a large bottom in a woman, a characteristic of African rather than European female anatomy.[5] The Creole word '*bunununus*' (or boonoonoonoos, as it sometimes spelt), which means nice, was often used to describe fat and attractive women. Miller (1969:87) found that school children born between 1951 and 1955 conceptualized the average Jamaican 'negatively ... in facial features and colour, but positively ... in terms of body build'. In other words, Blacks fitted the norms of beauty they had internalized with respect to the features of body parts below the head. All was not negative.

Despite the racialist attitudes, Jamaican peasants nevertheless held certain positive values with respect to their hair. From the time they reached the 'age of reason', girls were socialized to value and care for their hair. By the time they reached adolescence they would have internalized the weekly ritual of washing, oiling and plaiting, which as women they would do with the aid of a relative or friend. Long before aloe vera, known locally as *sinklebible* was discovered by the hair industry, it was widely used by peasant women in the treatment of hair. Until it virtually disappeared with the rise of 'pressing' and processing hair in the 1930s, hair styling in 'cane rows' was a practised art. It was later revived in the Black Power era. Women valued 'plenty' hair. A great tragedy it was for a woman to lose even her 'bad' hair, and an even greater one to cut it. The worst scourge of a girl was not 'bad' hair but that naturally short crop of hair known as *dry head*.

Perhaps no other aspect of hair practices is as universal as that pertaining to gender. Every culture has applied different, usually opposing, hair norms to males and to females. Only in very recent times, and only in the West, have these norms undergone such radical change as to culminate 'in androgyny ... and gender-bending' (Synnott 1987:400). The short-lived Black Power movement in Jamaica provided one such example in the *bush*, which lasted two or three years beginning around 1970. Males and females wearing this style were indistinguishable. Even in private the gender-bending was evident, for in order for the hair to retain its blown-out look it needed to be placed in plaits overnight. There have been other examples since then but there were none before. What females and males were allowed to do with their hair was determined not by gender alone but also by age status and by particular spheres of social interaction, as I shall presently explain. However, there were three definitely established norms based solely on gender:

Table 5.1   Gender-based norms for hair styles

Male	Female
Cut	Uncut
Short	Long
Natural	Cultivated

I have already described the pride women took in 'nuff' or 'plenty' hair, and the taboo against cutting it. Men, on the other hand, were expected to keep their hair short and to trim it. In the villages, the barber might himself be a small farmer, who on a Saturday evening or Sunday morning cuts the hair of his friends and acquaintances.

By use of the word 'natural' I do not wish to imply that males did not wash and oil their hair, but rather that they were expected to do nothing to it beyond what was necessary for good health and hygiene. Not so with females. As girls they learned the art of plaiting and decorating with ribbons and beads; as adolescents they underwent the *rite de passage* of the more intricate cane row styles or, once the curling fork was introduced, pressing. Passing reference above to the involvement of friends and relatives in the hair cultivation of a woman does not do justice to the social significance of the female hair ritual. More often than not, even the washing of it required the assistance of, and hence social interaction with, another female. Not to mention the plaiting or styling. Hair cultivation, despite it being 'bad', was an important part of a woman's female identity.[6]

One of the factors controlling gender differences in hair was age. Here the distinction is not just between the young and the old, but between children, young people and the mature and aging adult. One of the two operating concepts underlying the distinctions is a quantitative one, namely size, which is subject to both an absolute as well as a relative meaning. Children, or *pikni*, are conceived as *likl* (little); thus, *likl bwaai* or *likl gyal*. The word *likl* conveys the notion of being subject to the authority of others. Mature and aging adults, on the other hand, are conceived as *big*: *big man* and *big uman*, that is, people who are responsible for themselves and are subject to no one. Since authority is relative, *likl* and *big* are also used in a relative sense. With the strong sense of respect for age which marks domestic relations, an older sibling will accompany the punishment or reprimand of a younger with the words, '*Mi biga 'aan yu'!* (I am your senior). Sometimes also parents will taunt their post-pubescent children with expressions like '*Yu a ton big uman pa mi!*', meaning you are defying my authority, or acting like someone responsible for herself, or having illicit sexual relations, etc.

The second operating concept underlying age status differences is the young-old dichotomy. These were as much a matter of age as they were social categories. Thus, while clearly excluding the pre-pubescent, *young people* would include men and women as old as thirty-five and perhaps forty years old. It was their social activities which set them apart, as they asserted their independence from parental authority, began families of their own, involved themselves in sports and night recreation, and generally, like young people the world over, engaged in pursuits which nature allowed them. *Old*, on the other hand, referred to people whose physical age forced them to put away the style of living of the young and who, consequently, had become socially more settled and stable. The culture distinguished also between the productive and non-productive old, with the concepts *the older heads* and *old people*, respectively. The former expression also conveyed the notion of wisdom associated with experience; the latter connoted dependency on others.

One is thus better able to understand why females symbolized their passage to adulthood by adopting the styles used by *big women*. The greater attention and meticulousness now paid to cultivating the hair was a mark of their coming of age as women and, as women, becoming responsible for themselves. Announcing one's becoming a *big uman*, in this sense, could be accomplished also by pregnancy and recognized sexual activity. In either case, the declaration of independence symbolized by hair cultivation and pregnancy was marked by severe domestic conflict between mother and daughter. Young men had it easier, though they too symbolized their independence with departures from traditional hair styles. In the 1940s, for example, young men used to wear a style popularly known as *sab* or *sabu*, which retained a higher body of hair rising to a gentle peak in front.

While young people were allowed to deviate from traditions, with tolerance, Jamaican peasant society applied negative sanctions to those who, not belonging to the category of young people, tried behaving like them. Both male and female children trying to behave in advance of their age were reproved as *fuos raip* (forced ripe). Older males aping the hair style and clothing of young males, where these differed from tradition, were humoured as *young bwaai*, but older females doing the parallel thing were taunted as *mada young gyal*. One should behave as one's age status allowed.

Gender differences in hair culture in Jamaica were also determined by whether one was presenting oneself in 'public' or in 'private'. By 'private' is meant the domestic environs. 'Public' is here used residually, but excluding formal indoor situations. To the three points of opposition above may be added the following two:

Table 5.2 Gender-based norms for hair display

	Male	Female
In 'public'	Covered or uncovered	Covered
In 'private'	Uncovered	Covered or uncovered

The notion of public and private domains is strongly reflected in the folklore. The following proverbs capture the importance of guarding domestic privacy.

A no everyt'ing good fi eat good fi talk.
(Not everything one eats should be discussed outside)

Finger rott'n, kyaan cut i' off.
(A rotten finger is still yours)

Daag a sweat but long hair kiba i'.
(The dog sweats but its long hair covers it)

Proverbs aside, it was a grave offence to let the public know what one's family was cooking, unless it was to boast, and children were socialized into believing that what went on in the confines of one's house or yard was not for public consumption.

The public-private dichotomy was, of course, also reflected in dress. Both children and adults distinguished between *good clothes* and *jojin* (drudging) *clothes*, the former for going out, the latter for wearing around the yard. As an aspect of self-presentation, the hair of males could be covered or uncovered in public, and was a matter of choice, though certainly from the photographs taken of striking workers in 1938 the overwhelming majority appeared to prefer covering the head.[7] The rationale given for wearing caps and hats outside the home was protection from the elements. In private, however, that is at home, very rarely would one see a man with his head covered. The very opposite was true of women. In public they had no choice between covering and uncovering the hair: it was supposed to be always covered by a head tie, referred to as *tie-head*, or a hat. At home, she violated no norm if she went uncovered.

Given what I have said above concerning age, it should come as no surprise that young men and women went abroad uncovered, especially, in the case of the females, if their hair was recently done.

One could also observe male-female differences in religious rituals. Among the Revival groups the turban was an indispensable part of attire. The member of a band might be allowed dress other than the robe, but must always wrap the head. This custom, whose origin is not fully known, has come down to the present day. In fact, Revival members are sometimes called *wrap 'ead*. To my knowledge, the turban was first observed by the missionaries during what they called the 'myal outbreaks' of the second and fourth decades of the nineteenth century. As we know, by the turn of that century Myal had incorporated Christian elements preached by the Native Baptists, who were themselves converted slaves, and it took the name Revival at the time of the Great Revival of the Christian churches in 1860. One Revival song sings of:

> Working for a mansion and a robe and a crown,
> That is glory for me.

A plausible suggestion, therefore, is that the turban represents that crown.[8] Whether so or not, the fact is that the head was so wrapped as to cover completely the crown of the female, but to expose that of the male.

Among the Christian Churches, such as the Anglicans and the Baptists, the norms for head dress reflected European pattern whereby men uncover their heads in church, while women retain their hats. On the way to church, however, (in public, that is) the men wore hats.

Hair, because it is an outgrowth, may be regarded as an extension of one's person. According to Synnott (1987:404), it 'not only symbolizes the self but, in a very real sense, it *is* the self since it grows from and is part of the physical human body'. As such, hair is akin to other parts of the self such as nails and, among Jamaicans, the shadow and the footprint, as well as, by association, to personal articles of clothing. All of these may become the objects of imitative magic. For example, stepping on another person's shadow with evil intent was believed to be one way of harming that person. And so, even today, women after combing their hair will roll up the strands into a ball, which they then dispose of safely. Beckwith (1929:115) reported the following anecdote:

> An instance was related to me where a roll of hair thrown
> into the waste jar by a guest in arranging her hair so de-
> moralized a part-Negro woman of the better class that she
> was induced to pay a visit to an obeah doctor.

Safe disposal of hair could require burying it, but it never included burning, since this made one's hair fall off. Curiously, as far as I know, this practice did not apply to men. There was, however, one custom which applied to male children. It was thought that clipping the hair of toddlers retarded their speech development, or disposed them to catching colds through the fontanelle. Since female hair was never cut, it is clear that this taboo was aimed at protecting the male child. It was by no means unusual to see little boys in plaits. Once they began to speak, however, their socialization into male hair culture began with the regular haircut, performed usually by the mothers, until they reached the age when the ritual could be done by a barber.

Magical notions did not centre only on imitative magic. Hair could be intrinsically potent, as this prescription to prevent a *duppy* (ghost) from harming you shows: 'draw a hair from the middle of your head and put it into your mouth' (Beckwith 1929:92). One of my informants explained to me that he could destroy Kingston by shearing and scattering his dreadlocks in the 'four corners' of the city, while calling down the curse of Jah.

Sociologically, the person is an embodiment of roles and statuses, all of which combine to give him or her an identity. From the foregoing it is evident that gender, combined with age, plays an enormous role in the Jamaican's sense of personal identity. Were this a discussion of identity as such, attention would have to be drawn to other factors. Some of them, such as race and colour, have been discussed here; others, such as occupation, kinship, education, and a host of other dimensions, fall outside the scope of this chapter. There is, however, one which is of particular relevance to the theme of the discussion, and which I think may be regarded as the most basic of roles and statuses: that is, acting and being human, or as a social being. This may seem elementary, but the Ashanti, for example, never took this for granted. Among them an infant first had to acquire a name before it was accorded the status of a member of society, which came nine days after birth. Should the infant die before the naming ceremony, it was not mourned, since the kinship group had lost no one. Among Jamaicans the infant is human by virtue of birth, though the tradition survives in many rural parts of the country to name the child weeks, sometimes months, after birth. As soon after birth, however, as the infant begins to communicate with its eyes and face, it begins its socialization by its adult providers, whether mother, grandmother or other, into the kinds of behaviour regarded as acceptable. For example, it should learn 'not to want too much han', that is not to be overly dependent; or to be able to pass pleasantly from hand to hand so as not to become what Jamaicans call *selfish* or *spwail* (spoilt).

As the infant becomes a child and learns to speak, it assumes other roles and status, among them gender specific ones, such as those mentioned above. There is one activity which is specific not to one's identity as male or female but to one's identity as a social being, and that is grooming one's hair. Grooming sometimes involves washing and oiling, but always combing or brushing or both. When I speak, therefore, of grooming, the latter are meant. Children of both sexes learn this lesson quite early, learning in fact to endure with stoic fortitude the occasional but inevitable painful pull. Those who resist are called *nasty*, a designation which it would seem is deliberately intended to evoke feelings of pollution and contamination. Among Jamaicans, combing is one of the most elementary requirements of social life.

Table 5.3   Gender-based norms for hair in Jamaican society

Male	Female
Groomed	Groomed
Cut	Uncut
Short	Long
Natural	Cultivated
Covered/uncovered in 'public'	Covered in 'public'
Uncovered in 'private'	Covered/uncovered in 'private'

The non-grooming of the hair, on the other hand, placed one outside the pale of society. In Jamaica, up to the 1950s, non-grooming was a symbol of criminals, derelicts and the insane. There were exceptions, however, such as the farmer rising up early to go off to the bush, or the child sent in the early morning to buy breakfast items from the grocery shop. Even so, most times they wore headgear to hide the unkemptness.

By way of summary then, hair culture in Jamaica, leaving aside the privilege of youth, was one of gender opposition in all spheres but one.

The foregoing review allows us to make the following inference: changes in hair symbolism and meaning in the Jamaican context may reflect real or intended changes in the social order, on the one hand, and in gender relations, on the other. The question I now wish to deal with is what real or intended changes did the institutionalization of the beard and then of the dreadlocks among a group of Blacks reflect.

Institutionalizing New Meanings

The Beards

We have seen that non-Rasta males wore their hair short. I have argued that this was not purely a matter of style but something of a necessity, given the deeply rooted norms about grooming plus the fact that the production of grooming implements, particularly combs, were geared toward people with 'good' hair. In public their general practice was to cover the already low crop. By going along with these they symbolized their own conformity to the status quo, and, in the overall context, their own subordination.

The beard was to have been, for the first Rastafari who instituted it, the surety that God would part the waters to allow His chosen people to return to the promised land. It was, to those who wore it, the means for escape from out of the land of bondage, and therefore from out of the control of the White Establishment. But they instituted as well the practice of not cutting head hair, in violation of the convention among non-Rastafari Black men. The effect of both these measures was symbolic non-conformism and insubordination. They communicated the same message with unshaved and therefore luxuriant hair as the seventeenth century nonconformists in both England and America did with shaved and therefore short hair.

In reality, the Beards were in an ambiguous position. For they *groomed*, using the comb or brush, and they also covered the head in public. And since the daily grooming ritual was an essential, and head covering in public a customary, part of the presentation of oneself in society, they were in truth being inconsistent: conforming and non-conforming at the same time, one foot symbolically in the society it was their hope in the present life to leave, one foot symbolically out. This inconsistency was what the young Dreadfuls picked up. The initial campaign among the Youth Black Faith members was for the institutionalization of the beard as a requisite of Rastafari adherence. But soon their campaign turned into an internal struggle between those they called *Combsomes* and themselves, the *Dreads*. The dreadlocks was the symbolic instrument whereby the contradiction was resolved.

Table 5.4 Hair culture norms

Non-Rastafari	Rastafari	
	Combsome	Dreadlocks
Cut	Uncut	Uncut
Sparse	Plentiful	Plentiful
Groomed	Groomed	Ungroomed
Covered/ uncovered	Covered/ uncovered	Uncovered

Their hair uncut, ungroomed, plentiful and uncovered presented a dreadful image, indeed, but represented a total symbolic break with society. A position was reached of complete male opposition to the White-hegemonic Establishment, and this effect was achieved largely through the decision not to comb.

The Female Taboo

Symbolically, for the Dreadlocks, the rejection of the comb was also aimed in another direction. To repeat, if Negroid hair was allowed to grow luxuriantly in pre-Black Power Jamaica, the only way available to groom it was with the coarse comb used by females. The brush, which was also used to assist, was of itself inadequate, because it could not untangle hair at the root. Since by grooming, and thus conforming to society, the Combsomes had to make use of the grooming implements socially intended for women, then it is quite logical to conclude that for the Rastafari the symbolic bridge between being in and being out of Jamaican society was, as ludicrous as it sounds, *the female comb*.

Were the Dreadlocks conscious of this? Were they aware that in rejecting the comb they were at the same time rejecting an association with the female? Maybe not. But Rastafari men drew on the very folk culture they consciously despised in order to rationalize their ideological and practical ascendancy over women. It is otherwise impossible to explain the virtual disappearance of Rastafari women, except as spouses of Rastafari men, in the 1960s, in light of their strong, independent presence in the pre-Dreadlocks phase. Of my twenty-eight informants who had become Rastafari prior to 1938, seven were females. In describing the early Rastafari organizations informants mention that a significant proportion of the membership was female. This organizational feature continued into the 1950s. In the Claudius Henry group, for example (Chevannes 1976), one could count as many women as men. But by the time Dreadlocks had become synonymous with Rastafari, Professor Nettleford was taking note of the patriarchy among them as a possible reversal of the weak male image in the traditional family structure (1970). As I have suggested in Chapter 2, the complete ascendancy over the female came with ritualizing the 'negative' features of womanhood, in the Revival worldview, over her positive ones. A fuller elaboration is in order.

Woman in Folk Consciousness

Proverbs. There are a number of proverbs about women, and all seem to belittle the woman. *'Uman deceitful like star apple leaf'* uses the star apple leaf with its green upper face and brown underside to make the point. *'Uman an' hud neba quarrel'* means that women may be always made happy with sex. *'Beautiful woman, beautiful trouble'* needs no translation.

The Bible. Although the Bible is adopted in its entirety, the images of women most often referred to among the folk are Eve, Delilah and Jezebel. The last is used as a curse word,[9] the first two as examples of the power women have over men who submit to them. Not one of the more positive images, such as Naomi, Ruth, Sarah, Esther or Miriam is found in popular mythology, although they are used as personal names.

Drop pan. This is a popular numbers game, in which numbers from 1 to 36 are each given several meanings. Originating among the immigrant Chinese in the first two decades of the century, many of its aspects have been 'creolized'. Examination of the association of meanings reveals that the concept of womanhood is that of a receptacle, or a vessel (Chevannes 1989b). The woman is conceived above all as the bearer of the male seed, rather than as a person in her own right. Even the way references are made to a pregnant woman, 'Is huufa [whose] baby?' brings this out.

Nature. The moon is a symbol for the female, and like pregnant and menstruating women it is believed to have a malignant effect on crops during certain of its phases. For example, if reaped in the phase of the full moon, bamboo will be quickly eaten by termites. The moon is also thought to cause insanity if it shines on you during sleep. The sun, on the other hand, is a male principle, that of regeneration and strength. Staring directly into its light infuses one with its power.

The family. Without undertaking a discussion of the Jamaican family structure, which is outside the scope of this book, it would be fair to say that all authorities on the Caribbean family would agree that within the household the woman is the more dominant of the parental pair, even in male headed households. She is the manager of the domestic unit, a position which gives her a considerably greater depth of interpersonal relations. It has become quite a cliché to speak of the Caribbean mother who is also father to her children. But even where he is present and the head of the household, affectively he tends to be marginalized from the intense range of interrelationships. His role lies in mediating between the domestic group and the wider society, and this is perhaps why women at the turn of the century were content with this division of labour (Brodber 1986), and why eight decades later they may be still content to allow men the status of head of household though in effect it is they who run it (Powell 1986).

In Jamaican folk culture, the status of mother is the highest a woman can achieve. Motherhood is the goal of every woman, just as barrenness is a dreaded curse. One of the most searing insults is to call a woman a mule. Family planning experts believe that this value lies behind the drive of adolescent girls to bear children.

If the most penetrating insult to a woman is to be called a mule, the one most calculated to cause a bloody fight between males is to insult one's mother. Motherhood is also conceived metaphorically by the peasant, and *Mada* is a term reserved only for the most respected women in a community. Among the followers of Claudius Henry, his wife Sister Edna was until she died publicly acclaimed within the community of believers as 'Creation Mother' (Chevannes 1976). And she did function in her day to day role in the quasi-commune they began to build in Clarendon, as the nurturing mother of all, young and old alike.

Religious life. In Revival some of the leaders of great renown have been women, such as Mother Forbes in the 1920s (Beckwith 1929) and Mother Rita in the 1970s (Barrett 1976), alongside famous Revivalists such as Bedward, Fitzie and Kapo. All female Revival leaders are known as Mada, while their male counterparts are known as Captain (whence Kapo) or Shepherd. There is an explanation for this. Dr Wedenoja found that 64 per cent of female Revival leaders in a large area of the parish of Manchester were balm healers, compared to 46 per cent of male leaders. 'Spirituality and healing are largely associated with women in Jamaica' (Wedenoja 1989:87). If this is so, with what are men associated?

Wedenoja suggests that men are associated with obeah, sorcery and aggression, in contrast to the benevolence, care and trust of women. This may well be so, but it seems to me that this is only one aspect of the total picture, for if, as Dr Wedenoja himself observes, 54 per cent of Revival groups were female-headed, a significant 46 per cent would be male-headed. These could not all be obeahmen and evil. For an explanation I would like to refer again to the 'drop pan' game. The number 31 has as its most common meanings the penis, a piece of rope or wood and the pulpit. The number 29 is most commonly associated with parson, bull-cow,[10] ram-goat and the male of any species. Thus, the object most associated with preaching, the pulpit, is itself regarded as a phallic symbol, while the person most associated with the activity of preaching, the parson, is thought of as male. Taking Dr Wedenoja's conclusions into account, we can then say that at the symbolic level of folk consciousness in Jamaica, healing is properly a female activity, while preaching is properly male.

Menstruation. A menstruating woman is considered dangerous to certain crops. She is forbidden to pass through a field of ganja or corn nearing maturity, since the mystic power of her presence could endanger the crop. Although the most common expletive in Jamaica, *raas*,[11] refers to the anus, the most offensive is the one referring to the menses, *blood klaat*.

To summarize, in the semiotic life of the Jamaican folk, womanhood has both negative and positive values. The positive values are associated with motherhood, nurturing and the warmth of domestic interpersonal relations, while the negative values see woman as cosmologically dangerous. That the latter prevail so strongly throughout the society tells us the extent to which popular culture has been shaped by a male-centred outlook.

With this exploration of symbols, I believe one is better able to understand the compulsion among Jamaican men to control women. In the 1986 study of Jamaican males we found that submissiveness was the number one ideal trait men looked for in women (Chevannes 1986). The problem facing the men is the assertiveness of women, hence their frequent resort to physical violence and other forms of cruelty. Even access to birth control devices is denied out of the lurking fear of female sexual infidelity. They permit themselves, however, the privilege of extra-union relationships with other women. Most women rationalize their tolerance of these illicit affairs with the belief that they are natural.

During the Beards phase of the Rastafari, there is evidence that male adherents acted no differently from their non-Rastafari counterparts. Leonard Howell was reputed to have taken twelve wives during the Pinnacle years. Whether this was fact or fiction, it certainly was fact that Robert Hinds sired two children within a couple months of each other. Come the Dreadlocks, however, an entirely different approach was taken.

Briefly, what the Dreadlocks attempted to do was isolate the negative ideas about women, which were abroad in the culture, ritualize them, and by so doing establish ritual distance from the contaminating source of their confinement in Jamaican society, in Babylon. I say 'attempted' because, as in so many other ways, the effort was not entirely successful.

The Dreadlocks male hegemony

The Lion's mane. Dreadlocks became associated with the mane of the lion. Remarkably, Emperor Haile Selassie not only was the 'Lion of Judah,' but kept pet lions in his palace. According to Forsythe (1983:101),

> So engrossed are Rastafarians with this lion symbolism that they actually see themselves as bearing the face, countenance, power, dignity, beauty, fearlessness and whole-

some integrity which comes from the self realization that he has it within him to become like lion if awakened enough. His 'locks' are deliberately intended to symbolize the mane of the lion.

The dreadlocks/lion mane symbolism is seen by Forsythe as representing an alternative to the traditional self-concept, whereby the Black man sees himself as Anansi, the spider-hero of Jamaican folklore, who uses the wiliness of his intellect to deceive his way into dominance over the other animals of the forest. Forsythe is quite right.

But, note that this symbolism does not apply to females any more than Anansi did. By an act of nature, or God himself, the lioness goes without a mane. The dreadlocks as a male symbol was therefore divinely ordained.

Hair conduct. The relatively few women who became Dreadlocks from the outset up to the 1970s, and the increasing numbers since, must cover their dreadlocks at all times, at home or abroad, on sacred and profane occasions. Men, on the other hand, as I already indicated, were uncovered. A change took place, however, probably sometime around the middle to late 1960s, when men began to cover their locks in public with large woollen caps, knitted in the Rastafari colours of red, gold and green, but uncover in the privacy of the yard, in ritual smoking and on all sacred occasions. I do not know what prompted the change, but it should be noted that the period when it took place was characterized by what Nettleford called a process of mutual accommodation between Rastafari and the society.

Celibacy. At the time of my nearly two years of research in 1974 and 1975, some of the Dreadlocks I encountered had been celibate for many years. Their rationalization was that women were a tremendous source of distraction from the need to focus the mind on divine things.

Family life. Those who 'rather than burn' were forced into family life as spouses and fathers were the practical inspiration behind the new patriarchy for which Dreadlocks became known. In the traditional Jamaican household, the roles of the father/husband and mother/wife were like mirror reflections of the very roles Jamaican peasant culture assigned to the Creator God, Big Maasa, and to the Spirits. The former was the undisputed creator and master of the universe, the ultimate arbiter and judge. All lesser gods acknowledged him. But as far as the trial and tribulations of human life were concerned, it was the latter who counted, who possessed and were worshipped, to whom sacrifices were made. In his household, the Dreadlocks gave up the image of the distant God, retained the headship, but appropriated the nurturing role of mother. I cannot recall ever hearing of a case of physical abuse of his spouse by a Dreadlocks. Because he is the undisputed and de facto head, disputes which arise are settled by gentle reasoning and enlightenment. Naturally, if the spouse disagrees, she divorces herself. I also have never heard of a Dreadlocks applying physical punishment towards his children. Here, too, waywardness meets the same remedy as in the case of his spouse. Religious leaders and social workers familiar with the Dreadlocks have commented on the love which they exhibit towards their children. The concept of a good father among Jamaican men is of a man who *provides* for his children's upkeep and education. Once provision is made, however, it is the role of the mothers to do the actual upkeep and see to the education. Rastafari fathers, on the other hand, are known to take personal interest and be involved in the upbringing of their children, particularly their 'king man', as the males are called. All this is not to imply that female Rastafari give up their nurturing roles. As women, they are still mothers, a natural status in the lives of children which no male can alter. Besides, they are responsible for washing, tidying and other household chores. But compared to the non-Rastafari male, the Dreadlocks is an affective part of the household grouping.

Menstruation. The Dreadlocks' increased role in domestic affairs also stems from his relegation of his spouse as a result of the menstrual flow. She may not cook at this time, and in some households a red cloth is tied to a chair which she alone may use. For this reason many Rastafari never eat food cooked by women. Those that do generally take over the cooking when the woman is menstruating.

Among the Prince Edward Emmanuel group, known as the Bobo, women are secluded in a hostel for the entire period of their showing, plus twelve purifying days. Non-menstruating women attend to them. In the Bobo commune, cooking at all times is performed by the males.

Sacred rituals. The most common sacred ritual among the Dreadlocks is the yard reasoning. This is a simple discussion during which the holy herb, ganja, is stuffed in the water pipe, or sacred chalice, lit and passed from participant to participant, until all is consumed. Women are not allowed to partake. They also take no part in the formal ceremonies, except as onlookers. Only males may exercise the privilege of beating the drums. In the Bobo's Sabbath worship, all females, young and old, are strictly segregated on the left side of the tabernacle facing the altar.

Religious status. In the first twenty or so years of the Rastafari movement, women became converts on the strength of their own conviction. One of the tenets of the Dreadlocks is that only through the enlightenment of her spouse may a woman come to 'declare Jah,' that is achieve conviction.

Birth control. When family planning programmes got underway in Jamaica in the late 1950s and early 1960s, the Rastafari ideologized popular resistance to it as the White man's plan to kill off Black people. Rastafari women may not use contraceptives. The idea of 'ital' (natural) sex is still a dominant preference influencing sexual behaviour among the population.

Terms of address. No better word captures the submissive status of the woman than the term of address, *Daata* (Daughter). It refers to a female Rastafari, regardless of her age. While a term of endearment, it nevertheless reflects the fact that a 'big woman' is no more than a child, and that the male who uses the term is like a father. The term, however, seems to have been introduced as recently as the 1970s.

These are some of the ways in which the Dreadlocks movement established its total hegemony over womanhood and in so doing reinforced its separation from the world of Babylon. The concept of woman as a source of contamination was an extreme extension of negative ideas already reposited in the mind of the folk. It was necessitated by the contradiction which the Beards, or Combsomes, fell into, which they sought to resolve.

Conclusion

By contextualizing the rise of the Dreadlocks phenomenon in Jamaica, I have attempted to show that their matted hair was symbolic of stepping beyond the control of the White-oriented society. But it also was symbolic of their total ascendancy over the female, who was viewed as a force used to contain them within society. The female was contaminating, and therefore required ritual distance and control. In effect, what I am saying is that in at least this instance, long hair does not have to mean only phallic sublimation (Leach) or only freedom from social control (Hallpike), but both at the same time. Not only that, but both may be saying the same thing. Two things equal to a third are equal to each other.

What happens when the Dreadlocks is a female? By refusing to comb she also places herself outside the the pale of Jamaican society. But are her locks also a symbol of the phallus? Yes, I think so. By accepting that only *through her king-man*, as male Rastafari spouses are called, can she declare herself Rastafari, she acknowledges that her dreadlocks symbolically derive from him as well. The fact that it grows on her head does not make it hers, in the sense in which the matted locks of Sri Lankan female ascetics were the result of their own journeying and quest (Obeyesekere 1981).

With the increased numbers of women among the Dreadlocks, to a large extent the result of growth among the middle classes, many of the above tenets and practices are undergoing change. The Rastafari movement is not unaffected by the wider struggle by women for equal status. Rastafari women are taking issue with the taboos, such as those against contraceptives and menstruation, and public display of the locks, even within male presence (Tafari-Ama, 1989), and the right to speak in public and to participate on official delegations (Chevannes 1989a).

This is not the only aspect of the dreadlocks symbolism which is undergoing change. As a symbol of freedom from constraint it is also changing, as more and more it becomes normal to see Dreadlocks in professional positions, and as more and more Rastafari become integrated into the social fabric. In fact dreadlocks have become quite a fashion, beginning first among musicians and entertainers but now among the wider public. Without having artificial dreadlocks inserted, which is now commonly done, one does not have to be a Rastafari in order to dread.

Notes

1. See Jake Homiak in the succeeding chapter for a different 'dub version' of the orgins of Rasta talk.
2. Mongoloid hair is coarse like Negroid and straight like Caucasoid. According to Wendy Cooper (1971:23), 'The unifying factor is that all these hairs, of whatever type, are produced from little pockets in the skin called follicles'.

3. Black (hair type) students at St George's College in the 1950s were a minority. I remember well that male combs were part of the accoutrement of the Chinese, Whites and brown-skin mulattos, which many of them kept, visibly, in their shirt pockets to groom themselves at breaks. Strictly speaking, nothing prevented Blacks from bringing a comb to school. But to bring one which could really comb your 'bad' hair would make you a laughing stock; to bring one which couldn't really comb your hair would also make you a laughing stock. I don't remember any of us sporting a comb in school. Black Power changed all that. By the 1970s schoolboys were sporting Afro-picks or even the coarse female combs.

4. See, for example, Douglas Hall 1989. Thistlewood not only had a vigorous sex life with his African women slaves but was undoubtedly in love with one of them, Phibbah.

5. In research I carried out a few years ago among a national sample of Jamaican males (Chevannes 1986), one respondent had this to say about his ideal woman:

> I used to watch after special place on girls like dem bottom, dem hip, also the look of a girl face. That's my criteria: good looking, tall hair, big bottom, wide hips.

While there can be no doubt that 'tall hair' referred to a Caucasian type (in fact he was more explicit later on: 'light complexion, tall hair, straight nose'), the inclusion of 'big bottom' fits in with generally held male views of the ideal woman.

6. We need to rethink our assumption that hair processing by Black women reflects their desire to be 'white', to have 'pretty' hair. Many people who bemoan the demise of the 'natural' look of the Afro often attribute this to the low level of national and political consciousness among Black women. But the issue may be far more complex than that. For if there is any credibility in the argument that hair cultivation by Black women is related to their identity as females, then it is quite understandable that they would also be quick to make use of the latest in hair technology. I find it difficult to concede that many of the ardent fighters for women's rights in Jamaica wish to have 'pretty' hair because they cream or relax it.

7. See, for example, Richard Hart (1989). See also *The Daily Gleaner*, the week of 23 May 1938.

8. On the other hand, I observed the same practice in St Vincent in 1988.

9. The line *Yu ol' Jezebel* occurs in the popular ska tune *Kyar i go bring come*.

10. In Jamaican Creole *cow* is generic, like head of cattle.

11. Probably 'from your arse'.

6 Dub History:[1] Soundings on Rastafari Livity and Language

John P. Homiak

In 1987, a popular Jamaican deejay, Lt. Stitchie, hit the top of the island's charts with an irreverent parody of the Rastaman entitled *Natty Dread*. The song's success illustrated the extent to which Rasta cultural forms have become recognizable across the local Jamaican scene. It was also a powerful example of how easily outward sociocultural forms are severed from their underlying philosophical moorings as they are appropriated within the domain of popular culture. I draw attention here to the particular instances of Rasta dialect (known as 'Dread Talk' or *I-ance*) which occur in this song text and their resonance with a set of distinctive foodways practiced by the Rastafari. The latter, known as *I-tal*, are widely associated with a vegetarian, saltless, and fresh food diet.

In *Natty Dread*, the artist draws upon both of these signature elements of Rasta culture to develop a caricature of the Rastaman and his life-style. The scenario goes something like this. While traveling from his 'bush' (cultivation ground) to the market, a Dread finds himself challenged by a policeman, an agent of Babylonian authority: 'What yuh selling, Dreadlocks?' 'I-laloo, I-ppa, and Yunkin', responds the Rasta-mam. Apparently confused, the agent of authority rejoins: 'Mi said, what's yuh selling, me serious now!' The Dread responds, 'Mi Fadda send lightening and thunder to smite yuh!'. With this, the Dread is soundly cuffed and hauled off to jail where, now cowed, he is made to endure the abominations of Leviticus.

Natty Dread works as a piece of popular culture largely because the artist successfully trades upon the familiarity that Jamaicans now have with the outward trappings of the Rastafari movement. Many have, in fact, loosely appropriated aspects of the culture (such as the Rasta colours) as things that are authentically post-colonial Jamaican – even as they may be oblivious (or hostile to) the deeper philosophical outlooks symbolized by such cultural forms. A good example is the use of *I-ance* noted above. Jamaicans are easily able to decode 'I-laloo, I-ppa, and

Yunkin' (i.e., calaloo, pepper, and pumpkin.) Listeners may also appreciate the implied connection which these terms have to eating *I-tal* inasmuch as hot pepper is the preferred 'seasoning' in this food.

During the 1970s Jamaicans became increasingly familiar with *I-tal* cuisine through the appearance of local food shops run by small-scale Rasta entrepreneurs. Likewise, the 'battery of I-words' associated with the Rasta dialect gained wide currency with many younger speakers of Jamaican Creole. No doubt this diffusion of the Rasta lexicon was greatly assisted by the work of popular artists like Bob Marley who drew upon elements of this speech code in their music (see Bilby 1985:144-6). Despite the spread of these elements of 'Dread culture' outside the Rasta milieu, the broader society knows little about their origins or their meaning to those who authored them.

The gap between the superficial knowledge which most Jamaicans presently have of these codes and the local knowledge which would shed light on their origins can be illustrated with a brief example. Consider the following instances of *I-ance*: 'I-yuncum I-yoder' and 'I-yasta Yoolie-I'. I would imagine that these phrases are unintelligible to most Jamaicans as well as to a good number of Rastafari. Yet these are expressions which were widely used by the first speakers of so-called 'Dread Talk'. They are glossed respectively as 'The Nyabinghi Order has arrived!' and 'Rastafari!'. These were part of the I-word lexicon which first entered the soundscape of the Rastafari in the early 1960s. During this period, such phrases circulated as part of an evolving subdialect which was spreading rapidly throughout the Rasta camps of West Kingston. Moreover, the same cohort of Dreadlocks who were in the vanguard of developing this tongue were similarly the most uncompromising advocates of the *I-tal* dietary code. To appreciate how and why these speech and dietary codes developed we need to understand their systematic linkage to what the Rastafari call *livity*. Livity, glossed simply as 'lifeways', encapsulates an underlying philosophy, a blueprint for a total way of life.

In this chapter I outline the development of these aspects of Rasta livity and language by drawing extensively upon the oral testimony of a small cohort of Rastas who entered the movement in the 1950s. This group of Rastas – who called themselves the *I-gelic* House or *Higes Knots*, was central in establishing the foundation for the contemporary *I-tal* and *I-ance* codes. First, however, I discuss how such an account is even possible. After all, ethnographic work on the Rastafari did not begin in earnest until the early 1970s. In addition, scholars have recognized the problems linked to tracing ideological and cultural developments within Rastafari as well as the inherent complexity of these developments (see Bilby 1983; Hill 1983; Yawney 1985a:3-5; Owens 1975:89).

Dub History: Notes on Oral Tradition and Rasta Ethnography

In this essay, I use the term 'dub history' to refer to both the methodology through which I have gained access to oral testimony given by the Rastafari and the social construction of oral testimony as it circulates among the Rastafari. Let me first explain my metaphoric usage of the term 'dub' in this context. In Jamaican popular music, the remix of a song with the lyric track dropped out is known as a 'dub version'. The rhythm line remains to give the song a recognizable structure but the process of remixing may yield many versions. In this chapter I refer to 'dub' history to indicate the fact that particular oral narratives are constantly subject to revision-ing and are rendered in many versions as they circulate among members of a speech community. These are socially constructed narratives which reflect the contingencies of different settings and specific audiences. In short, any oral testimony is likely to depend upon the composition of an assembled group, on the relationships among those present, and/or on the intentions and volubility of a given speaker on any given occasion – as much as it may upon the presence of someone (like an ethnographer) who is perceived as an outsider. These factors underscore the contingent nature of oral testimony. They also implicitly deny the existence of a reified domain of 'oral tradition' comprised of widely shared or constantly voiced narratives that can be isolated for separate study (Cohen 1989:9-17).

My access to the oral testimony of the Rastafari began with fieldwork in Jamaica during 1980-81. Almost from my arrival in the field, I became involved in the 'yard life' of various Elders and began to participate in communal and recurrent speech events known as 'reasonings' (see Homiak 1987; Yawney 1979, 1985b). These are at once the primary form of ritual encounter, spiritual communion, and sociability shared by the male members of the movement and, as such, reflect a level of familiarity with its corresponding knowledge. It was primarily among the Elders of the Haile Selassie I Theocracy Government that my participation in these sessions was initiated and among whom it has continued. Through yearly or twice-yearly visits to Jamaica, I have, since my initial fieldwork, continued a close association with this loosely-knit ritual collective, also known as the 'House' of Nyabinghi.

The Nyabinghi House is a ritual community defined by its voices. The process I am describing is, from a sociolinguistic perspective, one in which I have been progressively incorporated into a community of speakers. This has meant acquiring familiarity with a discourse which is 'many-layered' (Hanks 1987:669-72). By this I mean that the Rastafari are men-of-words[2] who address themselves passionately not only to concerns of identity and ideology, but to concerns of communal morality and responsibility. They come together to fashion continuous streams of 'reasoning' in which 'Jah is praised', inspiration is received, and ideology is reproduced; they are also a collective of individuals who speak to each other, about each other, and about themselves and their experiences.

In the early stage of my groundings, Elders would frequently invoke personal testimony of their callings in the faith. I came to understand these verbal accounts simultaneously as performance genres and as oral versions of an uncodified history that provided important insights into the social organization and development of the movement. As my identity *vis-à-vis* certain circles of the brethren has been renegotiated over time, I have also acquired access to the 'backstage' of those yards in which I was grounded. In the ongoing dialectic between public and private discourse which takes place in these yards, I have been exposed to the personal biographies of various Elders, to their divergent views on the development of the culture, and to their ongoing critical review of the internal life of the 'House'. Much of what I am calling dub history circulates among these Elders in a continuous cycle of self-referential testimony. This confirms their sense of shared identity and constitutes an important part of the collective history of the movement.

In his own work on the links between the first Rasta preachers and the emergence of the Dreadlocks, Chevannes comments on the problems associated with using oral testimony to trace cultural developments within Rasta. He notes, for example, that the key informant who provided him access to the first generation of Rastafari directed him 'down a path trod mainly by [Robert] Hinds' group, and [he] therefore missed more of those who belonged to groups led by other founders, with their own alternative experiences, views, and insights' (Chapter 4, this volume). Factors such as this, coupled with the assessments which informants make of a researcher, constitute the problem of 'positioned utterances'. These are assertions which necessarily reflect the perspective, knowledge, experience, and intentions of speakers and of their evaluations and expectations of a given listener. We also know that speakers often privelege their own experience. They may adjust past biography to present practice, or they may pronounce bald conceits.

As a final point, I want to contrast dubbed testimony with certain oral narratives that have become 'authorized' among the brethren. By authorized accounts I refer to testimony which is specifically intended for public circulation and which may incorporate various distortions. Such narratives acquire currency for various reasons. They may have initially been voiced by a persuasive and charismatic individual whose supporters broadcast his version more widely. They may bear upon what are regarded as historic moments or events (for example, accounts of Emperor Haile Selassie I's visit to Jamaica in 1966 are virtually a genre within the Nyabinghi House). In some cases they may prevail simply because they remain unchallenged. Straightforward methods of oral history based on interviews are, I believe, particularly susceptible to the distortions found in the authorized account. Chevannes touches on some of these problems with respect to the testimony of Dreadlocks Rastas.

It is, in my view, only by hearing the same or related accounts 'dubbed' at different places and times that the ethnographer 'moving with Rasta' may assess these oral accounts as narratives. Even as the concept of 'dub history' destabilizes the quest for definitive accounts, it incorporates its own checks and correctives via implied access to a plurality of voices.

Within any oral culture there are no pure memories, only recollections. In this regard, there is strong evidence both in my own and Chevannes' work on the origin of the Dreadlocks to indicate that these oral accounts reflect important generational relations within the movement. This should come as little surprise to ethnographers who have worked in the English-speaking Caribbean. The constellation of values which Wilson (1969) terms 'reputation' are cited in relation to age-grading as an important organizational principle in West Indian societies (B. Williams 1987:82-3; R.T. Smith 1988:45). This holds true even more strongly for the Rastafari. The brethren with whom I have spent extended periods of time invariably come around to talking about their 'growmates' in Rasta. Yawney (1983:137) reports a similar experience in her work. She draws attention to the social construction of livity among small groups of male age-mates who 'come up together' through reasoning (Yawney 1985a:1). In my experience, this extends to the realm of dub history wherein age-mates, when gathered together, elaborate their own versions and ratify them as 'authentic'.[3] With these observations squarely in mind I now turn to the history itself.

The Nyabinghi House: The Generational Aspects of Livity

As Chevannes points out at some length, the foundations for Rastafari as a life-style were being laid within the movement throughout the 1950s and into the 1960s. The impetus which Chevannes attributes to the Youth Black Faith can be seen to have established a beginning for this process as early as the late 1940s (cf. Yawney 1985a:2; Homiak 1985:183-97). Their uncompromising ethic of cultural resistance, organized around the Nyabinghi concept of 'death to Black and White oppressors', has become a perennial touchstone for spiritual renewal among successive generations of Rastafari.

Those of the Youth Black Faith were not alone in their work. There were others of the same generational cohort. And, in the late 1950s, about a decade after the Youth Black Faith began, a younger generational cohort of Rastafari began to assert themselves. This was a transitional period and, reflecting this, a recurrent theme is evident in much of the oral testimony of brethren who arose during this period: that this was a time of 'heavy discipline' among the Rastafari. In part, I believe this reflected the attempt by older brethren, both Combsomes and Dreadlocks, to make young Dreadlocks conform to the protocols set in their yards. It also probably reflected their attempts to retain the prerogatives and the respect which accompanied their standing in an earlier stage of the movement. Following from this was the fiery nature of interaction among individuals and groups of Rastafari about which Chevannes comments.

Part of this discord may have ensued from the anti-Revival reforms which the Youth Black Faith sought to implement. Yet I believe there was something more. Many of the younger adherents who came into the movement during the 1950s, and who embraced the Dreadlocks covenant, rejected the exclusive authority of older Rastafari, be they Combsomes *or* Dreadlocks. Among other things, they contested the idea that the Bible and hymn-book, central to the 'street meeting era', should be the only source of inspiration for members of the movement. The solution required a deeper spiritual search.

This collective spiritual search was linked to the experience of an increasingly problematic social reality for the Rastafari. The period of which we are speaking, roughly the mid-1950s through the mid-1960s, was arguably the most difficult one which the Rastafari have suffered. The political developments noted by Chevannes coincided with Rastafari emphasis upon repatriation and with consequent deteriorating relations between them and the wider society. This was given impetus through public perceptions linking Rastas to criminality.[4] Dreadlocks were the official pariahs of Jamaican society. They were targets for police harassment and were scorned by the majority of society. They could not ride upon public transportation and were frequently subject to public humiliation by having their locks forcibly trimmed by the police. This history is well documented and is also vividly recalled by the majority of older Dreadlocks.

What is not so well established is the overall numerical standing of Dreadlocks within Rastafari at this time. They were, I believe, a minority who suffered disproportionately the scorn and abuse of the wider society. Bearing up under this with their faith intact enables us to appreciate just how activist was their role within the movement. Particular dubbed accounts which I have heard repeated convince me that Dreadlocks had not achieved ascendency, at least numerically speaking, by this time – the Dreadlocks delegate on the 1961 Mission to Africa notwithstanding.

On this point we can note that the Youth Black Faith, which a number of scholars have nominated as a vanguard with respect to the wearing of locks, actually passed through two phases which are often conflated in oral accounts. Originally this was a group of Combsomes among which a few younger members determined to 'carry locks'. It was only later, perhaps as late as 1958-59, that the Locksmen in this mixed group split to form the House of Boanerges, an exclusively 'Dread' solidarity (see Homiak 1985:183-85). Related to this time, Sister Merriam Lennox, an elder Rastawoman who grew up in Trench Town, recalls:

> At dat time in Abacka (Back-o-Wall) man spring up dem own different kinda Rasta ... different Rasta was still existing ... [but] is only after de (1958) Convention close date we have the springing up of de Nyabinghi Order. Dis is when de Locks-Dread form up and come right up. We (older Rastas) were talking of de Coptic House when dem man come and 'low-rate' Coptic.

> Those ancient bredrin (from before the Convention),
> some a dem 'fall dong' (leave Rasta), some a dem pass off,
> some still ina demself. Still, plenty of de old time Rasta-
> man couldn't tek de message of de Locks-Dread Nyahman
> . . . couldn't tek de message!

This kind of direct testimony should make us wary of published accounts that have inflated the Dreadlocks presence entering the 1960s.[5]
It should also force us to contemplate how far-reaching was the impact
of this Dreadlocks minority within a relatively short span of time.

Despite the difficulties of the late 1950s, the ranks of the movement
were increased by the addition of younger members. Concurrent with
these developments, camp life – associated with reasoning and Nyabinghi chanting and drumming – became increasingly important to the livity
of the predominantly male members of the movement. In fact, these
years marked the eclipse of the 'street meeting era' of Rasta by a yard
and camp-centred phase of cultural efflorescence (Jah Bones 1985:28-9;
Homiak 1989:2). What grew out of this phase was a particular style of
cultural resistance with younger militant Rastafari brethren in the vanguard. They challenged the taken-for-granted codes of the dominant
system *and* the older Rastas. This can be seen in the biographical account of Jah Bones (1985:22-37), a Rasta writer and poet who entered
the movement during this period. He observes that:

> Few people outside and inside Rasta livity know to what
> extent the process of creation, developman, and accept-
> ance of drednis as a life-style in Rasta has changed the
> character of Rastafari livity. Within drednis, not only does
> the hair style change from a combed Afro to an uncombed
> plaited flowing locks, but the talk or language changes, the
> food, smoke, clothes, dance, music, and so forth. Plenty
> Rastaman could not ovar drednis and rejected it. How-
> ever, most of those who had done so at the beginning em-
> braced it by 1961 and after.

Note should be made of the fact that most of those who came into Rasta
as young males in the 1950s draw a clear distinction between their cohort of age-mates who entered the faith as Dreadlocks, and the prior
generation (exemplified by the Youth Black Faith) who entered Rasta
as Combsomes and later became Dreadlocks. Another view of these
generational differences (which similarly distinguishes the activism of

the younger Dreadlocks from the inertia and conservatism of older bre-thren), is offered by Ras I-rice I-on:

> What really keep up de movements to dis day is de youth-ful generation. It was more a youthful generation, a new set of people come in now to carry on de Rasta move-ments different from de 'old-man-style Rasta vibes' (i.e., those elders who were preachers in the Revival mold).

The impact of these younger Rastafari during the mid- to late-1950s can be related to the organizational change in Rasta noted by Chevannes (Chapter 4, this volume) whereby formal membership was abolished. Indeed, one of the justifications which he cites for the Revival type 'of-fices' and postions which continued into Rastafari was the lack of lite-racy among the brethren and the corresponding need for individuals who could 'head the table' at street meetings by reading from the Bible or hymn-book (see Simpson 1955). I-rice, who is also one of the princi-pals in this history, links the eclipse of the 'old man style' to, among other things, educational changes among the increasing numbers of younger participants that began to swell the ranks of Rastafari:

> Ya see, it's a 'reading time', but some Rasta people don't send dem yout' to school. I is a type of person living in a *tatu* [shack], but when yuh come there yuh see a 'library' wid different books upon de [African] struggle. I could argue on international affairs' with anyone through I read de *Gleaner* and different books upon the [African] struggle. Those elderly sort a bredrin, because some of these bredrin hasn't been really brought through the school of knowing word-meaning, dey don't read dat . . . don't read nothing in de *Gleaner*. Dem elderly bredrin like Hill and Jew-Man don't speak wha we speak. Yet every yout' dat born and grow up in dat dispensation of time go to school so we know something out there. They would even want to get more education by associating wid other yout' outside [the home]. Who couldn't read and write much is de elders.
>
> Dat sort of administration is not wha' educate de yout' dem time, ya know. It was only kept among elders like demself. Because those people is people who want special

respect from de yout', and still have yuh as de yout' in colonialism according to how they were brought up!

We can surmise that as younger brethren dislodged themselves from
dependency upon those who could read and interpret the Bible text,
Rasta protest ceased to be wedded exclusively to prophesied events.
Certainly protest would no longer be limited only to social dramas like
the street march, the occupation of Kings House, or the capture of Vic-
toria Park or, for that matter, to solitary withdrawal into enclaves like
Pinnacle. The Rastafari did not, of course, entirely relinquish these
forms of resistance. Rather, mirroring the growing complexity of the
movement, resistance shifted significantly to a process of signifying
upon the authorized social codes that upheld the everyday common-
sense legitimacy of the system (i.e., physical appearance, dress, speech,
gender relations). This shift in orientation could be discerned in the
camp life as it was manifest among younger Dreadlocks during the late
1950s.

Warrior's Hill and 'Egypt': I-tal's Genesis

One of these camps formed in 1957-58 at the bottom of Paradise Street
between the General Penitentary and Bellevue Asylum. Its principal figure was a resourceful young brethren from Jones Town, Ras Maurice
Clarke (later known as *I-rice I-on*). The squatter site became an herb
camp which attracted Rastas and others who not only came to purchase
ganja, but to share in the social activity and quality reasoning at the
camp. One of those who *ground* with I-rice at the camp recalls that:

> I-rice is a bredrin who always carry a group ... not as a
> leader, ya know. When I seh a 'group', I mean like one can
> always visit him gates and spend all a week and eat every
> day and smoke every day. And is just pure livity and Rasta
> I-n-I reason 'bout. Differently now, yuh visit some man
> and him can't find food.

Through this, a small nucleus of young Dreadlocks began to *ground*
regularly with I-rice at that site. I-ney came from Allman Town, Rupert
from the West, Headfull from Bath in St Thomas. After a police raid in
1959 this site was abandoned. But the network of brethren that had

been established here proceeded, within a short space of time, to form two closely related camps, one in the East, the other in the West.

The first was on Wareika Hill, known to them as 'Warrior's Hill', the second in Back-o-Wall, widely known among Rastas at the time as 'Egypt'. Between 1960-64 this Back-o-Wall/Wareika Hill axis, until now peripheralized even in most Rasta accounts, gave rise to a unique chapter in the development of Rasta cultural expressions.

Those who grounded at Paradise Street and later moved to 'the Hill' were an iconoclastic group of individuals even within Rasta. After hearing three or four of this cohort witness about their sojourn on 'the Hill' I became curious about the following description of a Rasta camp published by Leonard Barrett.[6]

> At the foot of the long mountain range Wareika Hill, commencing from the KSAC[7] public park, at the end of Sligo Avenue, numerous members of the Rastafari cult eke out a miserable existence on the rugged hill slope owned by the Forestry Department. Among sharp pointed rocks and cactus they erect unsightly shacks out of cardboard, old wooden boxes, tree branches, and other materials with which the land is littered. The less fortunate ones, such as the newcomers to the settlement, live in shallow caves like animals. It may be hard for you to believe but if you take a walk up Mountain View Avenue, turn up Sligo Avenue, just below the Old Range, leading to that section known as the Quarry, what you will see there will surely upset your digestion. In close proximity to the public park at the end of Sligo Avenue, there are shacks which litter the whole area. They are dirty and unsanitary. The cultists live on land without any water. ... They engage in rituals unknown to other Rasta areas, and I have heard the cultists speak in a strange tongue.[8]
>
> I understand it to be a common language spoken by the 'Brethren'. To make a living, I understand that these hill people cultivate small gardens, in the back of their shacks, burn charcoal or supply homes with fence posts. To obtain their supplies of wood, or coal, or fence posts, the Brethren travel up the steep mountain range, barefooted and partially nude. (Quoted in Barrett 1968:5-6)

Barrett indicates that he visited this camp during his initial research. However, he mistakenly identifed the residents of this camp as members of the Rastafarian Repatriation Association on Adastra Road, a nearby group organized around the legendary Nyabinghi drummer Count Ossie. The young Dreadlocks on Warrior's Hill shared little in common with the Combsome group of Count Ossie. If anything, relations between the two groups were said to be antagonistic.[9]

The above account appeared originally on the front page of *The Star* on 9 April 1962. Complete with a photograph of one of the brethren, it was headlined as 'RASTAS ARE CAVE MEN'. Penned by a local observer who went under the name of 'The Saint', it was typical of the reportage on Rastafari over the years which reflected middle-class fear of the movement. By the time this description was published the core group that initially settled at this site had attracted a much wider circle of associates. The nucleus of its original inhabitants, however, remained a more or less tightly-knit group which continued to 'trod' regularly between Warrior's Hill and Back-o-Wall. Some 11 or 12 in number, the group included I-rice, Headfull, I-ney, I-ppie, Crucy, I-ston, Jackmon, Sekkle, Dizzy-I-yonny, I-yung-cum-P, Hy-a-whycuss, Hydow, and I-mes.

Despite the image of desperation and chaos projected by the newsmedia, the life-style of those on the Hill was quite consciously and deliberately constructed. It reflected a strict self-imposed ascetic code, the distinguishing feature of which was the ideological importance they attributed to the concept of 'nature'.[10] Many of these points are already rather well known. What is of particular note, however, is how developments within this small cohort formed a critical mass for the subsequent self-representation of Rastafari.

Chevannes is, I believe, on to an important point in noting that, with respect to hair culture, the Rastafari were not alone. They shared matted and knotted hair with impoverished derelicts who formed part of the lumpen strata of Jamaican society. Both remained outside the pale of 'respectable' society. But there was also an important difference between the two. Derelicts were stereotyped as madmen and controlled as such. They offered no collective commentary on their place or condition in society. While frequently labelled in the same way, Dreadlocks, by contrast, actively orchestrated a counter-discourse. They coupled the outward appearance of the derelict with innovative symbolic behaviours which signified upon the dominant codes of colonial society. Theirs was a multi-channeled process of signification which could not be easily bracketed or contained.

In this regard, Yawney (1985a:3) directs attention to the fact that the Rastafari have traditionally drawn upon multiple sources of authority in the social construction of their livity. These sources include continuities with African-Jamaican folk traditions, the Bible, and the ideology of the 'natural man'. Those of the I-gelic House drew prominently upon the latter. In their view, Dreadlocks reflected the way that the 'first man', the African man, appeared within God's natural Creation. This was imagery which harkened to a distant time and different place, and, as the Bible text showed them that what was 'in the Beginning' shall similarly be 'in the End', they reasoned that more was required of them than merely to 'carry locks'. It was incumbent upon them to realize again the primordial condition of the 'natural man'.

Their habitations, foodways, mode of dress, and ritual conduct were symbolic of this concerted effort. On the Hill, members of the core group lived in crude tatus or shacks made of boughs and thatch. These were little more than shelters for their few material possessions, since most slept in hammocks. On one occasion I listened as I-rice I-on, the first resident on the Hill, compared notes with another *I-tal* brethren on the austerity of their livity:

> You know how my gates stay? . . . whether through storm, rain, or anything? My house have no wall, ya know. It only have some stick jam up and a top of thatch. Mi sleep outside in a big hammock. Ya see, most a we just sleep outside every night. For three years mi only roof a de catafirma.

In addition to these *I-tal* gates, only items made from the natural 'creational' things at hand were used: coconuts and calabashes for bowls, and fired clay (rather than metal) for pots. Their garb was fashioned from crocus bags – or, in their 'dialect', from *I-rocus* which was tailored along the lines of the loincloths worn by East African tribesmen. That ganja, the 'holy herb', most often traveled in the same crocus bags was a symbolic parallel not lost on them.

For the I-gelic brethren, the Hill was liminal ground, a place of spiritual retreat and meditation. And in their rejection of worldly things they disdained all 'things of the flesh'. This covered two phenomenological categories: material comforts or indulgences, which extended to 'dealing with woman' (i.e., sexual relations or cohabitation); and meat products and items the manufacture of which required the slaughter of animals. These were the first 'strictly *I-tal*' Rastafari, vegetarians who

observed a total ban on eating meat. There was strict enforcement in related areas of ritual protocol as well. A visitor carrying a *cutlass* was expected to deposit it at some distance from the gates of a brethren, if
only because it was suggestive of a weapon. That fact that it could be
used just as easily to 'lick down' the birds around the area as to open a
coconut associated the implement with an aggressive intent. And, since
leather articles such as shoes required the slaughter of animals for their
hides, these Rastas chose to 'trod' barefoot as a logical extension of a
non-violent ethos. Others who came to sojourn in the camp were required to ritually discard their shoes in a fire pit. A similar taboo was
mirrored in their rejection of leather belts.[11]

Finally – and perhaps most noteworthy with respect to their place in
the wider Nyabinghi House, the I-gelic brethren exempted use of the
drums in their gatherings. Unlike others in the House who found a
powerful symbol of African identification in the *akete* (Nyabinghi)
drums and who made chanting and drumming an important aspect of
their livity, these brethren inveighed against using 'dead skin' (i.e.,
drumheads) to praise the 'Living Jah'. All of these observances represented logical extensions of the dietary avoidance of meat, the single ob-
servance which is today associated with *I-tal* livity.

Women: The Weaker Vessel

From the testimony of these Rastafari we begin to get an idea not only
about how they saw themselves as men, but how they saw themselves as
men in relation to women. Their asceticism extended to a taboo against
'dealing with women', an orientation which amounted to self-imposed
vows of celibacy. Virtually all members of this group include mention of
this principle in their personal narratives of 'coming up in the faith'.
Viewed in the context of cultural values associated with male behavior
and 'reputation' (Wilson 1969), this must been seen as a displacement of
prevailing attitudes toward 'sowing one's seed widely'. It should be
noted, however, that women had already become peripheral to camp
life among groups of Dreadlocks like the Youth Black Faith.[12] All the
same, celibacy was by no means a general feature of Rasta practice
during this time. A few Rastafari outside this group may have subsequently adopted this pattern, but among the I-gelic House celibacy
was enforced as a principle via peer pressure. Of the Back-o-Wall phase
at this time, I-yawney once proudly asserted that

Dem time in Abacka most bredrin nah really deal wid
dawta. It was a pure man trod dem ages. I man personally
spend seven year and nah deal wid ooman. One time mi
rest right between two dawta gates – hitch up mi hammock
right between dem gates, just untouchable.

Those of the original group, save for one of their number in Back-o-
Wall, adhered to this rule and vigorously enforced it among themselves.
Their abstinence lasted for periods of between six and ten years.[13] Although they broke temporarily with the aggressive masculine norm of
'sowing their seed widely', giving their separation from 'the flesh' a spiritual connotation, members of the group could still be seen to replicate
ambivalent Jamaican male attitudes toward women typical in the folk
consciousness.

I-n-I is not people wha lust! So even my baby-mother, mi
and she doan get along since she feel mi have no use fo'
ooman. Yet, within reasoning, de purpose of not dealing
wid ooman is because yuh need a time to guh in yourself
to reach dis (high) stage. Moses guh up a de Hill and
spend time, ya know. And when he come back down he
just deal wid people normal. De I seen? (I-rice)

. . . Ya see, dealing with a ooman, through she has ta see
her monthly period, dat is one of de chief problem. And
secondly, ya know dat after dealing wid a ooman in a 'creational' (sexual) form, she takes a certain amount of
strength out of your mind, out of your *goody* (body), and
she interrupt your meditation most time. (Headfull)

J: Like she cuts your nature?

No, she wouldn't cut your nature, but she interrupts de
spiritual entertainment because she would want yuh to
deal wid her naturally.

It should be pointed out that a number of those on the Hill came to
this camp with their baby-mother's children. It is difficult to say whether
the exclusion of women necessitated an independence in domestic matters, or whether, resolving to be independent, they decided to remain
apart from women. Reasoning upon the problem of the woman's 'issue'

[menses] (see *Leviticus* 15:19-20) and the potential pollution of one's food, I-rice remarks that

> ... it is no problem to eat from dem if yuh have an evidence of their condition. Remember, your mother is a woman. But in those time there wasn't any woman who would have to cook and give us anything – like maybe I siddong an wait till wha' a ooman cook before I eat. No.
>
> I first learn to wash mi clothes miself, and cook fo' miself, ya know what I mean? Because if yuh siddong and depend pon her at all times to guh through these section of livity yuh can be trapped.

At the same time, a number of brethren seem to realize that 'keeping a woman' (cohabitation) would impose domestic responsibilities upon them which might inhibit the expression of spiritual zeal they felt was necessary during this stage. Or, even keeping a woman within the gates yet vowing to remain apart would not be practical since she would not be inclined to accept the demands of their spiritual search. Headfull reasoned that:

> All she concentrate on dem time is ... like sometime yuh don't sex dem, they have a feelings 'pon yuh. And knowin' now yuh is a man, all dem is looking to seh is like yuh have another ooman outside ... and so much noise. So it cause a confusion.

Some may find these comments a bit puzzling in seeking to understand how the Rastaman has, as some argue, exerted a 'new found authority in the domestic domain' (Austin 1983:24). Strict *I-tal* practice, however, actually imposes upon the Rastaman domestic responsibilities not otherwise required of the Jamaican male. One can speculate that after this phase of celibacy was relaxed and the remaining observances of *I-tal* foodways were re-aligned with existing practice, this 'new found authority' continued to exert itself in other related forms.

I-tal I-tes: Rasta Foodways

A thorough treatment of *I-tal* food traditions would require discussion of this code in relation to issues of gender, class, household organization, and historical factors. This would include ideas about the social valuations placed upon certain types of food, the social relations associated with the preparation and consumption of food, and the ideological ends which food and food prohibitions (such as fasting or avoidance) can serve. Yawney (1985a) and McGarrity (n.d.) have already provided us with some important insights in this regard. The observations and testimony cited here complement a number of their observations.

Ideas associating food with ideas about purity and pollution as well as with spritual and physical fortification were already well fixed within the African-Jamaican milieu encountered by I-tesvar brethren. In early Rastafari, such implications for spiritual purification and physical well-being can be traced more or less directly to the racial eschatology and cosmology of the movement. The following passage in Howell's tract, *The Promised Key*, in which Whites are described as 'lepers' is revealing:

> The Adamic apple tree, my dear leper, your name is Adam-Abraham-Anglo-Saxon apple tree, that looks pretty and respectable to your eyes, don't it. Yes indeed – gross beauty is the Queen of Hell and royal leper Adam and Eve and Abraham and Anglo-Saxon are all White people if you please (quoted in Post 1970:201).

This view of Whites as diseased, as Austin (1983:23) points out, reproduces a deep-rooted concern prevalent among the Jamaican peasantry with the relationship between illness and spiritual states. We find this concern mapped onto the theme of Black Supremacy in the cosmology of nascent Rasta religion. Thus, a number of frequently voiced accounts of Haile Selassie's coronation draw upon the theme of illness in relation to White colonial power. The symbol of Black Supremacy and African power – mythologically represented by the biblical *golden sceptre* (see *Genesis* 49:10) presented to the Emperor in an act of obeisance by the Duke of Gloucester at his coronation – is juxtaposed with the supposed illness (variously leprosy or tuberculosis) of King George, the regnant figure of European colonial society (Smith, *et al.* 1961:19; Homiak 1985:169-70). This idiom of disease is used to symbolize, from a Rastafari perspective, the moral and spiritual putrefaction of the dominant White world.

By contrast, ganja, the 'holy herb' – the 'tree of life', which had already been embraced by the brethren as part of God's natural creation and elevated to 'the healing of the nations' – is conceived as central to a spiritual practice which separates them as Africans from this corrupt

world. It is not difficult to see how perspectives rooted in folk taxo-
nomies of the natural world could mature into individually expressed
ideas about purity and pollution, albeit ones without systemic application, whereby ideas about 'nature' are used to resist the dominant culture. In the African-Jamaican context where the natural world is seen as
alive with power, one can, as Yawney (1985a:4-5) suggests, appreciate
both the historical depth of the *I-tal* tradition as well as its creative re-
workings.

To most individuals familiar with Rastafari life-styles, *I-tal* typically
means 'vegetarian' (Landman-Bogues 1977; Owens 1976:166-9). Even
during its genesis, however, the 'strictly *I-tal*' orientation entailed more
than merely the avoidance of meat. In observing how the livity complex
is socially constructed among circles of Rastafari, Yawney (1985a:2-3)
makes note of the ideology of the 'natural man' as one among a number
of sources which Rastafari have to draw upon. This ideology was clearly
prominent among, if not actually innovated by, those of the *I-gelic*
House. All disdained store-bought, processed foods which, like other
Jamaicans, most Rastafari consumed. In this we can see a return to the
peasant context and the intertwining of rural and urban sturctures
which has marked the overall development of Rastafari culture. *I-tal*
brethren frequently obtained their fruits and vegetables from higglers
sympathetic to the brethren. They would tour Coronation Market late in
the day to see what, in fact, they might collect. Or, they obtained produce from the garden plots of the families related to members of the
group.

Not only did they, as Ras I-mes put it, 'lock off the shop' to avoid
dealing with commercially prepared or processed food in any form,
these I-talists also avoided the use of salt as a seasoning. And there were
also other discretionary observances at different times among those en-
camped on the Hill. This included a 'fresh food' tradition which forbade
cooking altogether for certain periods of time. During these phases the
preference was for raw fruits, peppers, and vegetables, some acquired
from higglers in the market known to them from their home parishes,
some grown on family land, and some acquired by foraging where food
like mangoes could be collected from open tracts of land. A number of
comments by I-rice I-ons and Headfull, respectively, touch on some of
these points as they related to the protocol in effect on the Hill:

> It start from Paradise Street in '58-'59 until I move to [Wa-
> reika] hill. Everyone come by we at de hill. Through de *I-*
> *tal* de I-gelic House start spread to Montego Bay, Steer

Town, Kusha Grung [St Ann] and dem place. *Once they is
amongst we, they see I-tal as a matter of compultry.*

Our chief delicacies use to be fruits, and pepper, and coconut. At a different stage ... we have a stage where we
never really cook ... but we roast – like we roast a bread-
fruit and we eat jackfruit and roast de seed which become
a 'bean' fo' we. Dat is a complete food in itself, ya know.
And yuh know is what we eat out of? De coconut dat
cut in two. Dat is our cup. And every one of our pot is
made out of clay. We were so I-tal we doan use spoon or
even bowl ... maybe we just eat off a leaf.

This turn to 'naturality' – which found expression in an opposition
between things 'created' and things 'made' – had a direct bearing upon
the attitudes and relations which the I-gelic brethren held toward
women. Eating *I-tal*, associated as it was with a preoccupation over the
purity of food and the possibility of pollution through association with
the woman's menses, provided further justification for excluding women
from male affairs. It may, as Yawney (1987:194) has suggested, also be
related to some of the ways 'brethren have co-opted the strengths of
traditional Jamaican women's culture and redefined the social context
so as to support patriarchial privilege'. We might consider the possibility that constructing one's livity as 'strictly *I-tal*' entailed a re-organiz-
ation of the household and domestic routines which appropriated the
partly 'feminized' domain of the yard (see Mintz 1989:248-9). This
makes sense in terms of Sherry Ortner's observations about the typically
opposed categories of male-female, culture-nature. With respect to
women's roles in the domestic domain she suggests that 'transforming
the raw into the cooked may represent, in many systems of thought, the
transition from nature to culture' (Ortner 1974:80). If so, the inventive
practices of the I-gelic House appropriated these ideas and the context
in which they are reproduced. The fact that *I-tal* food was originally
mostly 'raw' food is certainly consistent with widely held ideas among
the Rastafari which see cultural categories and practices in terms of
'naturality'.[14]

In addition to the implications of *I-tal* ideals for gender relations,
these practices also symbolized a determination among the brethren to
remain free from a dependency upon the hegemonic system. This went
hand in hand with independence from money and, by extension, the entire economic order which implicated Black people in relations of auth-

ority and subordination.[15] Reasoning upon the role of money at this time, they note that they

> would touch money, but I show yuh someting, Jakes, and yuh most really accept dis. Ya see, dere is people who maybe could sorry for us in a financial way according to how they see we 'pon de Hill. So, for instance, certain man come look fo' we there and when him was leaving him guh ina him pocket and tek out two pound and gi it way. And we seh, 'Fling dat 'pon de ground, man. Yuh haffi fling dat 'pon de ground.

> H: . . . so de earth bless it.

> I: . . . and de shop business was a thing I-n-I feel we coulda de without. It was someting to show we didn't need money – like looking into a more natural ting away from certain pollution dat mix up in dem food. We didn't touch nothing from shop – none a dem bread, bun, none a dem ting.

The exclusion of processed or store-bought food among these brethren predictably became associated with various customary rules and observances that continue among I-talist Rastafari today. *I-tal* brethren, as Yawney (1985a:5) observes, do not just 'eat from anyone' (i.e., allow anyone to prepare their food). They maintained collective responsibility for the quality and preparation of their food and sustained this concern through norms of commensality. To ensure the *I-tal* quality of what they consumed, each I-gelic brethren traveled with a large calabash to hold herbs and fresh food.

This attitude toward the purity of foodstuffs may be seen to reflect a broader concern with deep historical roots concerning food pollution and other untoward influences. In her analysis of the *I-tal* complex, Yawney (1985a:5) suggests that this concern over food may have a precedent in the widespread practice of poisoning in slave society and with the work of the obeahman. As least one assertion by a member of the I-gelic House suggests such a parallel. Ras I-mes, in reasoning about the origins of the *I-tal* code, linked it to what he saw as the practice of obeah at the 1958 Convention and prevalent among Jamaicans as well as older Rastafari. He remarks that:

Since I-n-I ages Rasta arise, is de Dreadlocks yout rise and stamp out de neo-Revival 'ting. Dat's why Prince Edward couldn't stay amongst I-n-I. De judgement was too stiff against dose (obeah) ting.[16] When I-n-I yout arise, dat is why we fling de clothes, de pot, de spoon, everything!

I is de first man dat 'throw away de pot', ya know [i.e., stopped cooking and began eating only fresh foods]. Just pure fruit and vegetables ... and I trod up in dat a good distance.

Two related facets of the food tradition which began on the Hill were the avoidance of salt and the copious use of peppers, both eaten raw and used to season pots of *I-tal* stew. There is no question that the austere life-style pursued by the brethren was construed as a form of 'testing' intended to separate the weak from the strong. A sojourn on 'the Hill' (in conformity with the norms that governed camp life) was a de facto rite of incorporation into the group. For those who could withstand its rigours the regime served to establish strong bonds. It should be noted that many brethren could not tolerate this regime (both with regard to smoking and eating). I-rice I-ons recalls, for example, those who would

smoke I-tal wid I-n-I but they complain. Say it affect dem stomach. And these people couldn't manage it. Like if a man come to visit us up there, ya see, most people can't eat [i.e., share our hospitality] because – Jakes, dis is not exaggeration – is all 100 and odd pepper, or 80 pepper we cook ina de pot. Good quality pepper like scotch bonnet ta raas! Or like sometime we is biting a scotch bonnet and eating a piece a coconut, and biting a bananna. Ya no know dem way?

Pepper, it can be seen, was substituted for salt as their seasoning.[17] There are, of course, precedents for food taboos such as the avoidance of salt in African-Jamaican traditions (see Alleyne 1988:104); and I have elsewhere suggested a cognitive explanation for why the Rasta's *I-tal* practice might have incoporated this feature (Homiak 1985:251-5). While some Rastas suggest a biblical explanation, I-rice I-ons, who was one of the principals in articulating aspects of the code, suggests a more direct and personally inspired explanation for his 'naturality'. One dis-

cerns in his remarks concerning the processes of nature an emergent
paradigm of 'the whole', of completeness:

> I use de pepper not because Lot's wife become a pillar of
> salt. For de big question is, if I gi yuh some green banana
> right now fo' cook yuh gonna put salt in it. But if I gi yuh a
> ripe one yuh doan add nuttin to it. Yuh know dem kinda
> way deh?
>
> In my spiritual research I was always saying that the
> Creator 'sweeten' and 'salt' dose ting Himself. So de
> mango doan need no sweeten, de yam doan need no salt.
> It doan need nothing, ya see, because nature is perfect to
> de dot. Dat is why we was de first man dat 'sweeten' their
> food wid pepper. So, as I seh, our naturality have always
> need respect.
>
> And when we get a jackfruit, is only de skin dash 'way
> after we done wid it. Ya see de seed of dat jackfruit – dat
> become a bean fo' we. We season it and stew it wid I-ppa.
> Same wid ginnep seed. I-n-I were so I-tal dem time we
> doan use spoon, we doan use (metal) pot. De pot we use
> were earthenware. And we doan use soap, cause we could
> guh ta Rock Spring and use ciracee or soap bush or some-
> time we use ackee skin.

Similarly, the sacralization of herbs that had begun amongst members of the Youth Black Faith was carried to yet 'higher' levels by those
who embraced a 'strictly *I-tal*' regime. I-rice I-ons' remarks define the
extension of *I-tal* into this domain of practice and associate it with a now
familiar lexicon in Rasta Talk:

> I-tal involve in de smoking same way. When I-n-I build a
> spliff we generally use corn trash because we condemn de
> paper. And we don't use cow horn fo' chalice. We doan
> tek de cow and cut off de horn. Doan deal wid nuttin
> name 'flesh'. We use a dreadnut [coconut] and de crotch
> of de oil nut [castor oil] tree feh we chalice.
>
> Within de smoking now, dat is where 'blindgarette'
> start. I-n-I doan use dem ting or de tobacco – which is de
> bac-o-tu. None of our bredrin ever smoke tobacco. Yet
> yuh still find some man would call it fronto to suit fo' what
> him was doing.

Herein was both a 'conscious' and austere attitude toward the things of nature – as with the roasting and eating of jackfruit and guinep seeds – and an 'emergent health paradigm', as Yawney (1985a) has noted elsewhere, of the *I-tal* orientation. Practices along this line included the copious consumption of *sinklebible* (aloe vera) which was peeled and eaten raw, infusions made from squeezed limes and the water from the chalices as a preventative against colds and a general wash for one's face and locks, and the use of coconut milk to shampoo the locks.

These practices were closely linked with an orientation of militancy toward the wider society; and within Rasta they were a means to publically announce the zeal of one's faith. By the mid-1960s as more brethren visited the Hill and to what had become an *I-tal* enclave in Back-o-Wall, these foodways and dietary practices began to spread, as Headfull recalls, well outside the capsule of West Kingston:

> De I-gelic House start to spread to Montego Bay, Kusha Grung, Steertown, and place like dat. Once dey is 'mongst we dey tek up de I-tal . . . and when dem gone home back dem carry dat.

I-tal held sway in many of the camps in Back-o-Wall: Brother Eric (later a well-known drummaker at Ferry) adopted the tradition and, whenever members of the group would pay him a visit, would respond with *I-tal* hospitality. Similarly with I-mes in Moonlight City and Stamp Out elsewhere in Back-o-Wall. What is significant is that these practices became part of a male-oriented and male-controlled sphere of activities, and served as part of the symbolic interface between this cohort and the wider movement (and, beyond that, the wider society). In its original genesis, *I-tal* became symbolic of an effort to reform Rasta attitudes toward the 'temple', the physical structure as the dwelling place of Jah. Younger Dreadlocks began to distinguish themselves in this way from many of those Rastafari who could be labeled as 'bellyswanger' and flesh eaters. Of these, I-ney explains that

> Dem man too much in dem h'eaty-h'eaty ways. Dem nyam any kind of flesh except fo' 'Massa Willy' [pork] and use all bac-o-tu. De I-gelic House was always preaching a more nutritional save-your-life kinda food, like health food. So we fight all de heap a meat eating and I-n-I find ourselves on de other side a dem like Bongo Claudy and Daniel who nyam flesh. Dem is man wha get dem terrible

mackrel from de middle a de barrel – de one yuh coulda
smell from a distant.
Man seh Jah live in him 'temple'. So wha yuh do man?
Yuh a defile yourself wid dat? Yuh a kill yourself wid dat?

In principle, most Rastafari could support these views. However,
many of the older brethren who were flesh eaters (and who were considered 'bellyswangers' by those of the I-gelic persuasion), felt in turn
that these younger Dreads were 'fighters' or fanatics who sought to be
unecessarily divisive. Many from this school counted those from the I-
gelic House as fighters whom they labeled as 'Absalom'. In a yard session with a number of *I-tal* brethren within earshot, Boboshanti, one of
the co-founders of the Youth Black Faith, used his testimony as an opportunity to 'throw words':

> It reach a stage dat I see a thing called 'food exploitation'
> ina de House from de one dat seh him I-tal. Well, when
> we check dat portion we feel so nice about it as another
> stage of de livity. But in an' among those dat really went
> on dat road yuh find a ting dat didn't exist among de
> general House coming up from such time. It bring a 'bad
> mind' ... man gonna exploit yuh because yuh eat a likle
> salt in you food. Yet when de 'binghi call him doan have a
> chant to hoist. Is de salt-mout man a de chanter, de salt
> mout man is de keteman [drummer]. He has been filled
> with de flavor dat are Rasta!

Another brethren, Stamp Out, who became an *I-tal* man in Back-o-
Wall in the early 1960s, recalls the contention that their practices engendered within the House. In my groundings, Stamp Out was the first brethren to offer an insight into the *I-tal* portion as identified with a
discrete grouping of brethren. His motives, I think were clear. He saw
my grounding as being influenced primarily by those outside the *I-tal*
ethos. He wanted to strike a point of balance. He remarked:

> In Back-o-Wall dem time yuh have dis session now, just I-
> tal Rasta, ya understand? No ooman no check dem ina de
> I-tes wha dem rest. And dem no check no ooman! Dem no
> check nothing fo' de world, seen? These I-tal man never
> use drum. They seh they don't use de dead skin and praise

His Majesty. So they chant a chant called 'Blackheart' without de drum.

So during dat I-tal session now it bring a 'tribal' [contention] between de I-tal man and these other set o' man coming off de same form [as Dreadlocks] who is fleshman. It bring a 'tribal' yet it was greater unity than even now! Well, dem man get de most beating from all these other Rasta (in the area) because all these man seh these I-tal man now a hold dong Rasta. Yet de I-tal man is de highest set of man these. De I-tal people was de I-tes of Rastafari.

Trodding in Higes Knots: I-tal Garb

The brethren who saw themselves as the 'I-tes of Rastafari' were unique, even awesome, in appearance – barefoot, with matted hair, cloaked in crocus bags, and armed with large rods. Their rods were themselves of note as they reflected the proliferation of organic metaphors among this group. They were crafted from small trees with the gnarled 'sprang' left intact to serve as their dreadlocks 'crown' and etched with the *I-ance* terms commonly used by these brethren to greet each other. Like the well known rod of correction of later Rasta history, these staffs served to convey an image of both power and defiance in a context where Blacks, most of all the Rastafari, were formally divested of authority.[18] The total ensemble was calculated to be an awe-inspiring spectacle.

The group coined a term for the act of appearing in public in this garb. They called it 'Higes Knots' (Higes I-yots) or 'Bags Knots', the word 'hige' being an archaic term in Jamaican English meaning 'to torment'.[19] The following statement by Brother Hyawhycuss is illustrative in this regard:

> My group, the Higes Knots people, were despised – even some brethren could not understand us. We were described as madmen. And there were special clothing dat we wore made from *I-rocus* [crocus bags]. And we would trod and 'torment' the blin'ty [city] to let de enemy know dat Rasta would stand regardless what dem try to do we. Dis was to show Babylon dat de Righteous would never

bow . . . fo' we went to de last stage of sackcloth. Even Babylon was afraid to come near we.

We didn't even wear shoes, We were like de barefoot
prophets of Ethiopia, it was so high. That is why many
people couldn't understand why young people like we
could 'disband' [abandon] all dese things, but it was *a way
of not appearing in the English style of dressing*, fo' we
didn't wear shirts and so on. We wear like an African
tradition in dose days, with our rod. . . . And when de rain
was falling, we wouldn't stop. We would just walk through
de rain and seh it was a blessing and just go on as a
prophet. And as one is moving through, people look and
seh, 'What is this in de rain?'

I-n-I were de main bredrin dat moved in de Higes I-
yots in its original stage. I am not saying dat bredrin did
not become Higes Knots afterwards, ya see. Or dat it is
different from Nyabinghi – fo' it is de same I-yabinghi, but
it is a stage [i.e., phase].

It was a high trod. Ya see, *we were searching to see how
far we could go go discover certain things.* (emphasis
added)

It is clear from this statement that the brethren were aware of how
their practice of livity could serve different functions. Thus, appearing
in Higes Knots (i.e., rejecting English dress) was a form of resistance to
the dominant culture while at the same time the self-abnegation associated with this phase was regarded as a necessary condition for spiritual
development. They were also aware that the extent to which they
flaunted the authorized codes of public appearance could serve to register outrage and fear as well as to communicate their intense zeal. In the
public perception, these brethren were seen as lunatics while within the
Nyabinghi House many saw them as the embodiment of an uncompromising 'never bow' ethic.

In the Back-o-Wall milieu, other brethren who were influenced by
this original core group came to refer to their form of austere practice
as representing the *I-tal* House. Much of their oral testimony reflects so-
cietal attitudes directed toward them (termed as 'Blackheart man') and
in this respect echoes the notion put forth by Chevannes that at least
some people made a conscious connection between (some) Dreadlocks
and madmen. It also reflects the perceived necessity to separate from
the defiling influences of Babylon. The visual codes which they shared

held no place for the evaluations and sanctions of the dominant society. I-rice recalls that

> Higes Knots was like a primitive 'first time' people. So yuh could imagine how people look 'pon yuh. Hicuss Hion and I wear dat and go through every part of de city, mek we family and friends see dat so we see who despise we. All kinda people was seeing yuh from your country [home parish]. They seh, 'Yuh see Maurice don't comb him head. Dem man soon gone a Bellevue, ya know!' Dat couldn't stop us. Ya see, it was a stage in de culture . . . a period of time for a certain amount of works until a next stage reach.

Yet it was not only the public which stigmatized these brethren; other Rastafari, as I-yawney recalls, chose not to endorse the Higes Knots livity:

> Nuff bredrin fight de sackcloth-and-ashes tradition. Dem seh we bring stigma 'pon Rasta. But I-n-I come wid de Higes Knots to purge out dis 'big suit' ting what some man wear. Like yuh gwaan like yuh can't go outa street without certain clothes. We bring dis to show man is not de clothes a do it. I-n-I of de I-gelic House just show ourselves publically in dat form to prove to man where de I-rits reach. Dat mean seh we dash 'way all Babylon vanity!

No doubt there were groups of Rastafari – both Combsomes and Dreadlocks – who saw the sackcloth tradition as unbefitting the dignity of a Rastaman. Some no doubt felt that the sackcloth livity made Rasta appear fanatical and played into the hands of those who wished to dismiss Dreadlocks as madmen and lunatics.[20] The Rastafari were quite consciously aware of how they were perceived, as I-rice notes:

J: Dey mus' seh yuh is madman dem time . . .

I: No . . . nah jus de *I-gelic* House. Man seh de yout [young Dreadlocks] dem a mad, ya know. Like man outa street seh, 'Yuh nah see who get mad? Yuh nah see Maurice walk up and dong ina crocus bag . . .' Dem regular use de

term 'lunatic' fo' we. But we seh is oppression mek de wise
man mad!

Such contradictory imagery has been apparent in Rastafari from its
inception; we have only to look to the Bible, or to the radical Puritan
tradition discussed by Roland Littlewood in Chapter 10, and the symbolic inversions characteristic of millennial prophecy. Recalling the
phrase of the Revival chant cited by Chevannes (Chapter 5) one could
be 'working for a mansion and a robe and a crown', yet accept with conviction that Rastafari will 'rise up the base things of the earth to con-
found the wise and prudent'.

Bloodfire on Babylon: Mystics as Militants

Despite the fact that some members of this cohort refer to the Hill as a
place of 'exile', they were not seeking to withdraw from society or others
within the movement. Rather, they were seeking spiritual growth
through a mystic alignment with nature and, from this, empowerment
with which to confront the dominant system. Quite consciously, they
made their site on Wareika Hill markedly visible to all in the surrounding area:

> Any part at all yuh there in Eastern Kingston – Windward
> Road, Rollington Town, Vineyard Town, Passmore Town,
> Franklin Town, all dem places – and look up, yuh can
> know which part our spot deh. Because there was an ever-
> lasting fire which never out! We always burn fire there and
> use a ting named carotee, mayflower. Every May it shoot
> out a ting. Ya see dat, de root of it, dat blaze and burn de
> whole night. Is a candle fo' we.

Nor were these brethren seeking to be inconspicuous when they left this
abode. Showing themselves publicly in the garb of Higes Knots was an
essential part of the tradition. Considering this as mandatory to their
witnessing to the faith they went out of their way to publicly announce
their presence to those in the area by 'trodding in Higes Knots' – walking barefoot in the middle of the street with their rods. Frequent movements between the Hill and Back-o-Wall provided ample opportunity
for them to show themselves. Moreover, it became customary for them
to walk a circuit as part of these movements calling down bloodfire and

destruction on Babylon. At times these public spectacles could escalate into social dramas. Headfull recalls that

> Ya see, when we in dem kinda mood there ... and we head fo' downtown. We pass through every police station on we way. We gonna pass through Giltress Street station, which in a Rollington ... de first station we blast it! Lightening and earthquake! Ya see, dem time I-n-I can't pass a police without drop a 'lightening' 'pon him. And den we walk guh on dong Portland road, guh dong Lacy Road ... and den we haffa 'trample' de Catholic Church a North Street.
>
> I: Yes, we gonna guh out a Cathedral a North Street, which is de island's capital fo' Catholic, and we quake dat too! Dem time now yuh did have Monsignor Gladstone Wilson, de Black Pope. Him name ina de history of Catholic in Jamaica. We blast there so. And we know which part him live too, ya know, and blast all there so.
>
> Everybody know and see we a come. Children run to dem gate and seh, 'Mummy, look who coming. "I-rie" a come'. And we call to dem when we pass.
>
> H: And den we cut dong back James Street and find we self dong back pon East Queen Street and haffa 'blaspheme' Central [police station]. And ya see when we coming back from Egypt [Back-o-Wall] later dat night, we have herb we get as gift from people outa respect fo' dat work.

Because of this the brethren on Warrior's Hill were seen by many in the surrounding community as a menacing presence. The result was that during 1960-61 two major police raids were carried out against the core members of the camp. The larger of these, which led to the arrest of 96 persons, unfolded as a public spectacle at the Sutton Street courthouse typical of the kind of spontaneous 'street theatre' that would attract numerous onlookers and curiosity seekers. Headfull and I-rice recollect the following:

> It was the biggest Rastafari case in de island dat time. In that case, we appear in court in African gown. When we

leave to de court, it wasn't from Wareika Hill, ya know. We guh to Back-o-Wall and is there – after we chant dat whole morning . . . cause we never guh to court yet without some heap a chant and I-ses.

H: It was like a procession leaving Egypt and going on . . . man walking in de middle of street. Dat is how we guh to court, ya know, not from a sidewalk point of view. And we is walking wid tall rod.

I: . . . not because we is violent . . . because to walk wid these tall rod, it 'militant' and one seem like dem don't know how to deal wid yuh. But is only de word we have as weapon . . . I-n-I never pig-gressive.[21]

H: . . . Yes, is tall rods wha carved . . . every one of us take rods and wear some tall gown. I have one dat write up wid 'Higes Knots', 'Blood and fire', and 'Blood touches Blood'. Nobody ever appear like dat in court before.

I: Is hundreds a people, ya know, when we pass through [Victoria] Park join in. It was like a parade . . . because before we reach [the courthouse] de police high command hear of us coming and set up barracades with riot squads and all dat. And dey come cross where we were standing wid big crowds on de other side of East Street – dat is when yuh reach on Sutton Street and East Street corner. And I remember dat dey start tek away rod from we because dey doan want yuh come in de courthouse wid rod.

Yes, dey tek 'way rod from Marcus and throw it dong de courthouse steps.

H: . . . and a lot of yout what follow we guh to jail too. Cause any yout dat seem like sympathizers . . . who leave school and [are] following . . . police was scraping dem up too. But we of we-self become untouchable because we were licking too hot wid de sound.

This militancy of the I-gelic House carried over into their interactions with other Rastafari during these years. For these, Back-o-Wall was their staging area from where they would travel to any and all functions kept by the House. Like I-ney, many of his cohorts complained that senior Dreadlocks expected certain deference from the youth:

> Ya see, bredrin like Puru and Wato seh dem is elder fo' we, so they never come 'mongst de I-gelic House neither 'pon de Hill or in Abacka. Yet we don't exclude dem, don't care how terrible de fight. When de House keep an I-ssemble I-n-I are everpresent. We guh amongst Prince Emmanuel, Wato, Duffos, Noel, Lloyd, all a dem man. I-n-I are de ones dat 'carry fire into de House' and really tek over certain scene. When I-n-I are there we control de chanting.

I-ney's descripton of 'carrying fire into the House' glosses a number of points. For this group the chanting of I-ses and the burning of fire were inseparably linked. The imagery of fire was, of course, prevalent within Rastafari prior to this. But the I-gelic brethren maintained it as a duty, both on the Hill and at their site in Egypt where enormous piles of tyres (collected from the JOS discards and carried into Back-o-Wall) were burned at their gatherings.

At a symbolic level, their practice of arriving at a grounation *en masse* and then proceding to take over the proceedings with their chants, symbolized an effort to 'burn out' the old colonial ways within Rasta. This introduced into Rasta ceremonies a new style of chanting which had been created by them on Wareika Hill: the repetitive chanting of the single sound 'I/ai' through a range of octaves.

In its inception on the Hill, what this reflected was first a disdain for the use of drums, the skins for which were acquired by the slaughter of an animal. I-yick I-on recalls that

> It was right after de Mission to Africa and . . . wha we do, we were stepping up in a special kind of I-yant. We just yant right through using our voice as music without drums. Dat's why yuh call it 'I-pper I-mes', fo' it set up in I-self. I-n-I create it without playing drums. Yuh would have so many voices playing de voice like an instrument dat it pull people to de area. Yuh could stay miles away and hear it.

Coupled with this was the effort by this group to free Rasta from sole dependence upon the Bible as a text (in its European form) and the usage, common among older-style Rastas, of the Sankeys or church hymnals to introduce or 'line-out' chants for the congregation (see Bilby and Leib 1983). Both of these practices the Higes Knots brethren saw as suppressing the 'creativity toward the culture' which had been inspired in them. In addition, they rejected the hymn-book form because it was too closely linked with colonial Christianity. Much, in fact, of what informed the ritual sensibilities of older Rastafari was seen as aligned with the colonial Christian source and derided as 'old-man-ism'. For example, I-rice I-ons observes that

> There is too much old-man-ism amongst dem. Some a those man come to Rasta as a big man so dem ingrafted wid certain colonial teachment and try to keep de yout under colonialism.

> Jake: Colonialism? How yuh mean?

> I: Everyting dem bring up at 'binghi come from de Church. Like dem woulda bring de same song book dem have in Church – wha yuh call de Sankey – to I-yabinghi. Is dat dem bring and sing after.
> So Puru and dem sorta elderly bredrin like Bongo Hill and Jew Man – dem don't speak wha we speak. De only ting dem coulda show yuh is de Bible. Dem can't argue nuttn widout dem bring de Bible. But please, when dem read de Bible, is a Christian interpretation dem give yuh. And when dem chant, yuh know wha dem chant? Dem use Sankey what dem use in Church of God. So it always cause a critics. When Puru tek dat out at 'binghi I-n-I put fire 'pon dat – 'Lightening pon dat ... dash dat 'way! Fire bun!' All a dem people wah yuh see a chant outa book and ting, dem burn out!
> De breda cannot give a prayers without de Psalms. Him don't have nuttn of him own dat him create as an inspiration to de culture. Ya see, certain movements don't fit de Rasta movements. Is de same ting transforming from colonialism back into de movement and it don't guh nowhere.

One of the ways in which these activists responded to this was, as I-ney recalls, to 'control the chants'. In their dialect, this meant chanting in *I-pper I-mes*, or 'stepping to the Upper Room'. At these assemblies,

the brethren would 'stand one side and chant in I-Hi-Hi ... I-yah-Hi
...', harmonizing to whatever chants were introduced. This they saw as
a means to 'rub out the Sankey and Christian hymn-book business'. In
their view, fixing upon the morpheme 'I/ai' as the cornerstone of a ritual
code, served to inscribe a communal sensibility and (like all ritual language) to objectify and externalize subjective realities:

> Dem time we had de I-hiya-I, I-ya-I, I-I-I ... a session of
> chants I-n-I call *I-pper I-mes* [i.e. 'the Upper Room']. And
> all chants like dem doan have no end. And no word! What
> I can show yuh is whenever dem have an assemble going
> on and we come there, they respect we but dey don't show
> we dat. Ya know is wha dem respect we for? Is because de
> I-gelic House is bredrin wha don't sleep. Ya see when we
> tek over now in our chanting, dat just a gwaan endless, ya
> know. Cause I-n-I gwaan like we have no responsiblity.
> We don't sleep, we don't worship food. And dem [the
> other brethren] love dat![22]

As the movement grew and diversified and as tight-knit cohorts like
the Youth Black Faith and the *I-gelic* House were assimilated within the
island-wide networks of Rasta, chanting in the I-sound came to have
pragmatic as well as spiritual significance. At island-wide 'binghi, those
who do not know specific chants, or who have a different repertoire of
chants, can easily follow the melody line in the I-sound.[23]

Their strict adherence to *I-tal* principles and the conviction with
which they enforced them warrants discussion in relation the common
practice of slaughtering a goat and holding a feast in association with
special *grounations* or 'birthnight' festivities.[24] Curiously, this practice is
little noted by other scholars. Those of the *I-gelic House* vociferously rejected the practice because it was perceived to contaminate Rasta practice not only through the shedding of blood, but also through connotations of 'science' via its link to Pukumina practice (i.e., the offering of a
living sacrifice to the spirits). Stamp Out recalls the following incident in
Back-o-Wall in 1962:

> It happen dat these man who would guh round wid de
> Nyah-Congo and chant, dem use to kill goat and cook pot
> and dem 'ting. When de 'binghi start yuh would see a man
> leaving wid a big ram and him put de ram ina de crowd

and one chop on de head and de ram drop. Well, it cause a combustion because de I-tal man seh 'No!'.

One day Duffus come from jail and Puru and Joslin now plan to have a goat feast round Back-o-Wall. And it happen a Sister want to celebrate her birthnight, so they look to kill a goat and feed up. Well, mi see I-ney man and some other bredrin leave dem gates and guh over there and seh, 'We want de murderer fo' de goat!' It cause a combustion, a terrible combustion dat it reach to where man gradually stop de goat business. From dat, man just gradually come into de faith and know seh, well, de praises of Rastafari didn't call fo' blood. It just call fo' a cup of herb.

By all accounts, the inclusion of goat feasts within the ceremonies of various Rasta groups was a prevalent practice throughout the 1950s and into the early 1960s. The intransigence of the *I-gelic* House toward this practice, especially anywhere within the Back-o-Wall enclave where *I-tal* brethren had become numerous, had a deterrent impact on this custom. By 1963-64 the practice had completely disappeared.

I-gelic I-yound: The Origins of Rasta Talk

Words live a 'socially charged life', as Bakhtin (1981:293) puts it, steeped in particular 'contextual accents and intentions'. Nowhere is this more apparent than among the Rastafari. It is clear from the preceeding oral accounts that a distinctive form of speech accompanied the *I-tal-Higes Knots* phase of witnessing among the brethren. The socially charged 'dialect' which they created was replete with words formed by substituting the morpheme 'I', 'I-yah', and/or 'Y' for the first syllable of the English form. It is this category of lexicon which has become the predominant and most creative aspect of Rastafari language (Pollard 1980:36; Alleyne 1988:143). Their personal testimony puts to rest a number of unanswered questions concerning the initial appearance and spread of the *I-ance*.[25]

Chevannes sees the development of this language as accompanying the origins of the Dreadlocks but is forced to concede that 'exactly which linguistic innovations among the Dreadlocks appeared when has not yet been established'. Similarly, Pollard (1982:20-1), who has drawn upon Chevannes' ethnographic work in her attempt to trace the development of so-called 'Dread Talk', suggests that while evidence for these I-sounds can be found in the 1960s, nothing is known of how they initially developed or how general their use became once they were introduced.

Chevannes is among those who argue that Rasta speech is historically continuous with the folk penchant for punning and experimentation with language. He isolates the Youth Black Faith for special attention in this regard, noting that the jargon presently spoken by the Rastafari should be attributed to a camp of young brethren 'who came together about 1949' (Chevannes 1978b:189; see also, Pollard 1982:20). This view seems acceptable only if we are to understand that the Youth Black Faith were among those who inagurated the process of remodeling the Jamican Creole along the lines of an 'anti-language' (see Halliday 1978:164). The emergent lexicon of I-words (which Pollard identifies as the most significant feature of Dread or Rasta Talk), was not, however, within the scope of their innovations. In fact, those of the Youth Black Faith and their age-mates are said to have been among those Rastafari most opposed to the *I-ance* at the time of its introduction. Yet it is clear that 'sounds' were developing among the brethren during the Youth Black Faith time. One of the co-founders of that House, Boboshanti, recalls that during the 1950s and even early 1960s,

> Dem time we neber use de term baldhead, or how man woulda seh now, baldtail. Dem is man I-n-I call *raas* plucky. For even within de Youth Black Faith is Comb and Locks mix up together before we step to de House of Boanerges. De culture was still developing up and dreadlocks was not compultry at dat time as a Rasta.
>
> And in those time not so much man use *chalice*. Is *cutchie* use in dem time. We don't call it *chalice*, we call it 'hot rod'. A pure *cutchie* I-n-I use dem time. Coming up the lineridge we step to *chalice*.

Only at the end of the 1950s did a 'battery of I-words', as Nettleford (1978:201) calls them, begin to appear in Rasta Talk; and then only among a small group defined by the *I-gelic* House and their associates. Some observers of the movement suggest the use of the term 'I', in the self-reflexive nominative case, among the Rastafari from about 1954 (Robert Hill, personal communication). This would reflect the obvious influence of the Bible. But until a more compelling claim is advanced by other brethren, it appears that the proliferation of remodeled words formed by substitution of the pronoun 'I' (and the cognate Y) must be directly attributed to that handful of young Dreadlocks who first grouped at Paradise Street and later established themselves on Wareika Hill. The founder of this camp, I-rice I-ons recollects that

> We exile ourselves to the hills where there is no noise, no bus, no pollution. Is a different meditation reach yuh there. Ya see, only a Bible and mi rod I tek to de hill. Eventually now, we guh into ourselves – into de 'higher mountains' as wha Moses did do for his meditation – in search of de Creator. And de Creator speak to I-n-I through de spirit and fix a new tongue in de latter days which is de *I-tesvar I-yound.*
>
> *See-knots-see-I, I-yah Kongo, I-yah-Yinghi-I!* ... *One Yantifull I-yound!* – those art words dat Headful I-on and I create – even up to *I-rie I-tes.* We started dat at Wareika Hill ... it never come from nowhere else. Well, after a time now we had to leave Wareika Hill to penetrate all dem *I-tesvar I-ses I-yasta Y-ool-I I-yantifull-I* into Back-o-Wall to form a group. Dat was de *I-gelic House.*

It can be surmised from I-rice's recollections that the *I-tesvar*, almost from its inception, featured creative constructions based not only the sound 'I/ai', but on the widely noted homonymy between 'I' and 'Eye' and the associated idea of vision (see Leib n.d.:16; Homiak 1987:225; Alleyne 1988:148; Hall-Alleyne 1984:143; Yawney 1979:170-72; Pollard 1982:21). Through this device Rastas derived the appreciation that the most positive force is 'perception', realized both physically *and* metaphysically through the 'I/Eye'. This gave rise to the proliferation of sounds like *See-knots-see-I* (Selassie-I), *see-var-standing* (understanding) and words that contained semantic inversions like *conspira-blind* (conspiracy), *pharma-blind* (pharmacy), and *blindgarette* (cigarette). The Jamaican linguist, Mervyn Alleyne (1988:147), has commented on this process of the remodeling of the lexicon, suggesting that it is an attempt to bring 'the form of the word closer to the (literal phonetic) meaning and to eliminate inconsistencies between form (i.e., sound) and meaning'. Rastas would certainly acknowledge such an *'overstanding'*, yet this does not account for such progressions and permutations as: understanding = ovarstanding = I-varstanding = Eye-varstanding = see-var standing; or babylon = *babylouse* = *lowbylouse*. In my view, the *I-tesvar* initiated a process, broadly conceived, of 'signifying upon' or 'on top of' the European-derived tongue while simultaneously dismantling it from within. This view, I believe, is more in keeping with the manner in which an interlocked complex of aesthetic codes (in dress, dietary practice, *and* speech) was deployed concurrently as an ideological commentary on personhood within Jamaican society. It also reflects a struggle within signification – these sounds conveying an attempt to decolonize and re-patriate Black people's consciousness from 'mental slavery' imposed upon it within the Creole hierarchy.

Judging from the predominance of the 'Y' substitution in the voca-bulary of these first *I-tesvar* speakers, they may have drawn (consciously or unconsciously) upon an African-derived dialect, archaic in Jamaican speech. Bilby (1985:145-6), drawing upon the work of Glenn Akers, de-scribes these words as Rastafarian adaptations of Bongo Talk (see Akers 1981:73-4), a dialect sometimes used in the recitation of Anansi stories.[26] Word formation is based on the substitution of initial conso-nants with the vowel 'y' to form words like *yood* (food), *yot* (pot), and *yound* (sound). Such words are frequently found in *I-tesvar* in addition to more complex parallels that would include, for example: *I-yasta Y-oolie I* (Rastafari), *I-yadda Y-ool* (literally, 'the Fullness of the Father'), *Y-ungo Y-ungo, Yanti-I* (Bongo-Bongo Shanti-I), or *I-ses I-yadda* (praise Jah). The frequent combination of 'I' and 'y' in *I-tesvar* through recourse to the more expansive 'I-yah' (as in, for example, *I-yah-yound* [sound]), may, in fact, represent a further level of modification on the speech by the first speakers of this code.

Whatever phonological and sociolinguistic continuities can be drawn between this speech and instances of Jamaican dialect, it must be em-phasized that the pragmatics of communication associated with this code served to reshape its semantic implications. This seems to be a dis-tinction largely overlooked by linguists who have commented upon the code (see Pollard 1980, 1983; Alleyne 1988:146-8). We might consider, for example, how it served to reinforce existing Rastafari constructions of gender. Here we should appreciate how the practices put into effect by the members of this group developed as a series of overlapping codes. In reasoning upon the significance of their abstinence from sex-ual contact, those of the *I-gelic* cohort linked this to the inspiration that produced their distinctive form of speech which was/is replete with I-words. Headfull remarks that

> By keeping away from ooman, dat's how de *I-tesvar* came
> into our mind. Ya see, dat is how we have got de spiritual
> gift. It is an inspired thing, we neber get it through educa-

tion. After a certain amount of years of expanding ourself
in de emotional powers of His Majesty, we leave out de
ooman altogether. Then de spiritual retreat start teaches
us.

Subsequent meanings which devolved from the pragmatics of communication in *I-tesvar* are similarly relevant to the gender issue. Note
the interchangeable usage of 'I' and 'see' coupled with the ideological
proposition that it is only the man who can 'sight up' Rastafari, that the
woman's path to Jah is through the man. And in actual speech usage,
the responsorial 'I' is not customarily used when speaking with '*dawtas*',
a term which can be seen to encode the subordination of women (Yawney 1987:2). 'I', for the Rastaman, is first person singular, masculine
gender. And use of the term 'I' (or cognates such at 'I-tes', as in 'Yes,
I/I-tes' or 'True I/I-tes') to affirm the statement of another individual is
typically reserved for exchanges among *male* speakers.

Another glimpse into the source of inspiration for these first *I-tesvar*
speakers is related to the effort of the brethren to learn to speak Amharic, a development which first began in the early 1950s. Headfull reports of his experience that:

> I started with Amharic words ina de '50s, for I use to have
> a book and I self-taught de Amharic. 'I-n-I' was really de
> first custom of our sound taken from de Amharical sys-
> tem.

Headfull did not explain the conjunction between the ubiquitous 'I-
n-I' and Amharic. However, the use of these sounds (i.e., remodeled
Amharic terms) suggests that quite early on, *I-tesvar* passed through a
phase of intensive elaboration. My experience with at least seven of its
originators leads me to believe that it was spoken on a continuum with
varying numbers of remodeled Amharic words (formed through
multiple substitutions of 'I', 'Y', and 'I-yah'). It was already the case that
Rasta speakers were conscious of the 'Queen's English' as being inter-
larded with phonemes that masked the true meaning of various words;
among some of those in the original *I-tesvar* speech community this recognition gave rise to a concurrent remodeling of Amharic words used
coterminously with the manipulations being imposed on English. Headfull again:

De word *I-ses* is praise. Like you'd seh, 'Sattamassa agana'
– in Amharic dat is 'Give thanks'. Now in de *I-gelic* House
dat is now 'I-yah-yatta I-yahmassa I-yah-yahyama'. That's
'Give thanks'.

Or tek, for instance now, in Amharic now you'd seh de
'sun' is Jammie barrie tasseyeh. In I-varic it was I-yammie
I-yarrie I-yasse I-yeh. De moon is 'karraca' which is I-
yahyacca. *Ya see, I-n-I at dat time was reasoning in de elements dat really holds up Creation.*

Considerable range of experimentation with this speech existed almost from the start. For example, some of the *I-tesvar* examples provided to me by Headfull and Hyahwhycuss Hyahkion indicate that gender and conjugation were employed in their elaboration of the code.
This was a usage which distinguished between active and passive
verbs/adjectives and masculine or feminine versus neuter gender with
reference to their 'high' and 'low' qualities. Thus, the idea that human
'activity' is something positive, and thus the term *I-hivity* or *Hi-I-vity*. By
contrast:

An inactive thing is something now which is not positive –
or *lowvity*. Or, Like how we woulda seh, 'We coming from
Stony Hill to Half Way Tree'. But we don't call it Half
Way Tree, we call it 'Piece-a-Way' Tree, for de 'half' is
just 'piece'. I-n-I would seh, 'I-n-I I-yodding I-yum I-yony
I-yill a [to] I-yahease I-hiyahyah low-eet'. Street now
becomes *low-eet* because yu'd a call it a neuter gender. A
neuter gender is 'tings like a car – *lowar* – doan have no
feelings, ya see.

During this period, the soundscape of the community was a contested domain. Like the sackcloth-and-ashes tradition defended by this
group, the *I-tesvar* was not favourably received outside of 'the Hill' and
in certain sections of Back-o-Wall. Most of those within the Nyabinghi
House – including cohorts such as the Youth Black Faith and the
Church Triumphant of Jah Rastafari, not only declined to endorse it as
a positive development, they condemned it as a 'strange tongue' and actively resisted it. One reason for this was probably the general attitude
which many brethren had toward the overall style of witnessing embraced by the I-gelic House: the sackcloth, the celibacy, the extreme
austerity, coupled with their general reputation as 'fighters'. One bre-

thren who came up under the tutelage of Boboshanti, Ras Shaphan, saw
them as outsiders to the House who refused to conform during a period
of 'heavy discipline'. He recalls that

> Dem 'big rod' man was some terrible fighter! They wasn't
> really trodding with de House. Ya see, when dem come
> which part we keep I-ssemble dey mash up de I-ses. Is
> only after a time deh come ina de House.

Resistance to this group may also have hinged upon their unortho-
dox approach toward daily Rasta interaction: the sounds they used ex-
clusviely in greetings. Dating to the time of the early Youth Black Faith,
greetings were important forms of Rasta social interaction. Particuarly
among the first generation of Dreadlocks, older brethren commonly
speak of never passing another Rasta who was anywhere within eyesight
without hailing him (see Homiak 1989:13) 'Rastafari' and 'Selassie I',
these were among the ambient sounds in the aural environment of Kingston. Particularly prior to the advent of dreadlocks, such exchanges sig-
naled the distinctive and separate identity of the Rastaman. As I-rice
and Headfull reveal, those of the I-gelic House 'forworded' with new
sounds which set them apart from all other Rastafari:

> In a stage, we doan seh, 'Haile Selassie', ya know. And we
> doan seh 'Rastafari'.
>
> J: Wha yuh seh?
>
> I-n-I seh 'I-sta-Yoolie-I'. So people was saying we de-
> nounce Rastafari. Because we would come on [to a scene]
> and man greet we wid 'Rastafari!' And we seh, 'I-sta Yool-
> ie-I'. And him seh, 'Wha de raas klaat yuh talking 'bout!'
> and come again with 'Rastafari!'. And I seh, 'I-ya-yinghi-
> I!'[27]
> Because we call out so much name in dat tongue. I-n-I
> greet everyone wid these sound. And dem guh 'way –
> same Rastaman, ya hear – dem guh way and seh we de-
> nounce Rastafari and we is coming speaking in strange
> tongues.

It should be noted that although an extensive vocabulary of 'I-words'
proceeded to diffuse throughout Rastafari in the ensuing years, few of

the greetings or related sounds that served as the public signature of these original speakers have acquired similar currency. Greetings such as *'I-yasta Y-ool-I'* and *'Yungo-Yungo Yanti-I'* (Bongo-Bongo Shanti-I), or exclamatories such as *'I-on shappan I-on'* (literally, 'man sharpens man', but a gloss for 'each-one-teach-one') or *'I-yuncum I-yoder'* ('the Nyabinghi Order has arrived') are in use only within a small subset of speakers.[28]

Older Dreadlocks who had established the groundwork for earlier linguistic innovations apparently resented these new developments. The linguistic process which Pollard (1983:21) refers to as 'stepping up words' (by which Rastafari can be seen to signify upon the dominant code at various levels), engendered, for a time, a certain amount of discord within the House. Speaking of his first groundings in Back-o-Wall (in 1958-59), I-yawney I-on recalls that

> When I-n-I forward in to de House dem time I hear de sound 'ovar' [overstanding], for bredrin seh dem leave de 'understanding' and step to de overstanding. Well, I-n-I de yout now seh we are not 'ovar' – I-n-I are 'Hi-var'. So I-n-I step to de *I-varstanding* and de *See-varstanding*. Yet within a time man get to realize it kinda cause a spiritual grudge for it come like a form of competition. Dem [older] bredrin a seh they set de foundation and they was defending wha dem create. According to dem is like de yout now come to change up a 'ting. So dem never really support it. Up to now most a dem don't know nothing about de *I-var I-yound*.
>
> Don't care wha a next man want to seh, ya hear. I-n-I of de *I-gelic* House were de ones to full-first dis language.

'I/ai' became a cornerstone for Rasta Talk not merely because it is about the Word and because it implicates a speaker in the Godhead; it became a rejection of the colonizer's power to name, a point which is strangely unappreciated by all but the Rastafari themselves. A quote by Yawney (1979:219) is apt in this regard.

> Who is You? There is no you. There is only I, I and I. I is you, I is God, God is I. God is you, but there is no you, because you is I, so I and I is God. We are all each other and one with God because it is the same life energy that flows in all of us.

As with every other innovation in livity advanced by this group, the organizational framework which ultimately accomodated these new sounds was the principle of free association defended by members of the Nyabinghi House. This supplanted the idea of formal group membership which had existed among the Rastafari prior to the time of the Youth Black Faith. As Chevannes (Chapter 4, this volume) notes, this principle was institutionalized among Rastas as the idea of 'being free from constraint' and free to be accountable for one's actions (see also Jah Bones 1985:29-30). In relation to this shift, the original etymology of the term *I-rie* is revealing. Consider the testimony of I-yawney on this point:

> In those ages [1959-61] yuh have man saying 'I-man free'. I-n-I in de I-gelic House now tek dat sound and seh, *Irie*! So it just become a creativity within de I-rits dat I-mple and I-mple could full-first a language. Dat sound now gone throughout de whole creation to show de sound is positive.

While *I-rie* has emerged as a sound among the brethren to cover a full range of social purposes, that it should have emerged as such a recognizable sound within the Nyabinghi House suggests a pragmatic link to the fiercely guarded prerogatives of individual speakers. Perhaps more so than any single sound in the *I-tesvar* vocabulary, this word is implicated in both the semantics and pragmatics of communication among Rastafari. The brethren are following quite sound linguistic intuition when they assert that 'Yuh can write a book out of I-rie', or that 'I-rie is a complete coverage for 'nuff thing'. Any attempt to reduce this sound to mere referential meanings only impoverishes our understanding of how the code functions.

I-rie may refer to an existential state – as in a state of completeness. Or it may be used as a 'form of pleasantry'. But it is also used reflexively to qualify the state of a relationship which may exist between speakers or between a speaker and an individual/group being referenced. Of course, the range of meanings which *I-rie* can take on varies with the understandings of different members of the speech community. In some contexts it may be used by a speaker to express his/her individuality and to underscore the expectation that one's right to differ be respected. This sound, in effect, relates directly to Chevannes' observations about how the Rasta concept of a 'House' supplanted prior notions of membership and authority among earlier groups of Rastafari. That this principle – 'I-man free' – became encoded in linguistic usage tells us something about the importance of speech for establishing and maintaining a sense of community among individuals who share a wide range of ideas and practices.

The usage of *I-rie*, for example, can be related to how Rastafari orient and interpret their mutual interactions in terms of a system of shared differences. This applies to the continuum of cultural practices which exists among Rastafari as well as to cultural differences which exist between them and other Jamaicans. Thus, when a strictly *I-tal* brethren is offered a 'cup' (pipe) with tobacco or food prepared without his supervision, he may decline with the response, 'Man I-rie' (i.e., 'I'm fine – but I'm also free to decline'). We can also appreciate how the code serves to mark similar contrasts between the Rastafari and non-Rastas, seeing Rastas as members of a 'local egalitarian community' of men embedded within the hierarchical structures of the wider society (Brenneis 1987). Thus, the Rasta can import conventions which apply to their egalitarian ethos into non-Rasta settings to deflect the hierarchical rules for decorum. For example, in a setting where behaviour might call for a formal greeting (e.g., 'Good morning, Sir'), a brethren can use *I-rie*. This is so common now that Rasta has begun to colonize domains of interaction within the dominant society, although such usage by a non-Rasta middle-class speaker would more likely be intended to strike a cord of familiarity with the addressee. The point I wish to make is that the whole range of sounds in Rasta Talk constitutes a register with pragmatic meanings. Usage of the code says something about the relationship between speakers.

Although many of the first Dreadlocks generation, perhaps the majority, rejected these sounds, by all accounts the tongue began to spread quite rapidly among younger Rastafari during the early 1960s. Regardless of the context of its use, its power lay in its effectiveness as a ritual dialect. That is, recourse to this tongue enabled speakers to externalize and objectify an ideal – the vision of African divinity and redemption – that is highly personal and subjective (see Leib n.d.:16). The physical mobility of the I-gelic cohort coupled with the centrality of the areas where they grounded no doubt assisted its dissemination. In Back-o-Wall other brethren like Spree-man, Gabby, Wake-eye, Negus, Sonny, and Brother Eric became fluent speakers and innovators of the *I-tesvar* as did Jah Bones and his cohorts linked to the various Trench Town camps. Other age-mates like Ras Shephan on Foreshore Road had similarly picked it up and began to actively expound it by the mid-1960s. Intensive interaction among Rastafari (and non-Rasta) in all of these areas undoubtedly assisted its spread. And, since we know that both linguistic and ethnic self-identification remain critical to social interaction in Jamaican society, the fact that public scenes were inscribed with the *I-tesvar* would surely have lent it weight as a register of resistance and as a source of in-group identification. An example by I-rice I-ons will suffice to demonstrate this:

> 'Egypt' [Back-o-Wall] was a serious place a gaddering dem time. Yuh see, Egypt was like a court where reasoning and chanting is 'round de clock. Dat spot is nearby guinep tree ... an open space wid *tatus* around where every man haffa meet to lick out sound.
>
> And when de I-gelic House keep a meeting up a Egypt – when yuh look round ya see people form a 'fence'. Because from these fourteen parish, people meet in Coronation Market and people in Coronation hear about dis 'ting round a Back-o-Wall. Dat was a time when yuh stay out a market and hear de chant ... as far as it is, seen? And den, people and peasant wha come as higgler find themself over there and can't guh back [until] morning, it draw up their attention so much! So is all kind a different people reach up there and hear someting.

Similarly, Hyahwhycuss Hyahkion observes that 'Coronation Market is a place dat help carry out de sound. When yuh guh in there and block these sound, people carry it out to place like Duhaney Park, Rae Town, and all dem place ... even into country'.

All of this had taken place more or less by late 1963 when Crucy, one of the charter residents on the Hill, was murdered by a local resident. In 1964, after the Government's destruction of Back-o-Wall and various police raids upon 'the Hill', the Higes Knots cohort ceased to function as frequently as a group. Although there continued to be resistance to the use of the tongue from various quarters of the movement,[29] the *I-tesvar* lexicon had permeated the wide-spread networks of the Nyabinghi House and became well established among many circles of brethren by the late 1960s.

One notable linkage which occurred during the interval took place after I-rice I-ons moved to Fifth Street in Trench Town in 1967. There, on a more or less daily basis, I-rice was in contact with Bob Marley and Peter Tosh on Ninth Street. Around the same time, Marley also began to visit the site of the camp on Paradise Street (also influenced by the *I-tesvar* sounds) which had been vacated by I-rice and his peers in the late 1950s. I mention this because the reccurrence of words such as *yot* (pot), *yook* (cook), and *yuud* (food) in Marley's song *Dem Belly Full* as noted by Bilby (1985:144-5).[30] What can be noted at this point is that while on Ninth Street Bob Marley was in fairly frequent contact with I-rice and other brethren of the *I-tesvar* persuasion. It is conceivable that the words used in 'Belly Full' could have derived from a general Bongo Talk source; but a more telling instance of the *I-tesvar* influence suggests otherwise. This appears in a later song, *Ride Natty Ride* on the *Survival* album. Following Marley's use of a biblical proverb frequently cited by Rasta elders, there occurs a sound that has either been missed or simply dismissed as a bit of characteristic Jamaican word-play, as Marley sings:

> ... but the stone that the builder refused
> shall become the head corner stone
> I-n-I will not be abused
> We will never never never go away ...
> I-YATTA Y-OOL ...
> I said ride Natty Ride
> I said a guh there Dreddy guh there ...

Without Bob Marley to pronounce on his intentions here, we are left to speculate on its meaning. This phrase is of the type which generally occurs in the ideolect of certain *I-tesvar* speakers. Literally translated as 'Daughter full', it would make little sense in this context. With a slight shift in inflection (which may reflect the sung rather than the spoken words), however, it could become 'I-yadda Y-ool'. Rendered as 'in my Father's fullness' or 'in the fullness of Jah', this would, of course, make sense.[31] Whatever the meaning (or non-meaning) intended, the circumstantial probability of an *I-tesvar* source appears considerable.

The ultimate validation of this lexicon within contemporary Rasta Talk, however, need not hinge on attempts to trace its precise spread within and beyond the movement. Indeed, this would be impossible. What I argue is that the widespread currency of the *I-tesvar* must be appreciated at a more general level in association with the cognate symbols of resistance and identity that evolved as part of the livity complex. Seen as part of a series of interlocking codes, the predominant sound of the *I-tesvar*, the sound 'I' or 'Y', becomes an ethnic shifter. Metaphysically, this cornerstone of Rasta Talk is associated with a mystery of transcendent proportions, the origins of ethnic paternity and, moreover, of human creation that are universally linked with language (see Fishman 1977:19-23). As this sound became a verbal icon among Rastafari such meaning was inferred through the pragmatics of communication. Moreover, in the actual social context of its reproduction, this idea is/was no abstract, disembodied idea. It is/was phenomenologically linked to the creation of symbols and meanings which substantiate perceived notions of antiquity, primordiality, authenticity, and nationhood.

Rastafari doxologies on 'the Word' are, of course, legion as well as being among their most poetic pronouncements. Reasoning on this cornerstone of their code, I-yawney and Ras I-mes reminds us that

> T: I full-first language, and even our Amharic language – which is a part of our anciency – is being revealed to I-n-I now. And who art teking in such language cast away de oppressor language dat were taught us.

> I: In other words, instead of how you'd use de letter 'A' as a first letter of your alphabet, de bredrin chant 'I'. For I is de only word in the English language with one letter. And is a personal pronoun, in a maxilin [sic] gender, carrying a nominative case, having a subject of its own. So I-n-I use 'I' as de first letter of any sound dat I-n-I would be speaking. For if you take 'God' and turn it around yuh get 'dog'. But anyhow yuh turn 'I' is de said 'I'. *So is just One, so you don't have no word to shift from it or change it. Is just one word – and de name of the Almighty Creator must be perfect!*

> T: To even strengthen dat, remember in de time of Moses when de Most High did appear to him and tell him 'Guh into de land of Egypt'. Moses reply to him was 'Who shall I tell dem send I?' Him said, 'Tell dem dat I ART DE I AM dat send thee. So 'I' was de first fullness. *It is foundational.*

Bunny Wailer, in the more popular reggae medium, articulates a similar idea in his LP, *Blackheart Man*, the same 'Blackheart man' represented by the Higes Knots brethren:

> In the beginning there was only one concept
> And that's the concept of 'I'
> Then arose Apaleon the Devil claiming
> that its 'you and me'
> And from that day on
> There is trouble in the world.

Other examples could be provided. What I think is noteworthy is that the 'I' morpheme performs one of the most important functions of ritual metaphors. It signifies a 'return to the whole' (Fernandez 1986); it is about source, authenticity, primordiality, and completion. All of the related symbolism and interlocked codes with which this dialect originated serve, within a specific historical discourse (e.g., Ethiopianism, the Bible), to support this function.

Finally, given that ethnic and linguistic self-identification remains critical to so much interaction in Jamaica (and elsewhere in Caribbean), the success of this code should be seen in terms of how ethnic differences are marked within the wider society. As Drummond (1987) points out for another West Indian context, any attempt to understand ethnicity as a cultural system must take into account that the daily behaviour of distinct categories of people are ascribed to 'inborn qualities' and deeply held beliefs which, it is perceived, cannot be altered. It is not by accident that 'the I is foundational' and that the ideological construction of this speech and related symbols in the livity complex are associated with an 'inborn' pedigree.

Postscript

In this essay I have drawn on a collection of related dubbed accounts, with varying levels of interpretation, to frame a transitional period in the history of Rasta cultural expressions. It should be clear from the foregoing that both the *I-tal* complex and the *I-tesvar* were the closely related innovations of a small group of brethren. They were part of a complex of overlapping codes by which these brethren sought to achieve a number of related ends: to express opposition to the dominant culture, to ratify the overall expression of Rastafari livity, and to seek personal spiritual development.

Much of this oral testimony elaborates upon and confirms one of my initial observations of the Nyabinghi House and the *I-tal* complex. That is, that the concept of *I-tal*, far from its restricted denotation as a dis-

tinctive set of foodways and dietary practices, is, in its broader connotations *'the overall cultural aesthetic which [over the years has] suffused
Nyabinghi'* (Homiak 1985:246) and the livity of those within the House.
Of course, to speak of these codes as an aesthetic system is to imply that
they are part of a socially constructed evaluative mode of thought which
underlies behaviour. It is of some moment in this regard that these
codes developed in concert with changes in the social organization of
the movement. This was the shift which Chevannes notes from formal
membership and positions of authority within specific groups to loosely-
knit egalitarian circles of individuals who were 'free from constraint'. In
the latter context, the emergence of the livity complex was of profound
importance. It provided a set of guidelines flexible enough to accomo-
date a wide range of ideas and practices (and thus respectful of individual autonomy). At the same time it incorporated a strong moral basis by
which those who called themselves Rastafari could mutually evaluate
their collective thought and behaviour. I would argue that the innovation of these codes was thus not only part of an evolving worldview and
a concerted quest for meaning, but tied to a procees of collective self-
criticism which can be found in similar inward-looking communities.

Of course, the Rastafari did not create these codes in a social va-
cuum. The *I-tal* concept of naturality – and the corresponding ideological opposition between things 'created' and things 'made' – can be seen
as consistent with various pre-existent African-Jamaican cultural principles and forms. Among the Jamaican Maroons of Moore Town, for
example, there is a similar valuation of 'naturality'. As Ken Bilby (personal communication) points out, this finds its clearest expression in the
opposition between 'weed' and 'trash' herbs used by Maroons for healing and the 'oils' and 'powders' bought in 'doctor shops' and used by
outsiders as well as Maroons influenced by outside practices. Rasta *I-tal*
practice (its innovativeness notwithstanding) and Maroon herbal healing practices share an emphasis on the use of organic substances which
are seen as 'natural' and as part of the respective 'roots' of both traditions.

When the Rastafari practice of livity is arrayed on a continuum –
from 'strictly *I-tal*' at one extreme to a more relaxed practice at the
other – the *I-tal* code serves as a means to progressively demarcate the
social boundaries of the community. It also serves as an ideology of cultural resistance which can be situationally upgraded for specific occasions.[32] We can see a parallel here with other emergent forms of religious protest which have drawn upon paradigms of the natural world
(see Comaroff 1986:261; Littlewood, Chapter 10, this volume). *I-tal* and

I-tesvar, particularly as codes inscribed upon the physical person, serve to defy the penetration of the hegemonic system into structures of the 'natural' world.

Compatibilities found between the *I-tal* code and African-Jamaican principles might also be extended to the *I-tesvar* and the use of African-derived language in Jamaica. With its metaphysical emphasis on 'sight', *I-tesvar* binds Rasta speech to African-derived sensibilities about power. The idea that a form of 'sight' enables especially empowered persons to detect and counteract malevolent forces is prevalent across the African-Jamaican folk domain (Beckwith 1929:122; Simpson 1956; Lewis 1969; Bilby, personal communication). Rastafari linguistic usage reinforces this idea on multiple levels.[33] For example, the intellectual and social content of a discourse which is positively evaluated will not only meet with the ratifying words of assent such as 'conscious', 'collective', or 'soundable', but with 'seen-I/Eye', 'sight', or 'I/Eye-lah'. Noting that the concept of 'sight' is regarded as the most positive force in the Rastafari armamentarium, Hall-Alleyne (1984:43) comments that 'this is the power which the African priest, the diviner, and the herbal healer possesses, and which guarantees for him a privileged place in the society'.

Linked to this is the Rasta insistence upon words in their ontological status as 'sounds'. As ontological phenomena, they have the power to be and to manifest what they really are. Words must be used judiciously and precisely because, in Rasta ontology, 'word-sound' *is* power. Word-sounds, moreover, are conceptualized in a fundamentally African way as 'vibrations' (Peek 1981:22) which have the power to impact directly upon the material world. Thus, when the Rastaman says that Rasta comes to 'destroy powers and principalities not with gun and bayonet, but wordically', we gain a better sense of how the Rastafari conceive of the agency behind words.

This extends to ideas about the public and private self – for the conviction of Rastafari as an 'inborn conception' involves a recognition that something about one's essential being stems initially from an unacknowledged force, yet at the same time the realization of this 'essential being' requires an effort of self-definition (see Fischer 1986:196-7). Speech is a central form and agency behind this effort at self-definition which is to be found in the Rasta conviction that Man is, ontologically, 'living sound', the Word incarnate.

Finally, as to the content of the testimony cited in these pages, I reiterate that it should be seen as a 'version'. The way in which many of these narratives became accessible can only lead me to emphasize the conditional circumstances involved in reconstructing such versions. In-

deed, I had grounded with a number of these *I-tal* brethren for years before they ever chose to mention anything of their 'trod' within the *I-gelic*
House. It was only around 1986, after several delegations of Nyabinghi
Edlers had traveled abroad to witness Rastafari in the Eastern Caribbean and in communities of the 'second' diaspora (e.g., to Toronto, Canada, and to England), that their testimony became accessible. It struck
me that many of the accounts that I began to subsequently hear voiced
emerged almost as counter-versions to those of other ranking elders
whose status had been enhanced through their participation in these international 'trods'. More or less unsolicited, the Elders with whom I was
closest began to dub many of the accounts provided above during the
time that I was assisting them to travel to Washington, DC as part of a
cultural exchange program.[34]

Their collective testimony provides new insights into the cultural
creativity of the Rastafari and into the timing of important cultural developments within the movement. The data presented here, as well as
that presented by Chevannes, also provide new material with which to
consider how the Rastafari have drawn upon African-Jamaican principles and redefined the forms or social contexts in which they occur.
However, as significant as this oral testimony is for understanding the
history of Rasta cultural expressions, one fact – frequently voiced by the
Rastafari themselves – is certain: 'The half has yet to be told'.

Acknowledgements

I wish to thank Ken Bilby and Paul Stoller for their many useful comments, criticisms, and suggestions on the content and organization of an
earlier draft of this paper. I also want to thank Barry Chevannes for organizing the 'Rastafari Workshop' and bringing together the scholars
who have contributed to this volume.

Notes

1. I am indebted to Carole Yawney for suggesting the term 'dub history' to cover the way in which the Rastafari draw upon oral testimony in their ritual discourse.
2. See Roger Abrahams (1983).

3. A number of the elders who authored the innovations discussed in this chapter represented the Nyabinghi House on missions to New York and Washington, DC in 1988 and 1989. On the second trip they participated in the annual Festival of American Folklife sponsored by the Smithsonian Institution and incorporated a number of 'language workshops' as part of their presentations. Subsequently, seven of these individuals were recorded on the l.p., *Rastafari Elders*, by Ras Records (1990). This recording contains some unique examples of the so-called *I-ance*.

4. In 1953 Whappy King, a lengendary Kingston criminal, was widely linked to the Rasta movement after the murder of a young man along the Pallisadoes; in 1954 the Crown conducted a number of well-publicized raids on Pinnacle; and in 1957 there was the Coronation Market riot in which much of Back-o-Wall was destroyed. This was followed by the failed expectations of the 1958 Convention and, shortly thereafter, the Henry Affair (see Chevannes 1976).

5. The *University Report*, for example, cites the *Jamaica Times* of 8 March 1958, p. 1, noting that: 'The Convention, which had apparently attracted three thousand people, many of whom were Locksmen, seems to have ended without anyone embarking for Africa'.

6. A number of the brethren also personally confirmed this as a description of their original camp.

7. Acronym for Kingston and St Andrew Corporation, the governing body for the city of Kingston.

8. Depending upon the idiolect of the particular speaker, this 'tongue' was known variously as *I-tesvar*, *I-varits*, *I-yaric*, or *I-var*. Contrary to the pronouncement of 'the Saint' in his description of the Wareika Hill camp, this speech was not 'common among the brethren' (which is to say, all Rastafari), in 1962. It was, however, fast becoming a register of resistance among the younger Dreadlocks on the Hill as well as in the camps of West Kingston.

9. Had Barrett had any personal contact with the young Dreadlocks on Wareika Hill he would have realized the importance of the developments taking place there or at least have been alerted to some of growing hostility between older Rastas like Ossie and those of the Dreadlocks persuasion. Former camp members from the Hill indicate that Ossie's group figured prominently in orchestrating much of the anti-Dreadlocks sentiment that prevailed during the 1960s.

Moreover, it is alleged by members of the I-gelic House that Ossie's group sided with residents of the area to encourage the authorities to raid their camp on a number of occasions.

10. Continuities with Jamaica's African-derived folk culture must certainly come to mind. 'Nature', in various symbolic forms, can be seen as a prevalent category in the consciousness and religious practices of the Jamaican peasantry (see Chevannes, Chapter 2, Kitzinger 1969:169, Simpson 1956). It was recontextualized by these brethren with more far-reaching ideological implications.

11. This gave rise to a later development among the Rastas – the substitution of leather belts with knitted red-gold-and-green belts. These are now a fixed part of the Rasta ensemble. The knitting of such belts and tams have become part of a cottage industry among the Rastafari. Their production and sale to other Rastafari coupled moral principle with practical self-reliance.

12. Pa-Ashanti, a co-founder of the Youth Black Faith, described for me at some length how those associated with his group would go from their place of work straight to camp to burn herbs and reason. These sessions would typically last all night with men returning to their work in the morning. Shanti recalls that sometimes a week might pass before a man saw his family. Often, 'baby-mothers' would come looking for their men and would be expected to sit out by the gate until the men chose to deal with them.

13. There is a precedent for sexual abstinence among Revivalists preparatory to special rituals both in the Revival tradition (see Simpson 1956) and among Jamaican maroons when preparing for kromanti rites (K. Bilby, personal communication).

14. Note should be made of the distinction these brethren made between the categories of 'roasted' and 'cooked' food. Roasted food was associated primarily with 'the bush' and with food that could be picked/dug, placed directly on a fire, and prepared for consumption without the use of a pot or implements. 'Cooking' entails a greater degree of cultural transformation involving utensils, steps in preparation of the pot, and the like.

15. In the tongue of the I-gelic House, money became 'dunny', an ironic commentary on the petty wage of the average Jamaican which was 'done' almost as one began to spend.

16. This is a reference to the fact that Prince Edward Emmanuel, the convener of the 1958 Convention, is said to have thrown some 'powder and oils' into the ritual fire at this event. This, the brethren claim, provided provocation for a detachment of police to 'clamp down' on the brethren.

17. There is a precedent for the copious use of pepper in the cusine of East Indians in Jamaica. It is curious that this *I-tal* practice flourished in Back-o-Wall during the 1940s, the same site that had been occupied by large numbers of East Indians during the 1940s.

18. Shepherds' crooks, staffs, and rods of various descriptions are well known as symbols of authority in the African-Jamaican religious milieu. In addition, the image of Garvey armed with his walking stick is well known in Rasta lore (see Homiak 1987:229-31). These rods, however, were a unique re-contextualization of this symbol, featuring as they did the unadorned tree roots. One might see in this 'natural symbol' an iconic identification with the dreadlocks and the other 'creational' icons devised by the group.

19. Cassidy and LePage (1980:225) define the term hige as 'to trouble, annoy, bedevil, fatigue, or nag'. It is given as cognate with 'bag' and, in fact, was so used by these brethren.

20. One should bear in mind that these developments came about during the time of the most tense relations between the movement and the wider society. Certain members of the Jamaican intelligentsia had already moved to separate out and identify segments of non-Dreadlocks Rasta as candidates for 'rehabilitation' by folklorizing their cultural creations.

21. This is an example of the form of remodeling English words. In this case, the word 'aggressive' (spoken in the *patois* as h'oggressive) becomes *pig-gressive*.

22. Contrasting examples of the 'lining out' style of chants and of the *I-pper I-mes* style can be heard on the LP, *From Kongo to Zion: Three Musical Traditions for Jamaica* (Heartbeat Records No. 17).

23. Although Nyabinghi drumming and chants dates from the late 1940s, there is little published information on this musical tradition (see, however, Bilby and Leib 1983, 1986; Homiak 1989). What is apparent, however, is that this is a dynamic tradition in which new chants are constantly introduced and old ones discarded.

24. In his earlier work, Chevannes (1978b) documented the presence of this practice at Pinnacle and we could speculate on whether or not this practice reflected the incorporation of Howellites into the West Kingston camps following the destruction of Howell's commune or if it simply derived from the more generalized sources of ritual borrowing related to Pukumina practice (see Bilby & Leib 1983:6-7).

25. This term has acquired currency among scholars like Velma Pollard who has written on 'Dread Talk', but it originates from the work of Yawney (1979:170-2). During her fieldwork in West Kingston in the early 1970s, this is the term which she found in use among a specific circle of Rastafari.

26. Writing of Anansi 'tongue-tie' speech and Bongo talk, Akers states that 'in these speech forms, initial liquids (/l/ and /r/) are replaced by /y/, resulting in forms such as /yed/ (red), /yedi/ (ready), /yes/ (rest), /yo:d/ (road), and /yait/ (right)'. Although only liquids are normally subject to this process, Akers states that the pattern has become 'generalized' to other consonants in the case of Rasta speech. He writes (1981:73-74, n. 1), for instance, 'In initial position, r-less alternates are found only in highly marked productions which preserve this archaism, such as Anansi's "tongue-tie" and Bongo talk ... This correspondence also occurs in "Rasta talk" where it is subject to over-generalization'.

27. Note that the term 'Nyabinghi', and more particularly the use of 'Nyah' as a term of address, was still a contested sound among the brethren during the late 1950s. 'Nyah', according to my informants, was a term of derision used by non-Rastas and the Combsomes toward Dreadlocks.

28. Note that the greeting *I-sta Y-ool-I* (literally translated as 'Rasta Full I') encodes the idea of an active relationship between God and man. Of related interest is the term *I-yuncum I-yoder* or *I-yungo I-yoder*, translated literally as 'Bongo Order' (a Pukumina derivation). It was during this time that the Rastafari were rehabilitating African terms like 'Bongo', later used as an honorific term of address for an Elder. The interchangeable usage of 'Bongo' and 'Nyabinghi' at this time relates to observations by Bilby and Leib (1983:6-7) concerning the development of musical styles in West Kingston. They note that as different musical styles 'began to interpenetrate one another, a certain confusion of terms or labels resulted, or rather, there was some fluidity in their application'.

29. Carole Yawney, who has worked among another segment of Rasta Elders, notes that brethren like Mortimo Planno and Ras Napier did not support the *I-tesvar* or *I-ance*, as they termed it. They rejected it as something too much like a 'cult' language. In the early 1970s, these Elders promoted the learning of Amharic (see Yawney 1990).

30. Ken Bilby (personal communication) has drawn my attention to the fact that Marley's song *Dem Belly Full* was authored by Legon Cogil and Carlton Barrett, not by Marley himself.

31. There is a third possibility which is a shift in the meaning attributed to such phrases. A second generation speaker of *I-tesvar*, when questioned about its meaning in this context, interpreted it as 'fire burn'.

32. This is the case within the contemporary Nyabinghi House. Those who have spent time among members of this House will recognize that a considerable range of variation exists in the actual day-to-day livitical practice of individuals. Yet at full Nyabinghi ceremonies – occasions when those in the House come together to publicly renew their commitment to the central vision of the faith (repatriation) – it is the *I-tal* code in its most austere form which is observed. These ritual occasions, which are associated today with important dates on the Rasta calendar, serve to sustain the ideological importance of the code in its 'strict' form even though only a minority of the House may remain true to all its various strictures on a continual basis.

33. This occurs not only through frequent enunciation of the pronoun I/Eye, and use of the words 'sight' and 'seen' as affirmative ratifying sounds in discourse, but to oft-cited biblical passages: 'What is hidden from the wise and prudent is revealed to babes and sucklings'.

34. This program, entitled 'The Rainbow Circle Throne Room of Jah Rastafari', was organized at the grassroots level by Rastafari of the Washington, Baltimore, and New York communities. The Office of Folklife Programs at the Smithsonian Institution provided assistance in obtaining visas for those on the delegation.

7 The De-Labelling Process: From 'Lost Tribe to 'Ethnic Group'

Ellis Cashmore

In the 1970s, Rastas in Britain were regarded as the rule-breaking, taboo-breaking renegades of a new generation. Their radicalism and acerbic critique of the system they called Babylon endeared them to few, apart from those to whom they represented a proto-revolutionary force. Capitalism and racist exploitation, it was thought, were the Rastas' enemies; give them time and they would move beyond a contemplative stage to a much more active posture; they were harbingers of change. But the type of change Rastas seemed to require was seen as threatening to existing institutions. The police in particular reacted alertly to the growing presence of Rasta devotees in the inner-city streets of Britain. A puzzling combination of Christian theology, Black power and reggae music appeared to be a recipe for trouble and the West Midlands police commissioned a piece of research in the Birmingham district of Handsworth, which was becoming something of a Rasta capital. The mass media had taken their cue from a report by the Reading *Evening Post*, which, in June 1976, disclosed details of a 'West Indian Mafia organization called Rastafarians ... an international crime ring specializing in drugs, prostitution, subversion and blackmail'. Its syndicated members were said to favour fast cars, wear their hair in 'long rat's tails' and 'walk about with "prayer sticks" – trimmed pick-axe handles'.

The police report, entitled *Shades of Grey*, was published eighteen months later and simply elaborated on the earlier depiction. It described a 'criminalized subculture', comprising 200 hardcore 'Dreadlocks', habitually engaged in street crime and conniving against the police. Both national and provincial media picked up the message and amplified it in terms of what newspapers called a 'Terror Gangs Shock' (Birmingham *Evening Mail*, 25 November 1977). 'Streets of Fear'; 'Lost Tribes on the Warpath' and 'Wave of Terror' were some of the headlines that preceded stories purportedly about the emergent Rastafarian movement in Britain.

In 1979, my book *Rastaman* was published. The atmosphere in which it was received was influenced by the hysteria prompted by the police and the media. As the book offered an utterly different interpretation to those already existing and as it had the benefit of being based on empirical research stretched over two years (as opposed to the two *weeks* of the police research) it was given a decent hearing. It was the first of a number of other publications which were to understand Rastas in a completely different light to what was then an orthodoxy. The orthodoxy was: Rastas were a serious menace to the streets, to public order and to race relations in general.

In 1989, there was a significant change in the British race relations legislation. Rastafarians were officially recognized as an 'ethnic group' under the terms of the 1976 Act. As such, they were afforded the same kind of legal protection previously enjoyed by such groups as Sikhs, Gypsies and Jews. They could no longer be discriminated against on grounds of their belonging to their ethnic group, so, for example, a prospective employer could not refuse employment to a Rasta because of his or her dreadlocks, as the distinctive hairstyle is part of the ethnic group's identity.

The case which brought about the recognition was precipitated by Trevor Dawkins, a London Rasta, who was turned away from an interview with the government's transportation agency because he wore dreadlocks. He took his complaint to the British Commission for Racial Equality, which, in turn, asked me to demonstrate publicly that Rastas did meet the criteria for an ethnic group laid down by the House of Lords in a previous case. The case was fought and won, the law was changed, and Rastas became legally enshrined as an ethnic group.

The change came about within ten years of the publication of *Rastaman*, an astonishingly short time for a group to transform its status from that of menace to cultural contributor. Social scientists have devoted much attention to the process of becoming 'deviant' – of getting labelled. In Rastas, we have an example of the virtual opposite: getting 'de-labelled'. In just a decade, Rastas were removed from their position as a threat to race relations and the Dawkins decision became only the last of a series of actions, all of which have pointed towards the acceptance of Rastas.

In many schools, children wearing dreadlocks have been encouraged to praise Jah and enlighten others in the religious aspects of Rastafari. Correctional services have allowed prisoners to wear locks, observe die-

tary restrictions and worship as they feel appropriate. Even the orthodox Christian churches have extended their arms to Rastas. The actual
integration of Rastas has been a phenomenon itself. We have examples
of groups, once considered dangerous and unwanted, becoming gradually accepted. Even if they are still seen as unwanted, they may be tol-
erated as co-existors in the same moral universe. But the sheer *pace* of
the change in reaction to Rastas is quite another phenomenon and one
which I want to explore in close detail.

This necessitates looking not only at broad changes that have hastened different public perceptions of Rastas, but changes in Rastas
themselves. Ten or fifteen years ago, Rastas gave no reason to adopt the
dominant values of British society, which, as they saw it, offered them
nothing. No matter how they tried, they got no nearer affluence or success. Their repressed rage seemed to have erupted against those who
surrounded them. Their parents were derided as 'puppets of Babylon'
and White society was blasted as an evil continuance of a four-hundred-
year-old system of oppression. The fact that a young Rasta, like Dawkins, was prepared to go to the Commission of Racial Equality – itself
an agency of Babylon in the eyes of many Rastas – signifies a suspension
of cynicism and a willingness to co-operate with a machine that older
Rastas would scorn.

So there are two sets of factors to consider when analysing the process in which Rastas have shed their deviant status and become 'respectable'. External factors combine with internal factors in my interpretation, so separating them is a rather artificial exercise: the
interaction between them is all-important. But, for clarity's sake, I will
handle them in terms of *external* and *internal* changes.

External Factors

The Political Promise

In the mid- and late-1970s, some warmly applauded the appearance of
Rastafari in places like London, Birmingham and Manchester. In Rastas, there seemed to be the first genuine signs of a radical streak in the
African-Caribbean population of the UK. A variant of American Black
Power had flickered briefly in the 1960s, but nothing resembling a fully-
fledged movement devoted to opposing White domination had arisen
since. Black Power in its overtly political form might have captured a

few minds, but couldn't secure the hearts of enough young Blacks to command a serious following.

Rastafari, by contrast, phrased its political critique in a religious form. It successfully linked Christianity, as practised and preached by local denominations, with the vast system of European imperialism that had reigned for the past three or four centuries. Christianity did not spring up fully-formed and imprint itself on people's minds, argued the Rastafari. It was interpreted in such a way as to act as a convenience for Whites. In particular, the central concept of salvation was transparent to Rastas: to inculcate people into believing that their salvation would come in an afterlife amounted to telling them to endure the material suffering and impoverishment of their day-to-day lives. What's more, the concept of God as somehow 'out there' was too convenient for Rastas' tastes. Believing in a deity who, in practice, could not do anything to change life in the here-and-now, was an essentially fatalistic and conservative concept. 'We know and understand Almighty God is a living man,' sang Bob Marley in 'Exodus' (Rondor Music, Island Records, 1977). The meaning of this lay in the Rastafari concept of I-n-I.

I-n-I refers to the unity of God and all Rastafari. God inheres in people: not the spirit of God only, but God as a total force. Dualisms like 'you and I' became useless and irrelevant to Rastas; all people are united in essence by God. In one version, this may have replaced one type of conservative belief with another. But, in a different version, I-n-I could have been seen as a mandate for action. If Rastas themselves felt disorientated and frustrated enough to go out and change the world themselves, then this, in no way, denied God a role. After all, God was *within*. Rastas doing the changing were the implements not the prime movers.

This augured well for a mobilization of Rastas inspired by the belief in I-n-I and committed to wholesale social – and ultimately, moral – change. But, if this was the promise inferred by radicals, then Rastas were ponderously slow in delivery. They showed no penchant for involving themselves in formal political discourse nor in mass action of any kind, save for their own assemblies.

While this may have been disappointing for some, it was a source of relief for others. The prospect of Rastas bursting the banks of their own frustration was daunting for the 'guardians of order' who had seen in Rastas a devilishly troublesome presence. By commissioning a report in 1977 the police indicated their concern over Rastas. If they were going to become disruptive, the police wanted to be ready.

In the event, 'false alarm' was all that flashed – no political activism, no taking to the streets, no mass violence. Occasional conflicts with the police were commonplace, but the expected threat never materialized. Indeed, gradually, the police were able to establish a rapport with Rastas, and by the mid-1980s, the political intentions of Rastas could, to a large degree, undergo assimilation.

By staying within politically tolerable limits, Rastas lost the support of the radical left who urged them to more secular deeds; but they eased the worries of institutions that might have feared the movement's developing revolutionary schism or even its turning into a more coherent political unit.

Larger Threats

Odd though the Rastas' lack of political appetite was to many, they still inspired agitation, though not in the predicted way. The concept of a gigantic conspiratorial plot to disengage Blacks from the political system and to render them submissive was always central to Rasta philosophy. But, by the early 1980s, for more and more young Rastas, Babylon was no longer an obscure reference to the ancient capital of Mesopatamia, or a term of abuse. It was a cogent and vivid description of the world that lay about them. They were *in* Babylon itself; but did not desire to be part *of* it. The city riots of 1981 bore testimony to this. Black youth did not opt for the more politically comprehensible targets when they began launching their petrol bomb attacks. They virtually imploded, destroying the houses in which they lived, the stores where they shopped, the cars they drove. Looked at another way, the youth were attacking the symbols of Babylon: reminders of their restricting circumstances; their targets were simultaneously the tangible evidence of Babylon and its effects.

Some Rastas were involved in the riots, but, as a movement, Rastas were eclipsed by the events. Prior to 1981, they may have been regarded as threats to public order. But, as we have already seen, their threat was mysteriously hollow. Now a new enemy had risen up; this time it bore no hallmarks, except for its blackness, had no affinities except for other Blacks, preached no gospel apart from sheer havoc. Young Blacks reared themselves as a potent enemy to the social order. Rastas were also Black, of course, but they looked quite tame alongside the more general young Black population which had no affinities and was therefore more difficult to identify.

Within four years of the 1981 riots, another series of major uprisings helped push Rastas further down the scale of public watchdog priorities. The 1985 disturbances were larger than their predecessors and more costly: lives were lost. This time, young Whites were heavily involved in the disorder. All manner of inquiries and policy reviews were enacted in the aftermath of the riots; and all this served to over-shadow Rastas. By 1985, the threat they had apparently posed to race relations had disappeared: attentions turned to the altogether more serious spectre of militant Black youth. The problem was compounded by high unemployment and physically decaying inner-cities.

New Panics

Panics and hysteria are common to all societies: the appearance of phenomena that seem to strike at, or undermine values, is often a useful reminder about rights and wrongs, about moral boundaries. During the mid-1970s, Rastas served as precisely these type of reminders. Yet, in objective terms, Rastafari were never the threat to race relations many thought they were, nor did their overall development suggest they would become so. Their actual impact is less of an issue than were beliefs about them.

The other main panic of the 1970s came from the Pedophile Information Exchange, which catered for those with sexual preferences for children. Punk, the predominantly White youth subculture, leaped into the headlines from 1976, but its allegedly damaging effects on the nation's young never materialized. Within a couple of years, it was virtually integrated into the mainstream.

My point here is that there were relatively few sources of panic available – relative that is to the veritable treasure house that opened up in the late 1980s, when the source of panic was less frequently people who seemed bent on constructing their own new moral order than more sinister, and often unseen, malefactors that were actually claiming lives.

In global terms, the AIDS pandemic superseded all other problems – with the exception of nuclear warfare. The rapid mutations of the HIV virus keep it one step ahead of medical science. The spread of AIDS provided much copy for newspapers and kept the mass media generally very occupied.

Linked to the spread of AIDS was drug abuse: the most affected groups in the North were those who habitually used 'hard' drugs and males who engaged in homosexual intercourse. Drugs have been an issue since the 1960s, but their association with disease and death was never so firm before the advent of AIDS. The emergence of the highly addictive cocaine derivative, crack, was not seen as a coincidence, of course, and the combined problems of AIDS and crack produced a hysteria that gripped not only Britain, but most of the world. These *were* threatening in an objective measurable sense. To reflect that Rastas had once occupied centre stage is almost laughable: the threat many suggested they posed seemed absolutely benign from the vantage point of the late 1980s.

Not that ethnic minorities have totally escaped the attention of panic-mongers: the chains linking AIDS to drugs in general and crack in particular extended into the British ghettos, where they met the 'Yardies', another mafia-style organization supposedly engaged in the production and distribution of crack. Whether the Yardies existed in the organized form suggested by police and newspaper reports is less important than the coverage they commanded. They were given virtually the same treatment as Rastas were in the mid-1970s: criminalized and given form, or structure, by being depicted as a vast organization with members, hierarchies, routine operations and overseas connections. The Yardies themselves – if they ever existed – are not of too much interest here: the point is that they both replicated and replaced Rastas as the central criminal element amongst the African-Caribbean population.

The Paramilitary Drift

Since 1981, the character of the British police has changed, its prime function switching from law to order. It has stripped away its service duties and revealed itself as a paramilitary unit, equipped with state-of-the-art technology and trained in a specialist way to deal with events that threaten order.

The paramilitary drift, as Gerry Northam (1988) notes, began after the 1981 riots and has proceeded through the 1980s and into the 1990s. It has the police force retooling itself: acquiring specialist training and riot control gear and, at the same time, de-emphasizing its law-preservation role. At first glance, this seems to contradict the police's attention to good community relations and its restoration of the 'bobby-on-the-beat'. In fact, it complements it. Community policing has been in the eyes of many cynics the velvet glove that covers an iron fist. While the police has redoubled its efforts in patching up relations with the communities – relations, I might add, that were shredded in the 1970s – it has spent inordinate amounts on preparing for confrontation.

The identification of target groups was part of the police's effort to maintain order; it entailed giving special attention to groups that seemed potentially troublesome. African-Caribbeans, militant trade unionists and women anti-nuclear protestors were among their targets. Rastas were included only insofar as they were a part of what seemed an unruly young Black population. But much more threatening to public order were Muslim fundamentalists who protested against Salman Rushdie's book, *The Satanic Verses*, which, they alleged, blasphemed Islam. On two separate occasions in 1989, police deployed riot gear to disperse Muslim protestors. They also used riot equipment to raid a public house in Wolverhampton and an 'acid house' party! The abuse to civil liberties entailed in the police's liberal employment of riot tactics needs no expansion.

In gearing up, the police ensured that it was equipped to deal with virtually any contingency. Alarms called in the 1970s would not have made much impact ten years later, when police were able to handle the most extreme situations. The effect of the paramilitary drift was to neutralize any residual threat of Rastas. The very idea of the 'Lost Tribe on the Warpath' would have been dismissed by the high-powered paramilitary police of the 1980s.

A Confusion of Morality

At the risk of sounding sanguine and liberal, I venture to suggest that there has been a type of moral confusion over the past 15 years. Rastas, when they first reared themselves with tales of the evils of Babylon and the imminent deliverance of Black people, seemed bizarre to many. Yet, many of their messages have been 'decoded' and integrated into academic, if not common knowledge. For example, the Rastafarian notion of '400 years' no longer seems a strained interpretation of the historical experience of Blacks. Scholars now acknowledge that it is impossible to understand the contemporary issue of racism without a deep consideration of its historical development, especially in relation to the European colonial expansion, beginning in the sixteenth century.

Racism itself, said Rastas, was not so much a product of Whites' individual prejudices, but a function of a vast system that operates to maintain White superiority and instil in Blacks a subordinate mentality – 'mental slavery', as Rastas call it. How different is this from what Marxists call 'hegemony'? Modern accounts of racism attend to its social construction, rather than its psychological foundations. Racism is not a purely individual phenomenon. Rastasfarian ideas in this respect, have become quite conventional.

The general pantheistic thrust implied by such concepts as I-n-I and I-tal has found a ready ally in the green movement, which embraces much the same anti-consumerism as Rastas. The effort to return to natural products and to spurn many of the conveniences of the modern age has caught on amongst people who would seem to have few affinities with Rastas. Many are unlikely to have sympathies with Rastas in most respects. Yet the basic imperative is similar and it gives further evidence of the incorporation of Rastafari themes into mainstream thought.

I talk of a 'confusion' of moralities to suggest that ideas that Rastas originally espoused no longer meet stony ground, but actually engender serious discussion. 'Were they right all along?' is a genuine question. 'They said the position of Blacks was rooted in the experience of slavery, that racism persisted to the present day and was perpetuated by the social system, that we were growing dependent on an environment we should really respect'. Now, all but the closed-minded at least give these ideas serious consideration. Rastas' moral and practical ideas no longer seem the lunatic ravings of escapist rebels. Most people think about them.

These then are a number of factors that have occurred outside the movement and which have affected public perception of Rastas. There have also been changes within: Rastas too have changed. Perhaps motivated by self-preservation, Rastas have moved to an accommodation with the wider society, as we will see in the following section.

Internal Factors

Rastas of fifteen years ago asserted their detachment from the society they called Babylon. 'Rasta don't want no part of Babylon', I was told by a Rasta, who was summing up the entire ethos of the movement. Today, they have evolved into a group ready to negotiate a presence; the Dawkins case illustrates that they have been granted one. I use 'evolved' though this suggests a glacial movement, but in fact, the shift in Rastas' position has been relatively sudden. It is not so long since they were regarded as estranged, alienated and effectively beyond the pale. Nowadays, their actions indicate something rather different.

Strengthening of Attachment

So heterogeneous is the Rastafari movement that one hesitates to write of a strengthening of the attachment to society's main institutions. Many Rastas spurn all associations and opt for a type of self-sufficiency. Yet, it also seems reasonable to suggest that many Rastas, who were either born into Rastafarian families, or who have practised their faith for ten years or more, would have by necessity forged links with major institutions. Contacts with the media, local politics, national health system, department of employment, education, the law and so on are absolutely unavoidable. Because they exist in modern society, they must deal with these institutions, and while they may not be convinced that such institutions are working to their advantage, they must also recognize that this contact is not crushing them. This is not to deny that racism continues unabated in Britain and that equal opportunities have yet to become a reality – indeed one of my own studies (Cashmore 1987) suggests that, if anything, the effects of racism are, if less overt, greater today than they were thirty years ago.

One result of this attachment is that Rastas have tended to mute their demands for change. Presumably, they are not so inclined as to risk putting pressure on their institutional links. For instance, police liaison committees may be window-dressing but they have led – in some areas at least – to less severe policing. This makes for a more comfortable existence, 'a quiet life'. Even the cynic must concede that, as a short-term measure, links with the police have eased the pressure on residents of some ghettos. This does not exaggerate the importance of Rastas' attachments; it simply explains why Rastas may not wish to strain them by taking actions that might disrupt what is, for now at least, a convenient arrangement.

A Stake in the System

In my recent book, *United Kingdom?*, I argue that the act of rioting by young Blacks signified a certain faith in the system. The act of rioting is not a purely spontaneous outburst: it has an element of political calculation. Put bluntly, there is no point in taking violently to the streets unless you think somebody, somewhere, is going to take notice of you and possibly take action as a result. Within the calculation, there is a gamble, because the reaction rioting precipitates may make life even more intolerable than it already is. In the case of the 1985 riots in Britain, my guess is that there have been a few benefits.[1]

I am referring here to a 'stake in the system'. People who protest in a vigorous manner, protest within a system; they make demands on that system, demands they hope will be met, at least partially. Young Blacks did not cry out for revolution, for a new social order to replace the existing one. They cried out for a bigger piece of the action in the present system. I believe this same mood pervades the entire young Black population, including Rastas. The fervour of early years and the fine dreams of a new heaven and new earth has given way to more pragmatic considerations – how best to survive in Babylon.

Paradoxically, Mrs Thatcher and the politics of the 'New Right' in the 1980s gave clues: self-improvement via small business enterprises. The same philosophy that encouraged individualism helped many Rastas envision a path for the future, not one that led to Zion, but one that led to a limited self-sufficiency, a greater independence. The whole of Babylon had to be embraced, but purely for reasons of survival. Many Rastas formed their own businesses: workshops, musical instruments, arts and crafts initiatives, and those who prospered, even minimally, made a degree of investment in the system they despised. Many Rastas took advantage of business loans, initiative grants, enterprise allowances and so on. Even if they wished to deny it, this meant that in a technical, if not moral, sense they had a stake in the system. The have, almost by default, become committed to Babylon.

Involvement of the New Generation

Since the start of the 1980s, a whole new generation of Rastas has grown up in a society of *relative* tolerance. I stress relative, for the continuing evidence of racism in the UK reflects a far from ideal situation. The fact remains, some understanding of the Rastafari, their beliefs, life-styles, ambitions and morals have been achieved and this has manifested itself, especially in schools. Young Rastas go to schools where children are no longer sent home if they wear dreadlocks. Quite the opposite: nowadays, in many schools, young Rastas are urged to talk about their faith and to compare it with those of other children.

For these children, their parents' perspectives may appear distorted. 'What's all this about Babylon and oppression?' a young Rasta may ask his or her parents who talk in terms of a vast system radiating hostility. Children have a different experience. The change instigated by the Dawkins decision means that they may have a more accommodating time when they leave school too, especially with the rising demand for labour. Their parents confronted a brick wall of unemployment. They may not.

This is not to suggest that racism will mysteriously evaporate in the years to come. It will not. But equal opportunity programmes, operating in conjunction with the changes that specifically affect Rastas, will create a multicultural context which young Rastas will find contrasts with that described by their parents. It is a context in which young Rastas may become involved in society to a degree their parents will find incomprehensible.

Internal Control

It is a feature of many social movements, especially those based on a critique of and protest against a social system, that they either splinter or solidify. In the case of Rastas in Britain, there have been traces of both, but the dominant tendency seems to be in solidifying. This means introducing a greater structure of organization and coherence of beliefs. Rastas are still a long way from becoming a sect comparable, say, to the Nation of Islam. I would argue that the movement will never assume such a form: its dynamic is in its heterogeneity of commitment and expression. It will never have a single leader charismatic enough to impose a definition of what is to be accepted as gospel and what is heresy. But, there is some evidence of collectivities of Rastas, such as the Twelve Tribes, attempting to create more enduring bases of organization by delegating positions, having regular meetings, staging events and so on. This has opened up the possibility of a crystallization of beliefs. No one will ever create a definitive version of what Rastas *should* believe. The reasoning process to which the movement owes its freshness will ensure constant dispute and debate. This is very healthy for the movement. Beyond this, however, there are signs that at least some Rasta groups are endeavouring to establish a framework for their beliefs.

However, the trend towards organization and crystallization will give rise to stronger mutual ties which are likely to engender greater internal control. Some control is currently exercised by Rasta elders, but more formal mechanisms may develop. This is likely to affect entire groups. Behaviour that is liable to bring Rastas into disrepute, for example, is already discouraged. In future, it may be sanctioned, perhaps even formally.

What I am pointing to here is an awareness that Rastas have reached a *modus vivendi* with society and a hesitancy to allow this to be upset. Rastas may have got a 'bad press' in the past, but their image nowadays has been polished up sufficiently for them to secure a foothold in society. Individuals who threaten this will be subject to control and this control has been made possible by a redrawing of boundaries to demarcate who is and who is not a Rasta. I should mention that the distinction, which was never clear-cut, has been made even fuzzier by the adoption of Rasta styles, mannerisms, expressions, not to mention ideas, by individuals who would not necessarily identify themselves as Rastas, but value at least an association with the movement.

These then are the factors involved in the process of de-labelling. Obviously, it would be absurd to argue that Rastas have totally shaken off their former image of urban devils. Nor are they beneficiaries of a tolerant and enlightened outlook. Rather, they have been eclipsed by greater and seemingly more threatening icons of modern times. In the 1990s, Rastas seem rather innocuous. But Rastas, while not striving for respectability, have through an almost natural development, acquired an attachment and commitment to, and an involvement with British society that would have been impossible ten years ago.

The irony is that Britain, in the same period, has grown more selfish in its individualism and ruthless in its enterprise, hardly the type of culture one could have thought conducive to good race relations. The fact is that race relations have not improved significantly: they have merely changed, or, more specifically, racism has mutated. Rastas are no longer the supreme enemy they once were; they have ceded place to what are seen as greater threats.

It is by no means certain that all Rastas enjoy their new status. Some feel compromised, especially by the Dawkins decision: the image of dread has been virtually smothered. But, the majority, including younger (say, under-22) Rastas have adjusted to Babylon in much the same way as it has adjusted to them.

This is not a conservative evaluation of the movement; it is an evaluation of a movement that has tended towards conservatism as its early ardour has quietened and it has passed to a second stage of development. What of a third phase? We face a fascinating possibility in the second half of the 1990s when the 'second generation', who have been brought up in Rasta ways and educated in multicultural schools, reach their teens or early twenties. Will they rebel against their parents in the same way as their parents rebelled against *theirs*? The possibility cannot easily be dismissed; cycles move on. Black youth may find Rastafari less relevant than their parents did: they may find the critique at the heart of the movement plausible, but less attractive; they may find the cultural baggage that a Rasta carries cumbersome. Alternatively, they may be drawn to other, perhaps newer and – to them, at least – more vital affiliations, just as their parents were in the 1970s. A different interpretation would hold that Rastas will continue the tradition, creating a further generation of affiliates, their bonds and beliefs stronger than ever.

There is room for both in the future, of course, and I expect there to be developments along both trajectories. What seems certain, however, is that Rastas will not rediscover the stirring and zeal that made them a blazing critical force in the 1970s and early 1980s and that they will continue to stabilize in a society that has learned to tolerate, if not accept them.

Note

1. See Cashmore 1990 for an expansion of this idea.

8 African-American Worldviews in the Caribbean

H.U.E. Thoden van Velzen

Dr Chevannes' discussion of the Rastafari worldview could very well be one of his most important contributions to this area of study. Chevannes lists as major elements of Rasta worldview: 'word power', 'contamination of death', 'women as a source of evil', 'man as God'. This chapter presents an account of the worldview of another African-Caribbean group, the Ndyuka Maroons of Suriname. Most of my examples are taken from one turbulent stage of Ndyuka history, from the days around 1890 when the *Gaan Gadu* cult brought turmoil to villages in the interior by its witch hunts. My purpose is to demonstrate the fruitfulness of the perspective suggested by Dr Chevannes by analysing Ndyuka worldview along three axes: namely, 'ideology', 'ethos' and 'collective fantasy'.

Surinamese Maroons and the Economy

The Ndyukas and the Saramakas are the two main Maroon groups in Suriname's interior. In 1900 each perhaps counted 5,000 members. Matawais, Paramakas, Kwintis and Alukus, the last residing mainly in French Guiana, are the smaller groups. Around the turn of the century none of these smaller groups exceeded 1,000 persons.

Most nineteenth-century Ndyukas, like most Maroons in Suriname, worked as independent lumberers, felling trees, squaring logs, and floating these, tied in rafts, to buyers on the plantations or in the capital, Paramaribo. During the first half of the nineteenth century, hundreds of Maroons left their villages in the interior to build settlements along the rivers of the coastal plain, closer to their customers. During the late 1880s, new economic opportunities opened up. Rich deposits of gold were discovered in the hinterland. Maroons abandoned the lumber trade to offer their services as freight carriers (river transporters) to gold companies or individual gold-diggers.

Around 1890, the *Gaan Gadu* cult erupted in Ndyuka villages on the Tapanahoni river, a tributary of the Marowijne (Maroni) river, the border river of Suriname (or Dutch Guiana, as it was then also called), and French Guiana. The cult soon spread to Maroon villages along other rivers and to those Maroons who had settled in the coastal plain. *Gaan Gadu's* priests were responsible for the first great anti-witchcraft campaign that swept through Ndyuka villages. The movement also demonstrated strong iconoclastic overtones. Its priests burned shrines of African-Surinamese deities and destroyed countless fetishes and amulets by throwing these into the river. In less than a year *Gaan Gadu's* priests had exorcized hundreds of spirits, bringing the religious activities of all but one of the Ndyuka spirit medium cults to an end.

The *Gaan Gadu* Cult

In the early 1890s, the Maroons of northern Suriname were restive. From the Ndyuka heartland, the Tapanahoni, far into the interior, word had reached them of the appearance of a powerful God called *Gaan Gadu* or *Gaan Tata*.[1] This God, they were told, would wage unrelenting war on the witches. The corpses of such nefarious persons were to be dumped into the undergrowth along certain creeks where carrion birds would pick out their eyes and caimans tear out their bowels. All possessions of those who, upon their death, were believed to be witches were to be confiscated by *Gaan Gadu's* priests and carried to a sacred forest shrine on the Tapanahoni river. Messengers from the Tapanahoni urged Maroons in the coastal zone to partake in this struggle against witchcraft. They also demanded that Maroons destroy all their cult shrines of African-American extraction, most of which had been in use since the settlement of Maroon society in the eighteenth century. All places of worship were hereafter to be dedicated to *Gaan Gadu*. The ancient obeahs were to be thrown into the river or burnt.

Commotion and excitement must have been widespread. From eyewitness accounts it is known that hundreds of Ndyukas, and many from other Maroon groups of Suriname as well, took part in great religious feasts, lasting several weeks. In Maroon societies such celebrations herald the coming of a new movement or a new religious leader. By 1893 the new movement had established itself as the dominant cult on the Tapanahoni river and in Ndyuka communities of the coastal plain. Soon it made inroads into the territory of other Maroon groups as well. For a few years before the turn of the century, the newly established ritual centres dedicated to *Gaan Gadu* were drawing scores of followers from the Saramaka Maroons. In 1893, *Gaan Gadu* priests were making converts among the Matawais – no small accomplishment as this had been the first Maroon group to embrace Christianity a few decades earlier. In 1895, in the west, even the small and remote group of Kwintis came under the spell of *Gaan Gadu*. Christian missions organized expeditions to preach against the 'false god' and in this way attempted to undo the impact of *Gaan Gadu's* message on their Matawai following. Despite their efforts to wipe out the cult from what they considered a Christian preserve, the missionaries were only partly successful; a quarter of a century later *Gaan Gadu* was still worshipped in secret in a few Matawai villages.[2]

The Political Environment

Perhaps surprisingly for a colonial society, the Ndyukas were to a large extent 'masters of their own house'. Almost all male Ndyukas, using dug-out canoes, worked for the gold industry in Suriname and French Guiana, enjoying a near monopoly over river transport. As is to be expected under such conditions, earnings were high. Market forces dictated the setting of prices and tariffs in the transport industry, and the Dutch political overlords of the Ndyukas in the capital were unable to alter that situation. Managers of gold industries repeatedly implored the colonial government to restrict the economic freedom of Maroon river transporters, and not leave wages and tariffs to the capricious play of market forces. After 1925, when the supply of boats outstripped the demand, they advocated the reverse, a demand government personnel found far easier to accommodate. But before 1925, when gold companies and government officials combined forces, attempts to reduce freight prices tended to be futile. When Maroon boatmen felt threatened by such policies, they reacted with strikes which, in most cases, guaranteed that the market would not be tampered with. The colonial authorities could not, and in some cases for political motives would not, oblige. Pressure could only be brought to bear on a few paid headmen, not on the average river transporter.

Rich and Poor

The overall economic picture was one of affluence and full participation of most male adults in a booming industry: river transport for gold companies and individual diggers. However, while doing justice to the major economic parameters this brief statement glosses over the crucial fact of inequality. Not every Ndyuka, nor every Maroon for that matter, profited equally from the bonanza. A rift was to open up between the wealthy and the poor, between the *patrons* (boat owners) and those who worked for them, but more strikingly between those who were employed in the transport industry, and those who were not. The new affluence was far from universally shared. Women formed the majority of all those who could not participate in the transport industry. Men over fifty also could not compete with younger men in carrying barrels holding ninety kilos of salted meat, or pieces of heavy equipment, over the slippery stones in the many rapids that blocked boat traffic in Suriname and French Guiana. The older men were not equal to the task of paddling and punting a canoe with a two-ton load against the current of the river for two, three or sometimes even four weeks. Many Maroons were incapacitated by illness in a society lacking adequate medical care. A small group of healthy men was unable to participate in the transport industry as a result of mourning obligations. Those Ndyuka men who had lost a spouse were most strongly restrained in their movements. They had to spend months in their deceased wife's village, as virtual prisoners of her matrilineage. As these people depended for money and various kinds of assistance on the boatmen, this whole category will be called 'dependents'. They needed clothes, salt, soap, household utensils and so forth, and the women also had to rely on male assistance for felling the giant trees of the rain forest. Without this help – which, due to lengthy periods of absence by males, was often not forthcoming – it was well-nigh impossible for them to clear new gardens. Thus, these women had to revert to farming on easily exhausted older fields or tracts of forests not sufficiently regenerated. A decline in agricultural production ensued.

Most of the new wealth was hoarded by the boatmen or spent on fancy goods. With a considerable number of boatmen staying away for periods of many years and choosing their mates from among the Creole women of the coast, the flow of goods to Maroon women slowed to a trickle. More seriously, the time-honoured mechanisms of lineage redistribution, so successful in the earlier society of male lumberers and female farmers, no longer functioned smoothly.

In short, the lucrative transport trade opened up a rift between freight carriers and dependents. For the Ndyukas of the Tapanahoni river, the inequality between the boatmen and their dependents was marked and, because of their continuous presence within the same geographical area, glaringly conspicuous. Travellers on the Tapanahoni noticed both signs of an astounding affluence and of starvation. Beneath a surface of prosperity, the gap between rich and poor had actually widened considerably.

Boatmen in turn-of-the-century Ndyuka society were rich. They owned the chief economic resource, the boats. They could circumvent relationships of interdependence with their own and their wives' matrilineages (owners of swidden plots) by buying their food elsewhere. They were not dependent on the labour of their kinsmen. In brief, boat owners had a position to defend, certain economic courses to advocate, and were in general in a position to do so. When such conditions exist, cult teachings will be coloured by the ideological positions of those who control the society's main economic resources.

Ideology

Ideology is one of the oldest and most useful tools we have for understanding our own and other people's cultural expressions. 'Ideology' in my definition stays close to the orthodox Marxist views, namely a set of ideas guiding and justifying actions within the socio-economic arena.[3]

The chief ideological tenet connected with Gaan Gadu is the defense of prerogative and, linked to this, mistrust of the weak and the disadvantaged. This need not surprise us, as the origins of this cult are to be found in the emergence of the new class of boat owners working as river transporters for gold mining. The new ideology of the 1890s reflected the basic concerns of the boatmen, propagated economic individualism, and cultivated suspicion of the poor. The *patrons'* distrust of their less successful kin betrayed itself in the specific ways witchcraft beliefs were elaborated and defined. People who met with adversity or debilitating illness were suspect, but even those who lacked the opportunity to earn money were not to be trusted. At the end of the nineteenth century, such witchcraft notions were radically novel. Most of the last century had presented a different picture. The victims of the witch trials prior to 1890 seem mainly to have been selected from among a small group of fairly successful males: a few headmen and a larger number of entrepreneurs growing cash crops for the city market. Noteworthy is that whereas formerly men had been persecuted – burnt at the stake before 1860 or 1870

– in the last decade of the nineteenth century women were the prime suspects. In this age of prosperity older women, particularly those who had been dependent on charity for extended periods, had little chance to escape such verdicts. This idiom of witchcraft was but one of the vehicles of ideology, but probably its most efficacious. It defined the social categories most likely to produce witches, and it presented a theory on the chief motive of witches: resentment. Barring a few exceptional cases, witches were not believed to be driven by an inherited constitution that could predispose them to such crimes (van Wetering 1973:84). Rather it was felt to be a state of mind seducing humans to harm the interests of relatives and neighbours. A witch was jealous of success, good health, a neighbour's partner, another man's fortune, a sister's numerous offspring; in brief, a witch coveted that which did not belong to her or him. A poor person has a motive for committing the crimes of witchcraft: a rich man has not. The poor person will compare herself (or himself) with others, and be reminded every moment of the day of his own inferiority. Envy and malice will get hold of his soul and gradually drown the psyche's other voices. Such at least were the points of view of turn-of-the-century Ndyuka boatmen.

This aspect of their worldview, this type of ideology, is absent entirely from the world of the Rastafari. Resentment and envy do not seem to figure among the evil forces unleashing Babylon's horrors. No wonder, when we learn about the preponderance of poor rural migrants among Jamaican religious cults. These destitutes had other concerns on their minds.

Ethos[4]

When persons holding strategic positions in the economy propagate an ideology, the advantage their economic transactions command is not hard to discern. The cluster of ideas surrounding the communion with *Gaan Gadu* is a case in point. Around 1890, when the dread of witches had sunk into the minds of boatmen and *Gaan Gadu* was called upon to safeguard his people, Ndyukas had to enter into a covenant with Him by drinking his sacred potion. This ordeal, called 'drinking of God' (*diingi Gadu*), was considered to be the new cult's main sacrament; at the same time it was believed to be a test separating the sheep from the goats. Those who fell ill within a week after undergoing the ordeal stood condemned as witches; those who remained healthy had proven themselves worthy of God's protection.

Two significant differences with the past come to light here. Whereas formerly the drinking of the sacred potion had been reserved for a few suspects, and once every few years for representatives of clans who, in this way, renewed the oath of allegiance to the Paramount Chief, after 1890 it became binding on every adult. Equally important, the rites were no longer defined predominantly as an oath of allegiance to the Chief; after 1890 they became binding on every adult. Soon, moreover, the rites were no longer defined predominantly as an oath of allegiance to the Ndyuka nation and its Chief, as supplicants from other groups were also encouraged to undergo the ordeal and in this way conclude a covenant with *Gaan Gadu* to uphold his most sacred command; never to have recourse to witchcraft. One's first loyalty now was to *Gaan Gadu* rather than to the deities of a particular group.

While the institution of oath taking was ancient, its redefinition was radical. It reflected both the rising fears of witchcraft and the fact that Ndyukas, Saramakas, Alukus and Matawais were now living and working in the same river basins of Suriname and French Guiana, sharing forest camps for night stops and assisting each other when passing rapids. A good man was no longer merely a trusted kinsman who properly fulfilled his obligations towards his relatives. Virtue now could be defined according to a 'universally' valid standard whereby a person demonstrated his/her moral stature by being immune to the temptations of power and revenge which the arsenal of witchcraft offers. Successful submission to the poison ordeal, taking some drops from the sacred potion, proved a person's purity, so that he could henceforth move in wider circles. Cult members formed a 'security cult' (Werbner 1979:665) for each other. They were considered mutually harmless: the propensity for perpetrating evil had been tested and found absent. Safety had been lost when boundaries of traditional kin groups gave way, and when new fields of tension replaced the old bonds of ambivalence people had learned to live with during preceding generations. The *Gaan Gadu* movement attempted to restore to the faithful a sense of safety, through the introduction of a security code. This is one example of how the cult opened windows on an expanded world, and thus helped to boost the wider economic circuits that were emerging. It thus constituted another linkage between the world of material goods and social positions and the symbolic universe.

Sacred rites converted a professional group of boat owners into a security cult. But the group's ethos was more encompassing: it also stressed punctuality and good conduct toward one's colleagues. The ex-

planation for such an emphasis comes from the fact that Ndyukas, working within the same river basins with other Maroon groups, for the first
time in history came to depend on total strangers. Before embarking on
long boat trips and other expeditions, they voluntarily asked to be granted permission to undergo the poison ordeal. By taking a sip from the sacred potion of *Sweli* (a synonym for *Gaan Gadu*), and afterwards receiving a scarf, or God's chord, which distinguished the initiated from those
who had not encountered the poison ordeal, cult adherents knew whom
they could trust. Early Rasta groups (Chevannes, Chapter 4 this volume)
while in the camp also expected that their members form 'security circles' (good behaviour being highly valued) and take every precaution to
minimize the risks of being infiltrated. In many other ways as well their
ethos looks astoundingly similar to that of the members of the *Gaan
Gadu* cult. Precisely which conditions favour the development of such
a security cult, and of values that are at once religious and social, should
be the subject of further research.

Collective Fantasies

The first two dimensions just discussed, ideology and ethos, offer opportunities for comparison. The ideologies are clearly different, and for understandable reasons – devotees of the *Gaan Gadu* cult and adherents of
the Rastafari faith occupied very different positions in society.

Due to the evasive nature of the phenomenon of 'collective fantasy',
a comparison of the *Gaan Gadu* creed with Rasta beliefs is harder to un-
dertake. A collective fantasy is a symbolic system noted for its visionary
images, for a 'philosophy' that ranges over and beyond the sphere of
practical action, for specific day-dreams and nightmares, and in general
for imagery unfamiliar to its mainstream culture. Given little space in social discourse under ordinary circumstances, and often presented implicitly, these elements, once brought into the open, may strike people as novel and powerful. A collective fantasy reveals itself in a fragmentary way,
through seemingly isolated pronouncements on the nature of a hidden reality and through covert culture.

Statements on the nature of collective fantasies vary from highly em-
phatic pronouncements to mere allusions. At the same time, attempts are
made, consciously or unconsciously, to conceal or disguise aspects of the
collective fantasy. Telltale signs may crop up in ritual and religious
thought: a deity's name, arbitrary sequences in rites, and traumatic episodes that surface when oral historians narrate a cult's past all can pro-

vide bits and pieces of data for a study of collective fantasies. Above all, a collective fantasy betrays itself through the heavy emotional charges that its images carry.

For example, the contamination of death is clearly a fear prevalent among Rastas as well as among Ndyuka Maroons. Ndyuka women threaten the power of obeahs by their biological processes. A man in contact with a menstruating woman, for example by accepting her food, or letting her stay in his house at night, jeopardizes his obeahs. Perhaps it is more accurate to say that she destroys them. But all these things could be the 'universals' of African-American culture rather than imaginary worlds specific to a particular cult movement.

Collective fantasies own whatever structure they have from a few dominant notions that overshadow all others. The key notions of the *Gaan Gadu* cult stress guilt and punishment, and the core idea appears to be that to reduce anxiety is to surrender to a punishing deity.

To turn to history once more. Around 1890, when the new generation of boat owners had won its monopoly over the gold industry's transport, they instigated an all-out war against witches. A stern, vindictive deity was the key element in the new collective fantasy of the 1890s. Once conjured up, such a notion, heavily charged with emotional significance, tended to define the territory of action and feeling. The 'Punishing Deity' notion restricted psychological space. Although meant to remove anxiety over witches and other malevolent forces threatening humans, it probably also caused other forms of anxiety. This key notion of the 'punishing deity' must have made cult follower's ponder the question of how closely they conformed to the tenets of purity as laid out by *Gaan Gadu*. His priests issued instructions for perpetual inner scrutiny. They also held out to the Ndyuka people that the world could only improve through regimentation and restrictions on privacy. To set their conscience at ease, *Gaan Gadu's* priests left one cargo of goods after another to decay in the wilderness. Each cargo consisted of a deceased witch's possessions. 'We wash our hands of it', the gravediggers shouted when leaving the witch's remains at the unholy spot in the forest. A feeling that atonement was required inspired the new generation of boatmen to conduct these remarkable rites. Before looking at these elements of the collective fantasy in greater detail, it is perhaps useful to listen to a Ndyuka medicine man when he compared the deity with *Agedeonsu,* an ancient sheltering and protecting God.

Gaan Gadu is vindictive; He gives you no rest; you always have to watch what you are doing, and even be careful about your thoughts. *Agedeonsu* is different. (. . .) he is of the loving type, ready to give solace, to protect the Ndyuka people from their enemies and from nature. He sees to it that the rains come when they are needed, and that there is plenty of sun in the dry season. Fish, game, good harvests, He sees to it all.

Self-Examination

One of the most important aspects of *Gaan Gadu's* creed was its puritanical slant. The deity's priests propagated a view of Man's destiny and of the character of the Godhead that was astoundingly novel and unfamiliar to Ndyukas in general. The deity watched their acts for traces of moral corruption, and scrutinized their thoughts and feeling. '*Gaan Gadu* is the deity who looks down into our hearts; and from whom we cannot hide our evil thoughts', it was expressed. Such divine monitoring was not limited to the period of contact when the sacred potion was taken: it was a continuing process, a permanent activity. It was a profoundly revolutionary notion, well adapted to the first priority of this creed, namely to ferret out the witches. However, as I will argue, the collective fantasy was developed beyond the point of instrumentality or 'ideological needs'. The 'strategic elaboration', as Foucault[5] would call it, had progressed far beyond such immediate aims.

Gaan Gadu's priests encouraged self-examination through constant exhortations. Witches were the great enemy of human society; witchcraft tempted everyone. Barring a few exceptional cases, witches were not believed to be activated by an inherited constitution predisposing them to these crimes. Rather, witchcraft was a state of mind whereby individuals were seduced to harm the interests of relatives and neighbours. Each transgression was believed to pave the way to successively graver ones. The propensity to practice witchcraft grew like a cancer in the body, feeding on it and ultimately destroying it. The process of gradual moral corruption often took years to reach its climax, by which time the depraved person was wholly determined to destroy human life, and indeed well-equipped to do so. But along the road to this final station stops existed, opportunities where the individual could resist further temptation and turn back. Hence a corollary of the omniscient God was the probing of one's conscience by the faithful. They were encouraged to search their hearts for feelings of envy, hatred, resentment, and long-harboured grudges. The notion of guilt was not foreign to traditional Ndyuka religious life, but the way it came to predominate over other feelings certainly was. The emphasis on the individual, who had to keep to a straight and narrow path under perpetual inner scrutiny was equally novel.[6]

Distrust in the moral qualifications of neighbours and kinfolk was enhanced by the account that was demanded by the priests when an adult died. The report had to be submitted after 'the carrying of the corpse', a posthumous divination that took place immediately after a death. This divination, of West African extraction, addressed itself to the moral stature of the deceased:

> *Interrogating a ghost*: Corpses are prepared for these inquests by wrapping them in clothes and tying them to makeshift litters. When this is finished, corpse and litter are lifted and placed on the heads of two bearers. The bearers stand motionless while a libation is made to the ancestors entreating them to assist the divination. The inquest, or rather the interrogation of the ghost, is conducted by carrying it though the village. The ghost communicates by moving the bearers. A forward move signifies an affirmative response, a backward or sideways movement a negative answer. Usually the 'dialogue' between investigators and ghost is much more complex than a simple 'yes' or 'no'. As soon as the interrogation is well under way, even simple moves might mean something different when placed in a larger context. Wild and chaotic movements of the litter are interpreted as revealing the ghost's discomfort and embarrassment at a particular line of questioning.

All deceased were classified as witches, sinners, or respectable persons and the circumstances surrounding the death were investigated. With more than half of all deaths attributed to witchcraft and with many others condemned as sinners the ordinary discourse among gravediggers in charge of the inquests could be likened to that of a group of judges who are convinced that their task is not to establish whether crime has been committed, but only to uncover it. Noteworthy, too, is the unfriendly manner of interrogation of a deceased's ghost; the pejorative words used in addressing the spirit, and the ostentatious display of impatience by interrogating elders. One got the impression that the deceased were considered 'guilty', unless they could prove themselves innocent. Such 'proof' entailed the successful passing of several tests. Posthumous punishment was severe. It included a prohibition to bury the corpse of the witch and the confiscation of all of the individual's property. The mourning ritual was reduced to bare essentials: the bereaved were to show no sign of distress, but rather were supposed to demonstrate their relief by gaiety and laughter.

We have an eyewitness account of what happened after the death of Donia, a woman from the village of Gaan Poowi on the Tapanahoni river. The death occurred during the early 1920s. Her ghost had 'confessed' to crimes of witchcraft. The eyewitness account brings out the intensity of emotions behind a witchcraft case. By moving the bearers in specific ways the ghost sends a message to the village of the Paramount Chief: 'that she could not fix the day on which to be 'thrown away',[7] as she had not yet settled her affairs'. But the chief did not agree with Donia's ghost and responded: 'that she must leave his realm immediately; her affairs will be settled by *Gaan Gadu'*. Donia's ghosts 'states' that she will obey her chief and fixes the hour on which she is to be thrown away as noon the following day. The eyewitness reports:

> During the time that the corpse is not being carried about, it is wrapped in a sheet and laid on the bare floor of the mortuary, to be cursed and mocked by the villagers and those who have come specially for that purpose from other parts. Nobody, not even her children, may mourn for a witch. Today, on December 30, a lugubrious feast is being celebrated at Gaan Poowi. Donia's corpse is being taken away. There is laughter and merriment because a wicked person has left the earth. At about noon all the villagers and visitors gather at the boat landing to be able presently to pursue the spirit with their jeers. The corpse, without a coffin, carried on the head of two men, is deposited in a large boat. Four oarsmen take their places. When they push off, there is a loud and general outcry: '*Heelu ooo, mi gi ju heelu, heelu, heelu, heelu ooo!*' which amounts to: 'I wash my hands of you'. This is repeated at every village along the way. (de Groot 1969:117-18)[8]

Apart from the capital sin of witchcraft, the deity would punish suicide attempts, most cases of physical aggression, adultery, and homosexuality. The taboos surrounding menstrual seclusion were considered even more sacred than before 1890: infringements were to be punished as grave misdeeds. In all these cases, the ultimate punishment meted out by *Gaan Gadu* was death, a sinner's death. The deceased would be left in a hurriedly dug, shallow grave – more than was granted to a witch, but still shameful. In addition, the mourning ritual which was quite elaborate for decent individuals, was reduced to a few libations and prayers.

The punishment meted out to those who showed lack of punctuality further enhanced the stern disciplinarian character of the new cult. Elders who were late in arriving at *Gaan Gadu's* services were flogged, probably as much to their astonishment (no one had ever been punished for such a trivial reason!) as to their discomfort. The priests tried to prevent divorces, squabbles between spouses, and wife beating. Divine laws seem to have been promulgated on the proper education of children and the inviolability of property, though for these latter cases I am unable to cite any examples (Burkhardt 1898:27). During the years immediately after the new cult's inception, the priests made sustained efforts to enforce a number of rules affecting many spheres of life (Schneider 1893:64). They managed to impress the image of a harsh and vindictive deity upon the faithful.[9]

The collective fantasy of the *Gaan Gadu* cult can be summarized in the following cardinal points. Self-examination was supposed to heighten moral sensibility, and distrust of one's own and other people's motives was sharpened through inquest and other forms of divination supervised by the jealous and 'punishing deity'. By promulgating a new set of restrictive rules and by conceiving the image of the deity in authoritarian terms, the divine disciplinarian depicted in the collective fantasy dominated the cosmos. It was a world without mercy, with ruthless, vindictive, and easily provoked powers that were difficult to appease.

Conclusion

Students of African-American cultures are often struck by the similarities in worldviews among such societies. For me at least it was an amazing experience to see ideas and sentiments prevalent among the Ndyuka Maroons of Suriname appear also in Jamaica, but to look at the areas of dissimilarity proved to be as useful an exercise. In this paper I argue the need to examine more closely the various aspects of 'worldview'. My suggestion is to differentiate between 'ideology', 'ethos' and 'collective fantasy'. Concepts such as 'ideology' and 'ethos' appear to be much more tied to the structure and processes of the socio-economic arena. The relations of production and the shape of social inequality seem to have a direct bearing on the realm of the ideological and the set of rules that govern human interaction in a particular group. The imaginary worlds that have been grouped together under the label 'collective fantasies' are a quite different matter. They hold a much more tenuous relation to the world of economic goods and power positions. Thus we have elements of a worldview that can be readily explained from the point of view of a sociology of knowledge. Other aspects, however, quickly exhaust the possibilities of social explanation. Collective fantasies remain largely intangible, evanescent and often ephemeral. Nevertheless they seem crucial in understanding a given culture's worldview.

Notes

1. The name *Gaan Tata* has fallen into disuse. This section relies on material from Thoden van Velzen and van Wetering (1988).

2. The reference to the Saramakas visiting *Gaan Gadu* shrines is found in Spalburg (1979:29-30); on the Matawais in the journal of the Moravian mission, *Berichten uit de(n) Heiden-Wereld*, BHW 1985: 12-42. I learned about the secret worship of *Gaan Gadu* in Matawai villages from Chris de Beet and Miriam Sterman.

3. Gould's definition is useful for my purpose: '*Ideology* is a pattern of beliefs and concepts (both factual and normative) which purports to explain complex social phenomena with a view to directing and simplifying socio-political choices facing individuals and groups' (Gould & Kolb 1964:315).

4. *Ethos* has been defined in various ways, often in an extremely general sense. For Sumner 'ethos' denoted '. . . the totality of characteristic traits by which a group is individualized and differentiated from others . . . '. For Honigmann 'ethos' 'refers to the emotional quality which an observer perceives in cultural acts together with the motivations postulated to underlie that quality'. And Kroeber 'tends to identify *ethos* with the values of a culture'. All quotes are from Honigmann (1964:246-7). I use 'ethos' in a much narrower sense as 'the norms and values that govern interaction in a social group'.

5. The strategic elaboration is – following Foucault – a number of largely unforeseen but linked developments of the 'apparatus', and

the social consequences that ensue from it. Measures of detention were considered rational and efficient methods to combat criminality. An unforeseen effect of this series of measures was the creation of a delinquent milieu. Foucault (1980:195-6) asserts: 'The prison operated as a process of filtering, concentrating, professionalizing and circumscribing a criminal milieu'.

6. Some of these theological notions smack of Christianity. Although very few missionaries visited the Tapanahoni during the nineteenth century, Ndyukas were well-acquainted with Christian ideas. One should be careful, however, to attribute 'self-examination' and related ideas to the teachings of missionaries. Acculturation is a much more complex process than the mere exchange of ideas or borrowing of cultural notions. I feel equally little inclined to ascribe the notion of *Gaan Gadu* as a divine disciplinarian to the proselytizing of missionaries. In 1890 these concepts were crucial to a new generation of boat owners who longed to have a better understanding of the world. After 1905, when much of *Gaan Gadu's* lustre and meaning seemed to have disappeared, many Ndyukas turned to the antinomian cult of *Na Ogii* (The Danger), rejecting the predominance of moral ideas and ridiculing the teachings of *Gaan Gadu's* priests as hypocrisy. Along with van der Elst (1970:183), we would caution against acceptance of superficial correspondences between Maroon conceptions of the supernatural and Judaeo-Christian theology as proof of syncretic origin. Ndyuka religion is not 'imitation Christianity'.

7. That is, to bring the corpse to the unholy spot of the forest. Here the translation of the Ndyuka word *towee* as 'to throw away' is too literal. 'Discarded' would be more appropriate. The gravediggers left the body on or near the banks of a creek, and covered it with a few branches. They did not actually 'toss' it into the undergrowth.

8. I have replaced several *Sranan* (coastal Creole) words with Ndyuka words. Here, this meant only a slight change in spelling. For 'landing stage' I substituted 'boat landing'. The quote from de Groot's book is a translation from van Lier's diaries; van Lier was a gold prospector, balata bleeder and government official working in the interior during the 1910s and 1920s.

9. For references, see Thoden van Velzen and van Wetering, 1988:152.

9 Demon in a Garbage Chute: Surinamese Creole Women's Discourse on Possession and Therapy

Wilhelmina van Wetering

The title of this contribution suggests two things: firstly, demons are not to be regarded as folkloristic relics of an almost forgotten past or of out-lying, backwards regions. They turn up where they are least expected. In the big cities of western Europe, among the migrants who look for a better future in the 'modern' world, demons are said to live in the waste-pipes of carefully-designed apartment buildings planned to house the elite of expanding urban centres. Secondly, the symbolism of a chute suggests that demons, as evil beings, dog our steps whatever humankind will do to be rid of them. Evil, the unclean matter to be discarded, is endlessly reproduced by our modern life-styles, perhaps in greater quantities than ever before. This is conveyed in the symbolism current among the Surinamese inhabitants of Creole descent who have recently settled in Amsterdam.[1]

A Surinamese Creole Subculture

African-American culture in its Suriname-based variety has reached the Netherlands only recently. The 1970s witnessed an influx of migrants from Suriname, a former Dutch colony that gained its political inde-pendence in 1975. Fearful of the new republic's future and rising unem-ployment, 10 per cent of the entire population migrated before this date (Cross and Entzinger 1988:13), and many have followed since. The refu-gees no longer were recruited from middle-class or elite groups only; a sizeable proportion were lower-class, semi- or unskilled, a section of the population that had been the proverbial mainstay of 'traditional', 'folk' or *winti* culture.

In the Netherlands, government policy aimed at integration in an attempt to forestall a concentration of migrant groups in ghettoes. Nevertheless, the Surinamese 'Black' or Creole population flocked to the big cities, primarily Amsterdam. There, a sizeable number settled in Bijlmermeer (cf. de Klerk and Van Amersfoort 1988:158-9), a newly-built neighbourhood which, like New York's Harlem, had been designed for prosperous indigenes. Soon, television shows boasted records of exotic rituals in this rather humdrum setting, showing respectable Black gentlemen changing white shirts and neckties for costumes traditionally associated with witchdoctors 'back in the bush'. They seemed perfectly serious about it. The audience was puzzled but intrigued.

In the large blocks of apartment buildings that dominate the Bijlmermeer, the high density of the Surinamese Creole population has created conditions favourable to the preservation of subcultural lifestyles. Apart from the many well-documented characteristics of lower-class culture, the new residents show a marked attachment to an array of traditional institutions: kinship and both orthodox and popular religious allegiances. The language, *Sranan Tongo*, is the first element shielding group life from unwelcome intrusions, and so is the concept of time. While informality, personal accessibility and chance meetings are of great value to all Surinamese, they hold especially great importance for members of this subculture. The distaste for scheduled programmes, written notices, fixed dates and appointments is immense and forms part of an attitude that balks at all restraints imposed by social superiors. Elusiveness about names, dates, addresses and plans is part of the subcultural code. Only very personal contact guarantees that one has received reliable information. This preoccupation with contacts in a personal networks goes far to explain why endeavours to move on into wider circles are rarely successful.

Lack of participation in the institutions of the wider society, a trait which Lewis (1969:47-59) has marked out as a first characteristic of a subculture, would hold for a great number of the Bijlmermeer Creoles. Nevertheless, social isolation is only partial, and many have established links with social services, health care agencies and educational facilities. Their long-term life orientations, however, are centred around kin groups and networks, the home country and social success as defined in these circles. Often, it is hard to tell who does and who does not belong to the subculture. Many hover near the borderline, alternately reaching outwards for contacts, and then taking refuge behind its screens when the need arises. The hard core, though not more than a small fragment of the total Surinamese population in Bijlmermeer, is conspicuous and makes itself visible by its ethnic activity.

There is one notable exception to the rule of non-involvement: participation in the church of the *Moravian Brethren* or EBG (*Evangelische Broedergemeente* or *Herrnhutters*). This congregation has a firm footing among common people, and a great majority of the heads of households, male and female, are quite outspoken in their allegiance. In the Netherlands, many Roman Catholic Creoles will participate in activities of the Moravian Church because of its ethnic Surinamese character. This does not imply that there are many active church-goers in the Bijlmermeer subculture, but in private rituals Christian and specifically Moravian elements loom large, as we will see below.

Although membership in a subculture is, by definition, partly involuntary, there is, at the same time, an element of choice involved. Some fall back on supportive networks when they find successful integration beyond reach. For others, particularly the elder people who never migrated to make a new start, keeping up networks is a worthy aim in life, since the re-creation of a whole ethnic entourage of food, clothing, music, parties and rituals tends to enhance their position. As has been argued elsewhere (van Wetering 1987), subcultural activities are like markets where self-created stocks in social capital are traded, and where those who rank lower in the social hierarchy perform services which are of use to the upwardly mobile. The elaboration of 'traditional' culture, the investments in time, money and energy will pay off in due time, as these tend to create an ethnic focus.

As Barth (1969:36) has pointed out, overt ethnicity and boundary maintenance will not lose their significance, as long as group members are dependent for security on the voluntary and spontaneous support of their own community. This would undoubtedly hold for the Surinamese migrants, who shelter many relatives and other guests who would like to stay in the country but lack proper papers. The politics of ethnicity are reinforced by economic considerations. The involvement in lucrative but illegal activities by many of the younger members of the Creole group contributes to the retreat into traditional and quasi-traditional forms of religion and kinship. Unable to realize hopes of financial betterment in accepted ways, many of the chronically unemployed have turned to opportunities opened up, for instance, by the rapidly expanding traffic in drugs (Buiks 1983). This has had some unexpected consequences. Ethnic solidarity requires the in-group to put up stoically with a rise in the level of violence and a concomitant weakening of norms that once regulated group life in the home country. To cope with these threats, all the conventional forces – kinship, religion and 'culture' – are called upon to bolster the minimum requirements of social order. For example, some of the earnings from illegal activity are laundered by sponsoring 'traditional' rituals, which, proverbially, both legitimize action and unify the group (van Wetering 1988).

Apart from these specifics, there are some general factors. For quite some time, the Creole group has been affected by erosion and dispersal owing to both horizontal and vertical mobility. This is not a recent development; labor migration has been characteristic of the Caribbean for a long time. The Creoles seem to have reacted by mustering all forces available to counteract tendencies to fission, by fostering ties of kinship, religion and other forms of 'traditional' culture.

Social Theory and 'Traditional Culture'

Anthropology is ill-prepared to treat as relevant those phenomena that it looks upon as outdated or as mere tokens of 'superstition'. Most students would therefore have predicted a rapid decline of beliefs in magic. Current views, whether based on assumptions about modernization, processes of state formation or encapsulation in a world economy, leave little scope for the resilience of beliefs and practices commonly referred to as 'animist'. Yet, recent studies bear out that any conclusions about an ongoing process of 'disenchantment of the world' are premature. 'Old' beliefs have been found to be highly adaptable to 'modern' situations and expressive of the predicaments people face. This assumption will be illustrated in this chapter by a case study of Surinamese Creole women who make use of 'traditional' concepts about demons to define and better their position in the 'modern' world of money and opportunities.

This is not to imply that Max Weber's familiar thesis on religious rationalization of life among the middle classes has lost its relevance; far from it. It most certainly holds for Surinamese Creoles. The majority of this group has no knowledge of, concern with or interest in anything related to *winti* (winds or possessing spirits), to which Surinamese traditional religion owes its name. Although there is a general tendency, in line with developments in the United States and the Caribbean (for example the growth of the Rastafari) to stress a Black identity, to bring the African-American experience into the limelight and to search for 'roots', the attitude to *winti* (or *afkodre* [idolatry], as the cultural heritage is also referred to) is highly ambivalent. To openly profess one's allegiance to *winti* is simply 'not done' among respectable Creole citizens. Although it is common knowledge that 'everyone', including those high up in the social hierarchy, will turn to a ritual expert in times of need, this is never publicly discussed. Secrecy about such matters is part of the cultural code.

The ambivalence often finds expression in humour. Traditional religion, preferably its practices of 'black magic', has a place in amateur theatrical plays, which are highly popular in Bijlmermeer. The director of the company writes his own script, as a rule. And the plot invariably is about the sex war: two women vying for the favors of one 'macho', an unreliable ritual expert or *bonuman* who is after money. The themes are taken from real life, and the people who come to enjoy themselves will, as soon as these situations start unfolding in the plot, shift from their relaxed mood to an anxious one. Many balance on a narrow strip between 'western rationality' and 'idolatry' or 'superstition'.

Discussions about *winti* are fraught with misunderstandings, and many refrain from discussing it at all, saying that they really know nothing about it. To an amazing extent, this is true. To the upwardly mobile among the preceding generations, *winti* was anathema. Children who grew up in well-to-do Creole families were strictly prohibited from speaking *Sranan Tongo* at home or at school. Yet, they often realized that the adults were secretly up to something about *winti*, so now many of the new generation growing up and living in the Netherlands are fascinated by the mysteries of the home country and the past. Books about *winti* are eagerly studied, and older people are finding their memories in great demand.

Home Rituals

There is only one exception to the rule of general embarrassment and this applies to the veneration of the soul, the *akra* or *yeye*. Though this is an essential part of the traditional belief system (Wooding 1973), many Creoles feel that this is not *winti*; it is not *hebi* (heavy), or charged with negative associations. To take care of one's soul is a sacred duty to all and its rituals are considered *oso sani* (home rituals), a part of private life where Christian and non-Christian elements are mixed to the adepts' delight.

The carrying over of religious practice from the public to the private sphere has given Creole religion its specific character. The move has had great advantages on both the individual and the collective level. It has freed them, as Christian believers, from unwelcome control by church authorities, while allowing them to maintain overt allegiance and church membership. The benefits of belonging are guaranteed, whereas dependence on large-scale organizations is greatly reduced. Also, this type of religiosity provides a link between elite, middle and lower classes. Particularly in a modern urban society with its prevailing individualism, the home, kin group and personal network comprise the relevant social framework. Private rituals, performed on occasions like birthdays and crises in the life cycle, often bring together kinsfolk whose stations in life caused them to separate. True of Paramaribo, and the whole coastal society of Suriname in general, it is also true of Bijlmermeer and the Netherlands. Home rituals were easily transferred to a new habitat and contribute greatly to the survival of an ethnic group. They loom much larger than the large-scale rituals or *winti pre*, although the latter are more frequently discussed.

Individualization

Although the cult of the individual soul has not been neglected in *winti* studies, its implications and social relevance have been underestimated. As a rule, *winti* religion has been analysed as the cult of a kin group. This view owes much to Wooding's authoritative study of the Paramaribo Creoles, among whom co-resident groups of kinsfolk honour the pantheons of deities as a collective. Each deity could be expected to take possession of one of the relatives, so the community would remain sure of access to all powers. In fact, ritual interdependence has been vital to keeping the group together.

However, in the present diaspora where it has proved increasingly difficult to bring a ritual community or a kin group together, the individual migrant has to carry a whole pantheon along within his or her soul. Theologically speaking, this is quite feasible in African-Surinamese religion, for it has been true both in Suriname, where it exists in embryonic form, and also in the Netherlands, where it is quite 'normal' for each individual to serve as a medium to more than one divine power at the same time. The *akra* (soul) is thought of as containing a number of guiding spirits or gods, called *djodjo* (Wooding 1973:125), which are identical to the gods of the pantheons. Each adept is thus able to entertain at least three representative deities of the major pantheons. Besides an immanent *Aisa*, or earth deity (mostly regarded as female), each person, male or female, will harbour one of the respected male deities, either

Kromanti (African) or *Ingi* (Amerindian), and one of the less trusted lesser gods that must be acknowledged in the totality of creation. In many Surinamese homes in the Netherlands, a sanctuary to the tutelary spirits is found, often in a small room. The old religious ideal – to be in harmony with all powers inherent in the soul – has not lost its hold. Whoever has reached this state is 'strong' and impervious to attacks by 'black magic'. Private rituals are performed with this aim in mind, and also because it is expected that one will do well materially only when one is on good terms with the gods. The sign that one has reached this blessed state is given in dreams. When the gods manifest themselves clearly and bring lucid messages, this is proof of their favour. The interpretation of dreams is one of the most important methods of divination. This is hardly surprising in a fragmented group that cannot readily gather for communal rituals. Whoever has dreams that contain messages for others in his or her network, can lay a claim to a position of informal leadership.

For people with great worries, this blessed state is seldom within easy reach, however. Many report more nightmares than beautiful dreams, and this is interpreted as a sign that demons are interfering, perhaps evil beings sent by a *wisiman* (witch). But benign deities may also assume a demonic guise, so it is often hard to tell what is the matter, in which case it may be wise to look for expert help from someone who has a reputation as a *lukuman* (seer). This person may also be a *bonuman* (ritual expert or healer). Heads of households, who feel responsible for the well-being of their loved-ones, often read signs in their dreams that there is *notu* (a sort of spiritual state of emergency), and that the time is ripe for ritual treatment.

When looking for a healer or ritual expert, those who belong to the Bijlmermeer subculture choose from their own ranks. They will often prefer a relative, but if there is no suitable kinsman or kinswoman at hand, they will turn to the trusted persons in the neighbourhood who have built up a reputation for never having entertained compromising relationships with the outside world and whose powers are thus untainted.

Routinization and Countervailing Forces

In Bijlmermeer one of the terms for demon, *bakru*, has become a household word, apparently deprived of all numinous qualities. It is scribbled by kids on walls, who tell that a demon haunts a certain elevator or garbage chute. The *yorka* 'shades' of the ancestors also are abroad. Traditionally, they have been linked to the demons (Herskovits and Herskovits 1969:106). But to imply an association of routine or loss of meaning would be deceptive.

Some demons are *hebi* (heavily charged) and these are rarely a subject of discussion. These are the *bakru* of the genuine devil's pact, 'bought' by the ancestors and now resting as a curse on the descendants. The ancestors referred to here would have belonged to the generation that had been gainfully employed in gold digging and balata bleeding around the turn of the century in the home country. Some of the fortune hunters did well but others returned down and out and estranged from 'traditional' morality. Present misfortunes such as drug addiction among the young and concomitant forms of criminality are often attributed to these *hebi bakru*. Of course, the possibility of more recently made devil's pacts is never mentioned at all. Invariably, it is the sins of forebears that are singled out as being visited now upon their descendants.

Some ghosts that hover around do remind of recent occurrences. An inhabitant in one apartment building tells a neighbour that she has heard a street-*bakru* screeching at night. The other replies that she also has noticed, and adds: 'This man just kept screaming'. This was caused, the women thought, by something he had 'seen'. A *bakru* had been knocking at another door during the night, but some plain ritual was enough to ward him off. The women think it was the ghost of a former inhabitant who had been sent back to Suriname because he lacked a valid passport and had been killed by a Hindustani there who had caught him red-handed at burglary. He was a relative of some people who still lived in the flat, and some of his clothes had been kept lying about. Perhaps the spirit had returned because of these personal belongings. Many residents give accounts of chance meetings with 'shades' and *bakru*. There is nothing especially frightening in this. The world is animated and full of 'beings'. They do not always convey a special message to a chance passer-by, or rather not everyone will see a sudden confrontation as charged with meaning. But 'shades' can be recognized as persons; they are concrete. The relation between their appearance and normal life can be ascertained.

As a rule, it is hard for a researcher to get any direct information about demons or other aspects of cosmology. Often, I overheard women laughing when a side reference to *bakru* was made. Mostly, it was impossible to get an inkling of what the story was about, the persons involved or the speakers' attitude. For as soon as I tried to take part in the conversation, the subject was changed or stifled in peals of laughter.

Once I caused hilarity by remarking: 'But I guessed that *bakru* is something bad, like *wisi* (witchcraft)', but I got no reply. Humour may be a perfect shielding mechanism. What I gained was that the notion has far more positive connotations than I had suspected. Only much later did I get some explanations.

Once I visited an elderly lady – I brought her a photograph I had taken – and found her behind the sewing machine. She was busy with all types and pieces of cloth that I had begun to recognize as sacred, dedicated to the various gods of the *winti* pantheon, of which the *bakru* are part. She was sewing a dress and was doing applique work: she adorned the hem of the skirt with a row of big neckties. 'It is in honour of a male spirit', she explained, 'A *bakru* is a man, after all. The gods should be treated with some attention: pampering is all'. Some pieces of cloth were lying about, in colours and designs dedicated to the mother goddess *Aisa*. 'Yes', she replied to my unspoken question, 'I am a medium of an *Aisa* spirit and of an Amerindian, an *Ingi*'. 'And you have got an *obeah*', I added helpfully, for she had told me so on one occasion. 'That is the same', she said, 'a *bakru* is an *obeah*, and a *bakru* is always involved'. 'Mine', she added, 'lets me know everything that happens, even where I am not present; he loves to rummage about. In a dream I once saw a girl carrying a basket on her head – it was Irma, the one who is a member of our club. Next morning I phoned Irma and told her: "Yesterday you performed a ritual". "How did you know", she answered. "It is my *bakru*", and the other laughed heartily'.

The *bakru* as a nosy child and a messenger is in accordance with prevailing views (Wooding 1973:193). There have been ample discussions about the characteristics of the deities. In the days of the Herskovitses (1969:66) it was hard to draw a clear line between the lesser gods and the demons. Nowadays in Bijlmermeer it is a hopeless task. Opinions vary, but generally three types of deities are recognized: higher female godesses, higher male gods, and lower gods that are invariably represented as naughty boys. I did not hear anyone speak about naughty girls. The common *winti* adept sticks to this threefold classification: high-ranking male, high-ranking female spirits, and a residual category consisting of various beings and forces of a male and problematical character. This is the most important classification in ritual practice. Interestingly, the view of human nature is basically androgynous: in every soul both male and female forces are active which demand and deserve respect. The forces that bring individuals into trouble are regarded as male only.

Often, the gods are almost equated with psychic forces, and human behaviour is explained by qualities attributed to people's guardian spirits. An untidy housewife, it is argued, should have a *Leba* (an African deity who often appears as a slovenly old woman [Herskovits and Herskovits 1969:68]) for a tutelary spirit.

References to the lower gods in relation to aggressiveness are so frequent that these are almost bound to lead to routinization. Character traits such as quarrelsomeness and ambition are often attributed to demons. Thus a hothead is told: 'So the *bakru* is afoot again'. Stealing is inspired by *bakru* (Wooding 1973:195; Stephen 1983:59). A *bakru* is represented as a child and associated with childishness. When an elderly lady appeared in white sneakers at a birthday party and a pink T-shirt with a Mickey Mouse in front, her *bakru* was blamed; people thought her grown-up daughters ought to have prevented this. Troublesome children are compared to *bakru*. The symbol of a small-sized, darkly coloured dwarf (Herskovits and Herskovits 1969:105), is thus entirely apt.

For all human qualities, a spiritual explanation is available. While psychological explanations might cause people to see through the symbolism and make the supernatural lose its magic, 'a well-understood God is no God at all' (Otto 1963:28). Despite attempts to reduce the divine to the commonplace, adepts regard the world of the gods as a *mysterium tremendum ac fascinosum*. But this is not a recent development. *Winti* has been withstanding the onslaught of profanity for a long time.

Ambiguity and Exorcism

But are the impish creatures being discussed here demons at all? Beings so utterly human can hardly be classified as really bad. Moreover, the Creoles do not seem to fear the *bakru* or to be deeply shocked by their appearance. In fact, the term *bakru* is applied to a variety of spirits, varying in character according to historical period and geographical area. As discussed above, the evil stirred up by previous generations that had recourse to 'buying *bakru*' is feared to a far greater extent than the contemporary demons entertained by one's fellows. Yet, the Creoles see a common element in both categories and make this clear by their choice of terms – an emic view.

There are other, related considerations. As Herskovits (1951:242-3) noted, the dichotomy between good and evil that is characteristic of European thought is absent in African-American cosmology. This would hold even for demons, commonly regarded as the very epitome of evil.

Wooding (1973:221, 230) corroborates this in an indirect way; a key element in ritual therapy is *'wasi prati'* (to cleanse by separating), in which the evil aspects are taken away and the beneficial ones are secured. This form of treatment is allotted to all invading spirits, demons included. This implies that exorcism – as a ritual meant to cast out an evil spirit, as is familiar among either Maroons (Thoden van Velzen and Van Wetering 1988:302, 351 ff.) or Europeans – is unknown as an institution among the Creoles. To explain this fact by pointing to cultural continuities would obviously not do. There must be social categories willing and able to sustain these ideas and practices. In the groups subscribing to *winti* beliefs, such a power differential seems to be lacking. Due to the processes of individualization referred to above and to the fact that people who climb socially tend to leave *winti* behind, the adherents who cling to their beliefs rarely have leverage over each other. In the Creole community there is no organization or institution that has a sufficiently strong social basis to stigmatize other people's guardian spirits as inherently evil. The viable groups are segments of kin groups held together by the female members, but even within these segments, only occasionally can consensus be reached. Particularly when an outsider is suspected of magical acts of aggression, female kin tend to band together and open accusations of *wisi* (witchcraft) will be voiced. To win support for accusations beyond the small circle of kinsfolk is nearly impossible, though. In the public sphere, the women have to content themselves with 'gossiping'.

Ritual Therapy

The case which follows supports and illustrates the general argument. Firstly, it shows how wide a gap there is between the 'discourse' of the Bijlmermeer subculture about social problems and disadvantages, and that of the social case workers entrusted with the task of promoting these clients' interests. The 'problem' singled out here for ritual treatment is that of education, a matter usually dealt with in other ways. This underpins the general idea that a preoccupation with 'the forces of the dark' is not linked to a general orientation of 'backwardness'. On the contrary, we see here how an older woman, with no interest in stepping outside of the boundaries of the subculture, attempts to better the chances of a very young granddaughter in the modern world by ritual means. She acts as a responsible head of a household and family, stating her 'definition of the situation' in a code that is well understood by the other members of the subculture, and enlisting the help of another woman in the apartment building, who has a reputation as a healer. Worthy of note is the mixture of Christian and non-Christian beliefs, characteristic of the private religious lives of Creoles. As we will see, the ritual is not without its psychological subtleties; the idiom may be 'different' at first glance, but the problem of decoding the message of the spirit world is not difficult. Also, the ritual seems to have made its mark. The reader may be interested to know that afterwards little Cynthia did rather well at school.

Confession at the 'Bear's Boat'. My presence at the ritual had been a pure coincidence; as a rule outsiders are not invited at private rituals. I happened to call at Ma Milie's door; she is a member of the Creole women's club I had joined (as an older and influential woman she is often addressed and referred to as 'Ma', mother). As a club, we had been invited to a birthday party of a woman whose address I did not know. I found Ma Milie just ready to leave. Fully convinced that all Creoles want a maximum number of guests at their birthday parties I confidently said: 'Very well, I will join you, let us go at once'. But she looked hesitantly at me and said: 'I do not know the exact number of the house and I have to call on someone else first, here in the building at flat number 'x'. I felt her reserve but said: 'In fact, that is where I want to pop in also, as I want to invite the old lady there to my birthday party'. She started visibly, looked at me inquisitively and said: 'Well then, come along'.

In the living room a company had gathered, among whom I recognized a number of women, fellow residents in the apartment-building and adepts of *winti*. The old lady I wanted to see walked out of the kitchen into the room. I greeted her and wanted to deliver my invitation, but she stopped me and told me to sit down. One of the younger women present whom I did not know nudged another and softly asked: 'What about her here, at this very moment?' Ma Milie overheard her and said: 'You never know what will come out of it'. By giving meaning to a coincidence, she placed my presence in a mystical perspective and the implicit criticism subsided for the moment. Ma Dina, the old lady and head of the household, took a seat next to the kitchen door and her six year-old granddaughter Cynthia sat on her lap. Someone solicitously put a rag on the floor, just to protect the floor covering. In the meantime, Ma Milie unpacked her ritual paraphernalia; apparently she had come as a therapist. Only then did I understand her reluctance to take me along, but, as a matter of fact, I was only glad that things had gone this way. She went round the circle with a small bottle, from which she dripped liquid onto each visitor's palms. 'Rub it into your neck, too' she called out to me as I had not yet done so of my own accord. Perhaps she also indirectely admonished other sluggards, or snobbish young relatives diffident of *winti*. This is a regular opening of any ritual. It is a libation in disguise, less conspicuous than a spilling of liquids on the soil. Also, it is a consecration of the person: the soul is carried into an atmosphere of sacredness and guiding spirits, hidden vital energies are called upon to be present. In fact, it was not the type of toilet water commonly used for the purpose, the 'florida water' sold in every Chinese shop in Suriname and Bijlmermeer. It was stronger and there was a hidden bitter smell in it. (Afterwards I realized that probably the demons had been called, too.) Then we were all invited to stand up; the Lord's Prayer was recited. Ma Milie asked Cynthia whether she knew it by heart. She said she did not. 'You ought to', Ma Milie said sternly, 'for everyone knows it'. Then Ma Milie ordered someone in the kitchen to fill a calabash with water and she started a libation on the floor, on the rag by Ma Dina's feet. She prayed to Ma Dina's soul while spilling a few drops as she spoke: 'A grandmother is more than a mother; at times she will notice things that will escape even a mother. First of all I pray to God, then to her (Cynthia's) *yeye* and all spirits guiding her. The girl does not do well in school. She is cheeky and will not do as the teacher tells her. She ought to pay attention in class. Mother Earth, I sprinkle cool water. I call upon your help, because she will come to nothing without learning things'.

Then Cynthia's other grandmother, her father's mother who also lives in Bijlmermeer, was requested to come, libate and say a prayer on Cynthia's behalf. Thus Ma Milie called upon all persons present, according to age, relation and position. The younger women were aunts. A man was called from the kitchen who was holding a baby there and feeding it with a bottle. He also offered his good wishes. I was invited too.

The bag was repacked. Everything had been on display on the table, next to the drinks. A bar of chocolate was attractively sticking out of a heap of sweets. Everything which is harmful to children's teeth and health is particularly suited to feed demons. There were also cigars. All participants were strengthened with a glass of gin or whiskey.

We then went out of doors. Again I overheard some nervous remarks among the aunts about my presence in the company. But Ma Milie repeated: 'You never know what will come out of it'.

We carried a plastic bag with some 5-kilo packs of sugar, a few bottles of champagne, and a copper bucket with a red piece of cloth attached to it. We went out by the back staircase. Apparently we were to go about our business unobserved, and without having to greet and talk to all and sundry in the hall. We went by dark and wet paths through the bushes; the public gardens had been designed to appear highly 'natural' and not conventionally suburban. It was November and dark at an early hour. We arrived at the meadow along the canal that forms a pond there, and made our way to a ramshackle jetty designed for fishermen. The young aunts had great trouble getting there on their high heels, and loudly warned each other of dog dung which we could not see in the dark anyway. They seemed less confident of the outcome of our ritual endeavours than the older participants. Ma Milie went in front; sweets were thrown into the water; a pot of honey and syrup was emptied. The next-of-kin were very close to her, and for me, at the rear, the words she spoke were not audible. By the splash I could tell they had taken water in the bucket. Later I was asked to carry it, so I was temporarily promoted to the rank of ritual assistant.

Between the apartment buildings is an open space and a children's playground with a climbing-rack in the form of a boat. 'The bear's boat' it is commonly called, after a popular T.V. program for the young. As is common knowledge among anthropologists, demons have their abode in conspicuous features of the landscape; rivers, rocks, waterfalls or high trees. In the local set-up, the bear's boat is such an object, and is well-suited to be graced with meaning. There, Cynthia had to offer a libation. This she did, emptying a bottle of champagne. She also was instructed to 'utter': 'I have to do my best in school, I have to obey the Lord Jesus and the teacher'. And she obliged, adding: 'Hi, miss pigglywee' (My knowledge of schoolyard invective fails me. Literally the girl said: 'Dag, mevrouw de koekepeer' – Hi, Mrs Koekepeer [nonsense word]. Conventional disrespect in Dutch primary school is: 'Dag, meneer de koekepeer' [male form]. Cynthia probably had a female teacher).

Ma Milie started to pick leaves and branches from shrubs and along the wayside, as we walked on past the apartment building where Cynthia had been born and where her grandmother had lived. All this was pointed out to me, but we did not stop there. We went to a dark place, a subway under the main road. This was the spot Ma Dina had had a dream about, some time ago. They still had not done anything about it, yet it had contained a warning not to be overlooked. Now that Cynthia was in danger of being demoted to kindergarten, the others thought it wise to take ritual action, as Ma Dina had proposed to do earlier.

Ma Dina had dreamt that Cynthia had met a frightful appearance, a White demon, on this spot. It had been a *bakru*, a White Dutchman or probably, Dutchwoman. Cynthia corroborated this when we arrived there: 'I have been here with two other kids, and the thing that gave me the creeps was there'. She pointed out the positions of herself and the being. Her second grandmother now took her to the water and washed her head with cold water taken from the canal. She proudly showed how wet her hair was. The girl had accepted the 'definition of the situation' given by her grandmother. 'The evil', the bad experience she had allegedly gone through, was relived, or, according to accepted standards of psychotherapy, the evil she had met with in class had been given form. She obviously was very proud of being the heroine of such a cosmic drama.

After this we returned home quickly, entering by the front door this time. The herbs Ma Milie had gathered were mixed with others and put in a copper basin. Some of the canal water was added but also florida water; the mixture smelled sweet. Hot water was added from the tap to make it confortable to be washed with. Now that the 'evil' had been brought back to the place where it had come from, there was one thing left to be done; to strenghthen and confirm good intentions for the future.

In this case the demon figured as the 'other' – alien both to group and to consciousness. To Cynthia the 'evil thing' probably had resembled a stern or demanding Dutch teacher; obviously an 'outer' danger. Yet, images of evil have an abstract quality, suited to encompass several aspects simultaneously. Surinamese Creoles often refer to demons as *ogri sani* (evil things) which may take various shapes. Cynthia's grandmother will have sensed another element, more akin to inner dangers. But precise information on such matters is not divulged. A reference to 'evil things' is well understood by all and needs no further explanation. Euphemisms like these are well-suited, on an ideological level, to keep 'belief' intact and ward off unwanted inquisitiveness at the same time. If we wish to know more about inner dangers, there is little use in direct questioning. A researcher has to be content to follow conversations patiently and wait for the demons turn up in discussions about dangers. In my case, I have had to listen to endless talk among older women to see in what way the topic would be broached.

Demons in Conversation

The sexual element in demoniac possession, often mentioned in writings on the subject, is also present in *winti*. The *incubus* is represented in the pantheon as an *Ampuku*, a forest spirit. These rivals from the spirit world are thought to be intent on spoiling a medium's relations with the male sex. An *Ampuku* appears in dreams as a darkly-coloured man who has intercourse with her. All kinds of disturbances, ranging from infertility to other disorders of the reproductory system, frigidity or any incapacity to entertain lasting relations with men are attributed to spirits of this class. These spirits are greatly feared but do not loom large in conversations. It is worth noting that men who act as traditional healers (Wooding 1973:232, 349, 376; Stephen 1983:54) have more to say about them than the supposedly afflicted women. I think that this has much to do with pride; no one voluntarily admits such weaknesses or shows a vulnerable spot. Spirit-caused affliction is thought amenable to treatment, and responsible heads of households would not readily concede to suffer from emotional disturbances or to have neglected important ritual obligations.

The *Ampuku* appears in various guises, and the *incubus* is only one. Aggressiveness and aspirations to wealth are discussed more often. A woman related a dream: she had seen a small Black man in a big shining grey car adorned with red white and blue streaks. This has been an *Ampuku*, was the expert judgment of the interlocutress. Another woman, medium of a different variety of forest spirit, an *Akantasi*, got the advice to offer the spirit a trip in a car. Like any other spirit, a demon also requires some pampering.

The fear of sliding down the social scale is not unrealistic, and this road is paved by demons. It is not fortuitous that demons often appear at the end of rituals. When all participants have been anxious about the outcome of a ritual and find occasion to relax, when, moreover, an impressive amount of alcohol has been consumed, the demons have a chance. These 'things' or 'beings', though uninvited, have been present all along, but lacked an opportunity to manifest themselves. Rituals often are longlasting affairs in Bijlmermeer. The sponsors feel their prestige is enhanced by the number and involvement of their guests. Those invited seldom have reason to leave early anyway, so people hang on in a rather unstructured situation, get tired and start to quarrel about trifles. Remarks intended as jests are badly taken, one word leads to another and before long the demons are afoot.

A demon in the tube. Ritual activities in the proper sense having been concluded, food and drinks are handed out and a lot of fun is made about demons. Florrie has had a great success with her trance of a forest Indian; her hair was hanging loose and she lit a cigar. Encouraged by the attention lavished upon her, her demon, called 'little Desmond' joins in the general merrymaking. 'How much is one plus one?' Florrie calls out amid enthusiastic cheers. Achievements in school do not loom large among the assets of those present. The demon receives an answer, as part of the consideration due to any spirit: 'Three'. 'Well done', Florrie yells out, flopping down into the lap of a buxom lady friend. A glass tumbles down and Desmond is reprimanded, which he resents. Another guest, who does not favour *mati* or 'lesbian' relations, has other objections: 'Stop the dikery here'. A third one comments that enough gossip has been spread about Florrie and that she ought to calm down.

A few days later we overhear that Florrie has been evicted from her home. A bailiff called and she has gone into hiding. 'She has got only herself to blame' is the most frequently heard comment. She had been caught for fare-dodging in the metro and had thrown a tantrum on the spot. Two ticket inspectors had held her to the floor. Then, 'they' had started to investigate, and it was found that she owed rent in arrears and was a moonlighter. She had got a summary dismissal and had lost both apartment and furniture. What had caused public opinion to turn against her was the fact that she had used the association's *kasmoni* (savings) she was entrusted with for personal ends. She had gone through other women's money fast to finance her private rituals. 'She is overactive in *winti* matters and the rituals never turn out well'; 'she gets into a trance state to all types of music, which can hardly be right'; 'she lets her demon get in control, so one can see what an unchecked demon will do'; 'the demon has caused her to fall into disgrace'.

The forces that would make for a routinization of *winti* beliefs are strong, but nevertheless their charisma persists. This can only be explained by the fact that emotional investments are at stake that are as strong as they are difficult to control. Factors like these can be put forward only if they can be called 'structural', that is, if they are reproduced on a continuous basis by social relations. One of the social forces that would apply is the obligation resting on heads of households to keep a group together and make ends meet. Assertiveness is a vital quality, basic to the survival strategies current among the underclass, but imperceptibly one can saddle oneself with demons and be confronted with the other side of the coin, namely the inner dangers that are less readily recognized than those that threaten from outside the group and from others. Unexpectedly they turn up in the guise of demons.

Relations Between the Sexes

As a 'motor' in this sense we may point to the relations between the sexes. A striking fact is that women inclined to scepticism where *winti* is concerned do have recourse to ritual countermeasures whenever they, their daughters or granddaughters are threatened by rivals. These emotions spring not only from anxieties about affective security or sexuality as such, but also from the great significance sexual relations have had for generations in the pattern of social mobility in the Caribbean. As Mintz (1971:28) has stressed, a sexual code of concubinage and the keeping of outside mistresses has made its mark on the middle class in plantation colonies. Patronage by a small group of affluent men provided a source of income to a large number of women. This seigneurial behaviour was adopted by the middle class and the lower strata; it has been democratized and accepted as 'normal' (Hoetink 1961). Among Surinamese in the home country (Buschkens 1974:154-5) and in the Netherlands, this type of patron-client relationship between sexual partners is common. As long as the mean income of men is twice that of women (Kruyer 1973:183), relations with men will continue to loom large in the aspirations of women. Although women in the Netherlands are entitled to social security cheques, for men this is cause to try and dodge their obligations to partners and children (Lenders and van de Rhoer 1984:90, 155).

From the labels of ritual objects sold in the market-place in Bijlmermeer we can gauge how strong the association is between sexuality and money: 'success', 'prospering', 'compelling', 'fun', 'come to me', and 'moni masra (master of money)', are marked on bottles of perfumed oils, incense and candles. Women are motivated to engage in sexual relations to get some extras. 'God gave me my pussy to work with', one of them expressed in no uncertain terms. The fear of staying outside the flow of money and goods makes her set aside any objections inspired by unfortunate experiences. This motive is generally so well accepted that a woman's visit to a traditional healer is readily interpreted as an attempt to secure a relationship with a man. Turning it around, men are on their guard. Although they like to play the macho role and are proud of the number of children they have fathered with several women, they often feel threatened. They will express jealousy of women who allegedly 'have easy access to everything', and fear that women are trying to 'tie' them magically (*kroi* is the term for this type of evil magic). Otherwise, they put up a good show in magical practice. Schoonheym (1980:64) mentions the fact that men will 'train' women to perform as prostitutes on their behalf. Illnesses and mishaps are often attributed to the magical acts of a jealous or resentful (ex-)partner. They like to boast about this. It is an important, widespread and accepted theme, which guarantees the speaker an attentive and sympathetic audience. 'This is what the world is like', everyone will agree. Even those who do not believe in 'all this nonsense' retain interpretations of this kind. It has become the stop-gap of this religion.

For women to whom it matters greatly to keep their self-respect but who, nevertheless, are dependent on financial assistance from men who often humiliate them (Buschkens 1974:154-5), this inner conflict is a source from which the inner demon arises – 'helpless anger', in psychological terms. For such women the demon is more than a symbol; it is a reality, a source of power as well as a danger.

Olga, a resourceful mother of eight children, two of whom had died in infancy, told with gusto how her husband, who had a steady job with one of the big lumbering companies, used to squander his money over his countless mistresses in Paramaribo. He would return home afterwards drunk and aggressive, while she would go to her mother's house with the children. After sleeping it off, he would then show up in front of her mother's door. At an excruciatingly slow pace Olga imitated the conversation that would ensue: 'Momma?' ... 'Yes, my boy' ... Behind the door Olga used to whisper to her mother: 'What are you doing? Did he ever give you as much as ten bob?' 'No, you are quite right. But what will happen when one of the children falls ill?' her mother would argue, 'The firm he works with will supply free medical treatment'. That clinched the matter, but Olga said: 'Then I felt the *winti* coming, and it created a scene. They all were afraid of me'. Looking back, this at least is a cause of great satisfaction.

These relations and the concomitant tensions and suspicions have repercussions for other relations. Not only (ex-)partners, but also mothers and sisters ask men for financial support. Sometimes mothers will be under strong temptation to undermine the relations of their sons with their partners, and go to considerable lengths to keep those of their daughters going, in both cases solely out of financial considerations. Interpretations of illness and misfortune are adapted to suit these motives. When Eva's new son-in-law, who wanted to divorce his first wife in order to be able to marry Eva's daughter, got involved in a car crash, she felt very sure that 'the other woman' was behind this, although she used to dismiss such interpretations on other occasions as 'mere superstition'. Rosa also thought it wise to have a ritual performed when the time for her daughter's confinement drew near. The women had found 'some messy things' in front of the doorstep and were sure that the ex-wife had deposited it there and that the dirt was *hebi*, charged with negative supernatural power.

Those who prosper always feel the pressure of poor or less successful kinfolk. Even if one does not acknowledge the claims as legitimate, the need is still there to justify the refusal: 'These people are always broke, it looks as if a *bakru* eats their money'. But kinship ties are not easily ruptured, however much conflict they might cause between partners. Louise was indignant about the jealousy of her husband's kinswomen; they always commented on her clothes which they regarded as too expensive. When they celebrated her fortieth birthday they had danced all night, till daybreak. It had been a wonderful party. But when she started cleaning up next morning, someone came to warn her that 'something' was lying in front of her door: 'Someone must have dropped an egg there by accident'. Louise thought it unlikely that the egg had just fallen out of a bag; its contents would have splashed in all directions. No, it had been put there intentionally. She approached it with bleach and talked to it: 'I do not know what this is, what you are or what you have come to do, but if it is for evil, get off then!' But she had been so upset, having been alone in the house at the time, that she fell into a trance-like state. Later on people told her anything might have happened: The *Ampuku* had run berserk.

Belief in magic reinforces itself. People who only partly believe in *afkodre* but get into a personal conflict situation will fall back on the cultural heritage and regard the apparently coincidental as 'intentional'. What is an act of magical defence for one is an attempt at bewitching for another. In turn, the alleged magical assaults will prompt the defendants to fortify themselves with magical precautions.

The mechanism will work, as long as the 'motors' are running. That is to say, this view of reality will be supported as long as the social relations people live in have not basically changed and people are liable to experience conflicts that have been ingrained in their social position.

Discussion

Where entertaining relations with men opens opportunities for women to obtain money and prestige, and rivalry is intense, the field is likely to be charged with magical dangers. This has been characteristic of colonial societies, and will continue to be so for groups originating in colonies, as long as social relations have not basically altered.

This data has been gathered by participant observation, by listening to and taking part in conversations among women. Often, women susceptible to possession are singled out by demons lusting after seminal intercourse. In the field of Suriname studies, this theme is well-known. Women acknowledge such powers, but are not overly preoccupied by them. For them, their own aggressiveness and rebellious tendencies, and their hankering after prosperity rank first. It is worthy of note that because these wishes are regarded as reasonable, demons are legitimized. Exorcism is non-existent. Demons are looked at with ambivalence: they are potentially useful, but the dangers they bring are acknowledged as well. The risks of being 'beside oneself', of coming to harm, or of bringing shame upon oneself and sliding down the social ladder are clearly real. In ritual practice, the aim is to take away the bad sides and establish the good. The *bakru* is regarded as naughty, not evil. To entertain a demon is something normal, for in every soul gods and demons are present – all powers will be needed at times.

Despite these differences, there are also similarities. As among Europeans or 'Bush Negroes', males were first to make contracts with the devil. Such men were held to be masters over the demons rather than their victims. Gradually women got involved with the devil, but their power over the evil spirit and their gains by the transaction were clearly estimated as of a lesser order (cf. Cohn 1975:233). Creole women seem to endorse this in symbolic language: they regard their demons as akin to those of the ancestors, but as less powerful and less dangerous. Yet, they make it clear that they do not regard themselves as the helpless victims of demons.

This is well in line with the fact that women, as custodians of the cultural heritage (cf. Herskovits and Herskovits 1969:9), enjoy a large degree of autonomy. *Winti* religion is mainly a private affair, an *oso sani* (house-thing). As heads of households and members of informal women's associations, women elders to a large extent control their own discourse. Apart from the dyadic relation between traditional healer and client, the kin group, the household and women's network are the only contexts in which reality about *winti* is structured. Unwelcome 'definitions of the situation', in which women figure as prey to sacred or profane powers, are not accepted. Women see themselves as actors who are responsible for the transactions they make in the material and the spiritual realm.

Note

1. The Foundation for Scientific Research (NWO) in the Netherlands has generously sponsored anthropological fieldwork in a modern urban setting. From 1984 till 1987 I benefited from a research grant to live in Bijlmermeer. There, I joined a Surinamese Creole women's club that strives for the preservation and promotion of 'traditional' culture and took part in the informal activities of the neighbourhood. Some of the data has been published (see van Wetering 1987 and 1988).

10 History, Memory and Appropriation: Some Problems in the Analysis of Origins

Roland Littlewood

Et seule l'histoire peut nous débarrasser de l'histoire.
(Pierre Bourdieu 1982)

The return to the past, the rejection of White values and technology, the identification of the Blacks as the chosen people, the White appropriation of the Bible, Christianity as colonial apologetics – many of the motifs and themes of Rastafari[1] are common to other movements of resistance among the peoples colonized or enslaved by Europeans. These too have frequently looked for a day of ultra-human intervention: the destruction of the colonial order and the restoration of traditional liberty.

Such movements have sometimes built upon existing precolonial apocalyptic themes, acted as the intellectual and organizational basis for new military initiatives, or else, faced with overwhelming White power, have become more 'individualized' and quietist, ultimately coming to resemble many contemporary Western religious sects.[2] The earlier the local reaction to the colonial enterprise, the more likely it seems to be associated with some type of pragmatic military response, to continue existing cultural traits, and the less likely to employ Christian themes, or at least to be interpreted by outsiders as confronting the ideological challenges of European Christian authority.

Those movements particularly intent on restoring a lost tradition (and which have been termed by scholars *revivalist* or *nativist*) have emphasized abandoning adopted or imposed European names, clothes, money, technology or institutions, and frequently carried out the destruction of representative objects. Thus the nineteenth century Shawnee, Tenskwatawa, known to us as Tecumseh's Prophet, counselled his people to avoid the Whites' foodstuffs and recommended barter in place of cash purchase, together with a return to traditional hunting techniques. Other groups may temporize with technology whilst awaiting the final, purifying redemption. Such movements provide an explanation of defeat: frequently military in the 'earlier' responses – defeat by superior technology or the force of arms. 'Later' explanations may involve the notion that the community was once a 'chosen people' but through sin (as with the Rastas) or through a mistaken choice (the Medang), this privileged status has been revoked by the divine power. Particularly in those 'late' responses where no effective military action can be offered, the explanation may actually incorporate and transform the White racist mythology which justifies European supremacy – such as a descent from Noah's son Ham – or indeed reject 'traditional' values altogether in favour of crumbs from the colonial table.

The expected redemption may entail the colonized people (or their whole world) in shedding an existing skin to reveal an original or restored world underneath, one which offers the conditions for a physical and social reconstruction of an idealized past. Restoration of a world now upside-down demands yet another turning around in which the current relations between Black and White will be again reversed. The Heaven of certain South African Zionist churches will be entered by the Blacks (the suffering Christians) but the Whites (the Foolish Virgins) will be turned away from the divine seat.

With the complete alienation of land by the Europeans a particular notion of 'Nature' seems to have developed. However much nature may have been categorized before colonization as being in opposition to human society, the colonized now becomes retrospectively identified with an idealized 'natural' state in which they had once existed in a balanced harmony with their (often 'female') environment.[3] In North America, the failure of the military Ghost Dance led to the development of 'Earth Lodges' where the identity of indigenous people and of land developed a new symbolic significance: the indigenous peoples become part of the land, in opposition to the European. As Smohalla, the prophet of the Wanapum movement, expressed it:

> You ask me to plough the ground. Shall I take a knife and
> tear my mother's bosom? (Lienhardt 1964:130)

Rasta values similarly prescribe for Black people, as the original race, a closeness to a Nature which is identified with the soil. 'We are an ancient people, We are a nature people' (Owens 1976:151). Many Rastas refer to the Earth as a sensate, feeling organism, identified with Selassie or else with men in general, while less commonly it may be a woman, a mother. They may sit by preference on the ground and refer to the communal consumption of ganja, meditation and reflection as *groundings*. Some celebrate the anniversary of the *groundation* when Haile Selassie set foot on Jamaican soil. Natural health is livity, harmony with the forces of Nature and God, while *nature* also refers to the sexual drive of men, a force of nature (Yawney 1985a).[4] The *bredrin* can achieve *livity* by living off the earth, cultivating it by hand and with respect. Like the Trinidadian Earth People, they criticize the mechanical exploitation of land as the cause of earthquakes and other 'natural' disasters, for 'the earth would be at peace with men if only man would leave it in peace'.

Any Rasta trope can, like *nature*, be pursued through a multitude of historical analogies and associations. Take the instance of the avoidance of salt. It is often used sparingly by rural West Indians. We know salt was avoided by African-born slaves (sometimes called 'salt-water slaves') specifically because it would hamper any possible flight back to Africa (Herskovits 1958:156). Certainly for the slaves from inland Africa, their first experience of salt water had been closely associated with their enslavement. Salt of course remains associated with the imported slave food, salt fish, preserved 'dead' food which still forms an important part of the rural West Indian diet. An alternative tradition found in both Europe and Africa links salt with the spirit world; in West Africa devotees of the orisha Obatala refrained from salt. Salt is needed to catch the *soucouyant* (vampire) in Trinidad, and salt in Europe is similarly associated with nature spirits (Kipling's *Puck of Pook's Hill*), while food prepared without salt was once offered to the African *powers* (Abrahams & Szwed 1983:156), and in the 1930s in Trinidad it was used thus in wakes (Herskovits & Herskovits 1969:263). In Guadeloupe it represents female sexuality (André 1987:183). Native Americans avoided it: to take it was a sign of European civilization or even of sorcery (Taussig 1987:97, 172). Salt is salient in Catholic doctrine ('salt of grace') and its manufacture from ashes might have seemed unseemly or even evil. In alchemy salt returns us to the earth, the mother and the body. Finally, 'avoidance' of salt among those of African descent may be related simply to their greater physiological retention of it, relative to other ethnic groups.

A series of prefigurings and analogies of this sort do not by themselves constitute an understanding. Can we determine the extent to which Rasta theory and practice are a continuation of existing patterns, the extent to which they are a set of innovative values?

The Persistence (and Resistance) of African Institutions in the West Indies

Innovations are of course only innovations within some continuing tradition. Chevannes, in Chapter 2 of this volume, calls for a 'new approach' to the study of Rastafari on the basis of its links of continuity with earlier African-Caribbean religious traditions and worldviews. This continuing existence of the past in the present has been an enduring concern for Caribbean writers (Austin 1979) in their consideration of a society historically grounded in a particular moment of Western capitalism, a process well documented since its inception.

The area of debate was first laid out by Melville Herskovits in 1941 in *The Myth of the Negro Past*, in which he developed its characteristic terminology: 'syncretism', 'retention', 'survival' and 'reinterpretation'. He postulated a continuum of African 'retentions' in African-American societies ranging from the 'Bush Negroes' of Suriname (maximum African retention) through Haiti, the British West Indies, and Blacks of the Southern United States, to those of the urban North (minimal retention). Herskovits himself attributed a greater number of contemporary patterns to 'survivals' than have his successors in the debate. Thus he argues the preference of African-Americans for adult baptism by full immersion as a persisting attachment to certain rites of initiation once derived from West African religions while engaging with American historians on the contentious issue of slavery in the formation of contemporary African-American societies: notably in his debate with Franklin Frazier, who maintained that no significant residues of African culture could be said to have survived slavery in the Americas.

The problems in postulating an African tradition is perhaps best approached through Herskovits, the scholar who has placed the greatest emphasis on the resilience of African patterns of life in the New World. As he himself pointed out, a major difficulty is that of the unit of analysis. Do we trace persistence of tradition through the self-conscious continuation of isolated names for foods and ritual objects or the organization of events such as funerals? Alternatively, should we follow the fate of such sociological abstractions as 'matrifocality'?

Not altogether surprisingly, Herskovits had difficulties distinguishing the original items of analysis both from their subsequent transformations and from the very process of transformation itself: 'The acceptance of new forms does not necessarily preclude the retention of an underlying value-system that derives from an earlier kind of enculturative conditioning' (Herskovits 1951:46). This recalls a form/content distinction and indeed he does employ a dichotomy of form and role; 'form' however (contrary to its usual employment in the nineteenth century German dichotomy) refers to the superficial, the 'formal', and not to an underlying structure. Thus, Herskovits' pupils, Simpson and Hammond (1960), comment that below form lie 'more significant psychological attitudes'. Whether these 'roles' are invariate is far from clear, nor is there any consideration of continuing function – how and why 'survivals' survive. Simpson expressly states that he is not concerned with the problem of a continuing function at all and takes it as self-evident that any social institution should provide for psychological satisfaction and meaning for individuals, solutions to personal problems, and so forth; his implicit functionalism inevitably leads to assumptions that certain patterns of local religion may be 'dysfunctional', a common conclusion in sociological studies of Caribbean institutions (Simpson 1980:108, 111).

A problem which concerns us more closely than that of vague theory involves what we may term 'the African baseline'. Herskovits, like many Rastas themselves, assumes a relatively homogenous and autonomous historical West Africa,[5] although the area had been in close contact with Europeans for three hundred years by the time slavery ended and many West African societies may be said to have been constituted through the European slave trade. The Western ethnographies often used as a reference point are derived from fieldwork in Africa carried out a century after the slave trade ceased, and the search for the common point of origin, the 'real Africa', has thus to be determined from earlier mission and colonial documentation. In fairness to Herskovits, it is worthwhile to emphasize that much of his data was derived from Trinidad with its relatively rich post-Emancipation contacts with West Africa, as compared to Jamaica or the United States.

Perhaps the major problem with the 'Africanisms' perspective is its failure to consider how and why retentions may be actively selected at specific historical moments. M.G. Smith reminds us that 'form is one thing, function is another; process, the third, is the ultimate goal of our analysis' (M.G. Smith 1960:41). Far from being a diachronic record of social change, the majority of studies on African-Caribbean religion are 'folkloric' collections of informants' own exegeses, taken to reflect current (or at any rate recent) practice, which are then rather crudely compared with contemporary West African material. As Ernest Gellner puts it in a not dissimilar context, their lives seems to be 'made up of

left-overs of which they have somehow forgotten to divest themselves'
(Gellner 1964:v).

Herskovits' 'survivals' range from complex socio-cultural patterns to
the relatively superficial, such as terms for the preparation of food. At
times he comes close to the racism he is concerned to refute: Shouter
Baptism in Trinidad appears 'more congenial to the traditions of these
people than are the other denominations. One need only cite such an
aspect of worship as the emotionalism of spirit possession' (Herskovits
& Herskovits 1969:181). For Herskovits, persisting Africanisms include
the 'polygynous family', the ease of parental separation, distant relations
between father and children, the 'ancestor cult', the 'feel for political
manoeuvre', the importance of the funeral and funeral societies, kin
terms and personal ('family') names and the distinction between sorcery
and witchcraft. Some appear fanciful in the extreme: the 'African' flog-
ging of children, or the preference of individuals to avoid certain foods
being seen as the survival of West African 'totemic' prohibitions.

Note that these are all measures of 'difference' from European
values rather than aspects of a self-contained society. While the persistence of the names of deities and foods, perhaps the two most frequently
cited Africanisms, seem relatively unproblematic, how helpful are such
notions as Herskovits' 'West African funeral complex'? Bastide poig-
nantly notes that the funeral was the only social institution left to the
slaves, for the plantation owners were not interested in dead slaves –
'the Negro doesn't die, he comes to an end' (Bastide 1979:129). Slaves
were frequently abandoned by their masters when incapable of work
and their 'death' (from the White perspective) might be dated to this
point. That the dying or incapacitated slave had, in a sense, already escaped from the plantation, and was thus about to return to Africa, was
recognized by the slaves.

Many West Indian patterns such as matrifocality are hardly unique,
but rather are common to other modern capitalist societies where a high
proportion of the male population continues to migrate or where there
is considerable individual mobility around the country to seek paid employment. The assumption that matrifocality was ever common during
the period of slavery seems derived from plantation records which
named the mother, but not the father, of a newborn child.

Radical Puritanism in the Caribbean

> We need not the rule of kings and crowns,
> Neither mansions with splendour enhanced,
> Thrones and prisons are part of a system.
> (Doukhobor anthem)

While many of Herskovits' Africanisms may be general characteristics of Creole or peasant societies (for example, the various patterns of co-operative labour), there is another aspect of Caribbean history which has exercised as yet little academic interest, that of seventeenth-century millennialism. Such Old Testament themes as Exodus and 'crossing over to Jordan' are part of a continuing common heritage of radical Puritanism common to Europe and America. Certainly, religious revivalism appears more characteristic of the Protestant anglophone than of the Catholic francophone Caribbean. The extent to which radical Puritanism in seventeenth century Britain had its own roots in perceptions of social deprivation is still debated, but its themes of personal redemption, Exodus, the chosen people, of the moral bankruptcy of the established churches, and the close and continuing relationship between divine and human, have continued to be articulated by the disadvantaged and dislocated.

Apocalyptic and utopian visions of a world upside down[6] are a recurring theme in the West, a radical 'countercurrent' to established power which has flourished since the beginnings of Christianity, now hidden, now bursting forth to illuminate whole periods, occasionally represented in dark antinomian acts or forming strange coalitions, and finally declared by Weber to be attenuated into the secular only to re-emerge yet again in the counterculture of the 1960s, in Rastafari, and among the Earth People.

It may be legitimate to talk of these fissiparous strands and short-lived enthusiasms as a continuing 'tradition' in that the radical millennialists themselves often referred back to earlier movements whose oppositional themes remain remarkably constant. As does the idiom. The Rasta term for the deity, *Jah*, has an established radical pedigree (see note 13) while *Babylon* represents the compromised secular state with its servants and technologies, as it has for the countless apocalyptic groups which have returned to the Book of Daniel for their inspiration. The eighteenth-century British millennialist, Richard Brothers, declared his followers to be the 'lost tribes' and London to be Babylon.

The modern industrial state was Babylon, argued both the Rappites and the Zoarites (religious communalists in nineteenth century America), as did the Commonwealth Seekers and Ranters of Britain, while for the competing sects of New York's 'Burned-Over District' in the nineteenth century the expression was reserved for Catholics or for rival evangelical groups. Enthusiastic Franciscans and Lutherans had both identified the Papacy with Babylon, Sodom, or the Anti-Christ of *John* 2:7, although some Protestant groups preferred the designification of 'Rome' for their opponents (as do the Earth People), or even 'Chaldea'.[7] Neologisms such as the 'Ninneversity' (Nineveh/university) of the New England Puritans recall those of Rastafari. Many Protestant sects in Europe have on occasions believed in a mystical flight to the Promised Land; that they were the lost tribes of Israel and should not eat pork; or that as the millennium was imminent, conventional law and morality were no longer applicable. All these themes were current among the West Indian slaves and are now found among the Rastas and the Earth People.

To trace a direct 'influence' of the early radical Puritan tradition in the West Indies is problematic. Certain themes such as an identification with the Last Tribes, or the avoidance of 'swine flesh', may perhaps be attributed to recent proselytizing by the Seventh Day Adventists (although a refusal of slaves to eat pork was recorded in the Caribbean in the eighteenth and early nineteenth centuries). We certainly know that Quakers and other Protestant radicals were established in the English-speaking West Indian islands by the 1660s as settlers or as transported felons (C. Hill 1972, 1984).[8] Millennial and political groups such as the Ranters and Anabaptists established utopian communities in Jamaica which were crushed after the Restoration, to be replaced by slave plantations; and Christopher Hill makes the intriguing suggestion that these groups, deist and democratic, may have contributed after their dispersal to the egalitarian floating republics of the Caribbean pirates, the Brethren of the Coast. The island of Providencia was settled by the Puritans in 1629-30 and was occupied by Spain in 1641 (on the third attempt) for the 'piracy' of its inhabitants. The first revolts of the Black slaves in Barbados were supported by White indentured servants, and Jamaica remained a centre of radical republican activity after 1660 (C. Hill 1984:2), as did Trinidad after its cession to Britain. Slave revolts were frequently attributed to evangelical preachers whose beliefs Michael Taussig has characterized as a 'radical . . . utopia, anarchist and egalitarian, founded in the sacred ways of nature' (Taussig 1987:46). From the period immediately predating the emancipation of the slaves, Baptists and other evangelical sects from the United States were conducting numerous missions in the West Indies: Troeltsch described such Protestant sects as egalitarian and radical, and Bryan Wilson points out that they developed not only in opposition to the established church but 'against the state, secular institutions of society or in opposition to or separation from public institutions'.[9] We have also to consider the esoteric but subversive Masonic, Hermetic and Rosicrucian teachings, still found in West Indian *high science*, or *conjuration*, which probably arrived in the English islands with the French refugees from Sainte Domingue.

Not only the beliefs, but the very 'style' of Rastafari closely recall that of the seventeenth century British utopians, and it may not be too fanciful to regard the Rastafarians as one of the latest flowerings of the radical Puritan heritage. It is unlikely there was no explicit 'underground' continuity in the repeated response to established power. Unlikely, but such a continuity is difficult to prove, even if we may agree with Donald Wood that the American Baptist ex-slaves who settled in Trinidad after 1812 fused African religions with 'the Puritanism of sixteenth-century Münster and East Anglia' (Wood 1968:22).

A suggestion of some presence of the radical millennial 'countercurrent' in rural West Indian life requires a brief consideration of its salient themes. Coherent tradition or not, its contours demonstrate values which continually appear in any radical Western 'oppositional ideology', whether represented in everyday 'strategies of resistance' or coalesced into organized groups.

Popular millennial expectations in Europe have always looked for a return to a purer original state (an apokatasiasis): 'When Adam delved and Eve span, who then was gentleman?' The very term 'revolution' implies such a return. Millennialists in Britain anticipated a return to Edenic purity, to the communalism of the early Christians (*I Corinthians* 10:24) or, at the least, to the restoration of the rights of the Anglo-Saxon common man. The radicals lived in a biblical present in which the Last Days were being enacted, for which they cited familiar Old and New Testament texts. For some, even their relationship to the Bible was equivocal, for in the eschaton its authority could only be temporal and compromised, faced with the Christ within and the imminent intervention of the deity: 'The letter killeth but the spirit giveth life'. At the same time, as with contemporary rural Jamaicans, they lived in a world whose explanations, idiom and style were to a considerable extent biblical. 'They will state that they have no Bible among them; yet to all questions put to them regarding their faith, they reply with words drawn from the Holy Scriptures' a visitor observed of the Canadian Doukhobors earlier this century (Maude 1904:20). Many groups recognized the British (or other nations) as the last tribes, and Jewish iconoclasm and the avoidance of pork recur constantly. The secularization of the radical millennial vision within what we now conceive of as the left-wing political tradition, from the seventeenth century onwards, propelled it away from this cyclical return into a linear potential of totally new human relationships, but the promise of removing those historically imposed constraints on the human spirit, to release its pristine dawn, remains to haunt both the libertarians' notion of 'nature' and the Marxists' 'alienation'.

Among the numerous medieval manifestations of the radical 'counter-current' were the Lollards, the Brethren of the Free Spirit, the radical Hussites, mystics like Böhme and Langland, and later the Neoplatonic and pastoral pantheism of the Tudor poets.[10] Whether peasant revolt or aristocratic poesy, the common arguments which continue to recur are the rejection of the established churches, their sacraments and priestly power; the pope as Anti-Christ; the communality of believers; the particular closeness of the poor and oppressed to Christ; the guiding inner light and the presence of Christ in all. The more radical groups which constituted what we might now term the 'left-wing' of the Reformation and the seventeenth-century radicals (Familists and Anabaptists, and in Britain the Ranters, Levellers and Quakers) added a rejection of state authority and of the established professions of law and medicine; pacifism; opposition to standing armies and to infant baptism; a radical restructuring of marriage, sometimes equality for women; the occasional suggestion that heaven and hell were of this world; an interest in astrology and 'correspondences' between humanity and an animate nature which led, in some cases, to frank 'pantheistical materialism',[11] and, in others, to opposition to any law, the communism of property, free love and the ultimate salvation of all people.

From the end of the sixteenth century when, according to Max Weber, 'man historically abandoned the garden of enchantment for means-ends rationality', these themes became transformed through Unitarianism and Transcendentalism, to Humanism, New Thought and Socialism. Less secularized, they persisted in the West Indies, and among the British millennialists and Romantic poets of the late eighteenth century, and in a number of American utopian and communalist projects. Shelley's poem *Queen Mab* presents a pantheistic female cosmos, an identity between spirit and matter, the notion that God and religion are man-made devices for legitimating tyranny of law and government, but that the Earth is physically changing to initiate a period when love will govern all.

Shelley dreamed of anarchist utopias – 'kingless continents sinless as Eden', and such 'counter-current' themes are common, indeed dominant, in the American experiments in communal living which involved over a hundred groups and perhaps a hundred thousand people in the eighteenth and nineteenth centuries. Many were closely associated with or assisted by the Quakers and gained their members from the popular 'camp meetings' during periods of general religious enthusiasm and revival. They varied from mystico-pietist groups with a strong Hermetic interest (such as the Woman in the Wilderness community), to Anabaptist and radical fundamentalist sects, to a 'rationalist' Owenite or Fourierist anakhoresis. Some emphasized rejection of the state, together with opposition to racism,[12] slavery and conventional marriage, with advocacy of pacifism and economic self-sufficiency. They were egalitarians, self-styled 'peculiar people', who fulminated against slavery, war, the criminal code, the treatment of the insane, and sometimes even the tendency to make left-handers behave as if they were right-handed. Today the Doukhobors of Canada still await the fall of all temporal governments when 'the complete unification of the nations would result'. Communitarians avoided 'social' titles and given names, calling each other Brother or Sister, and adopted distinctive and sometimes paradoxical modes of dress and speech (the Shakers incorporated glossolalia into the everyday hymns printed in their hymnals). Communal life devalued privacy and individual differences through formal debate and through confession, both public and private.

Let us take the radical transformations of language. William Blake's use of homonyms, paronomasia and polysemy immediately recall the inspirations of the Puritan radicals, as do his doctrines: 'Prophets in the modern sense of the word have never existed ... Every Honest man is a prophet'; 'Art is the Tree of Life, Science is the Tree of Death'. Some anticipate those of Rastafari and the Earth People: his opposition of Urthona (Earth Owner) to Urizen (Your Reason), Nobodaddy (God), morning/mourning, vale/veil, sun/son. Rastas, too, pride themselves on being more natural, honest and authentic, less devious and calculating than the *social* population: 'Man knows, Men [Babylon] believe'. Rasta idiom, often unintelligible to the middle-class West Indian, is essentially working-class Jamaican English with phonetic and semantic revisions, employing new words based on puns and sound values, or else changing the 'negative' associations of standard words:

> Within the word/sound structure of the Queen's English
> there exist subtle negative connotations ... Rastafarians
> are continually exploring these negatives and seek to sub-
> stitute and reaffirm more positive vibrations ... Within the
> words 'be(lie)f' and '(sin)cere' we can perceive the word-
> vibrations of 'sin' and 'lie'. In the case of 'sin' the 's' is
> dropped reaffirming the word, sound and power positively
> as 'Incerely' or 'Icerely'. (Faristzaddi 1982)[13]

Thus *(ded)icate* becomes *livicate,* and *to(bacc)o,* yields *frunto.* Any plu-
ral implies diversity and disunity so Rastas collectively are simply *man*
or *I-and-I, men* and *we* being appropriate only to Babylon. 'For Jerusalem is ruined and Judah fallen because their tongues and their doings
were against the Lord' (*Isaiah* 3:8). Inappropriate speech places one in
a state of spiritual alienation and physical *dis-ease.* (Rasta idiolect however is seen by some as only a transitory stage before returning to Amharic).

Resistance and Appropriation

The possibility of an *active* creation by African-Americans of a complex
of new values and behaviour specifically concerned with the White
domination has been ignored until recently. Thomas Webber however
has postulated a set of enduring values for Black life in the rural United
States, values rooted in an opposition to the plantation experience such
as Black group identity; antipathy towards Whites; and explanation of
'official' Christianity as merely the legitimation of White supremacy;
Black moral superiority as opposed to White political power; close family ties; the everyday relationship with the supernatural; the desirability
of literacy and the elusive goal of personal autonomy (Webber 1978).

    In his consideration of *les religions Afro-Brésiliennes,* Roger Bastide
dismissed Herkovits' 'passive syncretism' in favour of such dynamic and
individual patterns as appropriation and innovation, for 'Syncretism
cannot be defined by the mere juxtaposition or merging of civilizations
in contact: it is an activity of men united in divergent or co-operative
groups. It translates into dogmas or rites the very movement of social
structures as they came apart and are reassembled'. Similarly Clifford
argues that 'It is just as problematic to say that their way of life 'survived' as to say that it 'died' and was 'reborn'' (Clifford 1988:339). In his
consideration of what I have called 'the units of analysis', Bastide how-

ever comes close to Herskovits in giving considerable autonomy to 'religion' as opposed to 'society' and 'politics': 'Collective representations had to create new organizational forms in which to incarnate themselves and through which to propagate themselves in time'. These religious themes had to find 'niches' in Brazilian society (Bastide 1979:16-17). When describing change in the African-Brazilian cults, Bastide seems as syncretic as any popular cultural historian. His emphasis on the autonomy of the African themes leads him to describe the 'disintegrations' of these themes in terms approaching the pathology of the sociological functionalists: such 'denuded' themes become 'magic' through their too-ready conflation with personal needs, or else 'ideologies' through their employment for seeking political power in the social world.

Political response to White domination in the Caribbean before the 1930s did not take the form of mass secular organization for this had been impossible under slavery and largely rendered ineffectual under colonial status. Cultural resistance and reassertion for African-Americans has always been closely associated with religion. While the mere existence of some type of African religious practice in the slave compound provided an independent identity not derived from plantation life, slave rebellions in the Americas, most notably in Haiti, used the practical organization, beliefs and rituals of those nocturnal meetings when the disparate tribal traditions became welded together in *vodu*, *shango* or *umbanda*. Boukman, the Jamaican slave who led the revolt in Sainte Domingue (Haiti) in 1791, organized his followers through vodu-like rites. Many leaders claimed divine powers to protect their followers. Some preached a Black God. Those West Indian slaves who had been born in Africa and the descendants of the escaped slaves (Maroons) both believed that they would return there after death, and were buried with insignia which would be recognized in their native land; the planters argued that the persistence of such beliefs accounted for the high suicide rate in African-born slaves (Abrahams & Szwed 1983:6, 140, 163, 168-9, 201, 340).

Gradually Christian ideology was appropriated, even if its heaven was seen as a place where there was freedom the Whites themselves were perhaps unlikely to attain. Underground slave traditions maintained that the Blacks were the sheep and the Whites the goats mentioned by Jesus, or even that there was a 'real' Bible hidden somewhere which gave a true account of Black history (Webber 1978:82 and Chapter 6). Exodus and the crossing of the Red Sea provided a symbolic representation of the return to Africa, whether after death or as some future political event (and it is likely that these two alternatives were not so distinct). Ethiopia, the ancient Christian kingdom said to have been founded by Solomon and the Queen of Sheba, African but not (yet) colonized by Whites, appeared as a sign of dignity, independence and hope: the first Black Baptist Church in Jamaica in 1784 was named the Ethiopian Baptist Church and many self-help groups and lodges took the name 'Ethiopian' in the nineteenth century, perhaps influenced by an earlier European fashion for things Abyssinian (Bernal 1987). Organized missionary Christianity was regarded by some as merely a legitimation for the plantation system. Locally trained preachers continually left the mainstream churches to found fissiparous and sometimes expressly political groups, a pattern which still continues. Many revolts were led by 'assimilated' slaves – skilled workers or overseers – and in North America in particular leaders like Nat Turner and Denmark Vesey employed Christian themes of deliverance and Exodus to articulate their revolts, as did the 'Baptist Rebellions' of Jamaica led by Sam Sharpe, George William Gordon and Paul Bogle. What may be perceived as a 'religious' dimension continues to be integral to African-American political action, particularly in Jamaica and the United States, but it is most clearly manifest in Rastafari.

In their consideration of North American Indian religion, Clyde Kluckholn and Dorothea Leighton argued that in situations of cultural and political dominance an indigenous religion provides the obvious alternative system of meaning for the dominated, presumably because religion is usually less accessible to external control than other collective behaviours (it was the only form of aggregation permitted during West Indian slavery) and, while not reflecting existing political structures in the Durkheimian sense, it can provide the model for an alternative social dispensation at an appropriate time, keeping intact in the meanwhile shared patterns of meaning which remain in opposition to (or are at least radical reinterpretations of) those of the dominant group. The very notion of 'survivals' tends to miss this active principle of resistance and redefinition, whatever may have been Herskovits' stated intentions of refuting the notion of the passive slave.[14] The generation of Caribbeanists which came after Herskovits does acknowledge such a function of pragmatism and resistance. Thus Mintz describes the reassertion of African identity and the persistence of African patterns of agriculture almost teleologically, as if they were only a preparation for the free peasantry which developed in the West Indies after emancipation (Mintz 1974, *passim*).

Although one of the first Rastas, Leonard Howell, had served in the Ashanti Wars and probably learned some West African languages, African themes in Rastafari are transmuted through the Black experience in the Caribbean or are derived from the presentation of Africa in the Western media. It is only in recent years that a few Jamaican and British Rastas have spent time in Africa and fed this experience back into the movement. The most fundamental tenet of the movement however is that it is African.

Mintz warns us that 'It is one thing to perceive African sources, another to consider whether people see it that way' (Mintz 1974:25). Rastafari certainly does, even if the Africa which it reasserts and experiences is one, in part, secondary to European perception.

Rasta patterns are less 'survivals', discrete objects of analysis, than repetitions of relationships that persist through time. West Indian working-class life has always contained in *reputation*[15] what, following Schwimmer (1972:117-25), we may term an 'oppositional ideology':

> inversions or reversals of putative scale values on which the members of the disadvantaged group suppose themselves to be consigned to the pole of marginality or peripherality by those in the 'centre' ... One of the potent ways in which they appear to give meaning symbolically to their communality is by reversing the polarities of the scale to make their values central.

Such a series of pragmatic and individually functional values – including word play, satire, irony, *worthlessness*, masquerade, folklore, obeah – lie available for reconstruction into a unitary set of new 'central' values. An ascribed role become an achieved identity. This happens in Rastafari with its elevation of the *worthless* over the *social*, but to an even greater extent among the female leadership of the Earth People who have discarded male dominance, technology and Christianity much more radically. From the participants' point of view, Rastafari offers a reassertion, perhaps an overturning; no schema however can be so radical as to constitute a total change, and the point at which we may say that personal 'reassertion' of subdominant values becomes a 'reversal' of the dominant ones remains arbitrary.

Oppositional ideology is not a dull re-enactment of some aetiolated tradition. The *worthlessness* of the Black working class man is ascribed anew in each generation through economic power and educational disadvantage: acting through this subjectivity, whether in the carnivalesque *no behaviour* of everyday life or the conscious resistances of Rastafari, is a personal creation by each.

As I have argued, the ascription of a tradition – the 'organization of the current situation in terms of the past' (Sahlins 1987:155)[16] – and the perception and experience of actually living in one are rather different. A dominant European tradition may be identified through its own sense of continuity, its texts and institutions existing through time, its justifications and appeals to earlier figures. Here subjectivity and ascription correspond for individual members and social theorists alike. Dominated individuals – and here I am talking of Black people and, to an extent, women – seek control over their lives and their meanings in explicit reaction to the dominant group, through evasion, accommodation, denial, reinterpretation, resistance or just simply getting by, through a rhetoric of verbal indirection, masking, parody, and left-handed compliments (Gates 1988; Bristol 1985). If the dominant tradition, defining itself against them, manifests some coherence through time, then their own reactions will take similar forms (as a perverse affinity, not as a lineage). If as individuals they affirm and trace back through time some continuity of reaction then we can say they are living in a counter-tradition articulated through an oppositional ideology:

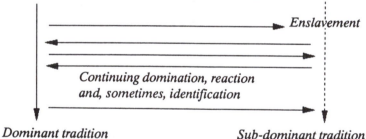

Dominant tradition   *Sub-dominant tradition*

For external observers, historians or anthropologists, the question of perceiving such a sub-dominant response as a 'tradition' whether among the poor of Europe or the Caribbean, is one of acknowledging the coherence and centrality of a self-aware, sub-dominant (or counter-)tradition against an endless series of individual reactions determined ultimately from the outside. If we do so, its form will hardly be that of the dominant ideology itself, internally consistent and marked by texts which signal a lineage through time. It will be a double-voiced tradition of response and of survival, of gesture and irony, of compromise and deception, ludic inversion and apocalyptic time.

Notes

1. And of other recent African-Caribbean movements such as the Earth People, a small group which established itself as a commune on the northern coast of Trinidad in the mid-1970s. While its founder, Mother Earth, had been an adherent of the Spiritual Baptists (and when young, had participated in Shango ceremonies), after her visions on which the group were based, she was joined by numbers of Rastas from Port-of-Spain. I am grateful to Cambridge University Press to allow me to quote here some passages from my book on the Earth People, *Pathology and Identity: The Work of Mother Earth in Trinidad* (1993). I owe a particular debt to my colleagues at the ISS Workshop for their critical comments on an earlier draft of this paper.

2. Passage between what the observer sees as 'political' or as 'religious' response may go in either direction. As with the 'quietist' response of the Quakers after 1660, in Trinidad both Rastafari and the Earth People were formed after the failure of the 1970 Black Power mutiny. Members of both say they are continuing the goal of Black liberation by other means. While neither of course are 'early' responses (comparable, say, with the Maroons), a 'military' response may develop out of an earlier 'utopian' withdrawal: as with The Move, the African-American sect whose members resembled the Rastas in some aspects – the use of dreadlocks and an emphasis on Nature – and whose beleaguered communal houses were destroyed in 1985 as the result of an air strike by the Philadelphia police department; or with the Black Muslims, who attempted a coup in Trinidad in 1990. Our choice of the term *movement* or *sect* as opposed to, say, *revolt* depends on an assessment of the continuation of a separate 'national' or quasi-national identity: the participant is likely to see a *movement* as constituting a *revolt* long after the sociologist has adopted the former, more neutral and 'religious' term.

3. Kenelm Burridge (1969:19) emphasizes the significance of alienated land in millennial movements and quotes a Maori in conversation with a White clergyman: 'Bishop, many years ago we received a faith from you. Now we return it to you for there has been found a new and precious thing by which we shall keep our land'. Contrast Aimé Césaire: 'My negritude is neither a tower nor a cathedral. It plunges into the red flesh of the earth'. Sam Gill however argues that such

identification with the pre-colonial earth is in part due to the popularization by Western anthroplogists of some sort of universal 'mother earth' concept (Gill:1988).

4. To lose your sex drive is in common West Indian parlance 'to lose your nature'. The shaking of the head causing the locks to whirl about is often suggested by awed observers to have an element of sexual display and threat. (Interestingly, in Arabic *ras* refers to the head of the penis [glans] as well as to the head residing on one's shoulders or the head of a community).

5. See such idealized accounts as Janheinz Jahn's *Muntu: The New African Culture,* Credo Mutwa's *My People: Writings of a Zulu Witch-Doctor,* or the work of the Trinidadian ethnologist J.D. Elder.

6. *Psalm* 149:9; *Isaiah* 14:1-2, 20-1; *Acts* 17:1-6.

7. The 'Babylon' of Daniel was itself of course allegorical, and represented the contemporary Jewish subjection to Antiochus Epiphanes. As a term for the spiritual enemy it goes back to the Sibylline Books. After Cromwell failed them, the Fifth Monarchy Men termed the Commonwealth 'Babylon'. For a recent use of the Babylonian theme, *The Two Babylons or the Papal Worship Proved to be the Worship of Nimrod and His Wife,* by the Rev. Alexander Hislop, London, Partridge, 1916, is worth a cursory examination. 'Babylon' continues to feature in the more extreme variants of Ulster Unionism. 'Rome' as used by the Earth People was an earlier usage of Rastas and Garvey. In response to Mussolini, Garvey wrote: 'The Rome of sin and human hate has plagued the world before'.

8. On Nevis, Quakers 'had the run of the island' (Lovejoy 1985:139).

9. Ernest Troeltsch, *The Social Teaching of the Christian Churches,* cited by Bryan Wilson (1973:11).

10. Not to mention Waldensians, Taborites, Amaurians, Spiritual Libertines, Bergherds, Beguines, Euchites, Flagellant groups, the Drummer of Nicklashausen, Collards, Turlupians, Spiritual Franciscans. Earlier millennial impulses galvanized the Gnostics, Montanists and Carpocratians, and 'mainstream' Christianity remained subject to occasional millennial preoccupations. There is certainly continuity between them, even if we might balk at describing them as a 'socioreligious chain' from before the Reformation to Marx, as Henri

Desroches puts it in his *American Shakers: From Neo-Christianity to Presocialism*.

11. Christoper Hill's term.

12. The Moravians intermarried with Native Americans, and the Shakers had Black members. During the period of ecstasy (Mother Ann's Work), Shakers were possessed by the spirits of Eskimos and American Indians. The Quakers (alone of Christian missionaries) on occasions actually encouraged such tribal millennial religions as the Puget Sound Shakers.

13. Similarly the American Father Divine would reply to 'Hello' with 'Other Place' and use 'Bless!' as a substitute expletive for 'Damn!' The procedures appear particularly to be: (i) reversal, as in *livicate*, *overstand* (also *iverstand*) from 'understand'; *man go* from 'I come'; (ii) omission as in *ble(sin)g*; (iii) substitution as in *I-range* (orange); *I-rit* (spirit); *I-nana* (or *free-nana*) from banana; *I-rie* (merry); *I-laloo* (callaloo); *I-tal* from 'vital'; *I-dren* ('bredrin'); (iv) use of biblical terms, as in *Babylon, Rome* (same meaning: 'nine to five church and society, the inheritor of the empire of Nimrod and the Old Babylonian Roman order'); *Judah* (one of the names of Haile Selassie); (v) other loan words, some from the Maroons, *esho* for 'water'; *Jah* for 'God', the Maroons taking this form of 'Jehovah' from the English Bibles used between 1539-1758; it was also used by the Jehovah's Witnesses, pre-Rasta Jamaican peasants (Kerr 1952:141), the Shakers, and is found in *high science* (*The Sixth and Seventh Books of Moses*, Arlington, Texas, Dorene Publishing Co., n.d., p. 97), and Masonry (Bernal 1987); (also from Creole *Dieu*?); Jahweh was an 'Akan' deity (Field 1960:48); (vi) deliberate and accentuated use of Jamaican English as in *yout* (youth), *bredrin*; (vii) nonspecific alterations to demonstrate the essence of something such as *Jamdung* (Jamaica + dung (down)); *Elizabitch* (Elizabeth II); and *Queen* (The Rasta woman, often found as in King Rasta and Queen Omega); (ix) semantic inversions, so *blackhearted* is the term of approbation. Many words have multiple meanings, particularly *dread* which refers both to any frightening or powerful event (similar to Standard English), thus to the oppression of the Blacks, the state of revolt this engenders in the Black and therefore anything connected with the power of Rastafari, particularly the *locks*. Similarly *Raas* may actually be used as a term of abuse probably because of its similarity to 'arse'; it is then only directed to outsiders as far as I have

seen. Key concepts may have many names, and *ganja* is variously known as *herb, i-shence* ('essence' and perhaps 'incense'), *kaya, strength, grass, colly, I-ly, tappie, sensimina, maka, Jerusalem bread, King's bread, Lamb's bread, Weed of Wisdom, Holy Weed,* or *Solomon Herb.*

14. Simpson (1980:309), the leading comparative authority on African-Caribbean religions, does not engage in a potential debate (which might parallel discussions of the influence of Methodism on the British Labour Party) as to whether the religous response facilitated or hindered the political response, merely pointing out that adherence to African-Caribbean cults has had the effect of strengthening loyalty to the sub-group while 'contributing to the continuation of the existing social order, including the political systems'. He thus appears to favour the 'hinder' alternative.

15. Peter Wilson's term for the primarily male demotic values, which are opposed to *respectability* (White values represented more typically in women) (Wilson 1973). Alternative names in Trinidad include 'no behaviour', 'worthlessness', or 'niggerways'.

16. 'Every actual use of cultural ideas is some reproduction of them, but every such reference is also a difference' (Sahlins, p. 153).

11   Afterword

Barry Chevannes

This collection was stimulated by a workshop organized around three papers I had written, which focused on the continuity in worldview between the Rastafari and the earlier Revival religious movements, notwithstanding the self-conscious and obvious (to the onlooker) departure of the former from the latter. Appearing on the urban scene from the 1930s, Rastafari presented and represented a new discourse, new symbols and new, freshly discovered truths. Their new way of cultivating first facial and later head hair went like an arrow of God to the heart of social conscience, with the intent of offence as carefully aimed as was the new doctrine that the Emperor of Ethiopia was the returned messiah, Jah himself. However – and this is the point, closer examination by the onlooker reveals that in many very important ways the discourse is not and could not be new, insofar as by the act of communicating Rastafari has to speak a common language. It is this language that constitutes the worldview. Rastafari is thus a restatement of the older, antecedent religious expression, emerging from and shaped by Revival, but at the same time it is a refashioning of that expression in the face of a changing reality.

'So what?' the reader may well ask. So what if there is this sort of continuity? What difference does it make to our understanding of the Caribbean peoples?

The reader might recall my reference in Chapter 1 to the low status enjoyed by Revival. Studies which have established its African roots by examining its structural, ritual and belief characteristics (Beckwith 1929; J.J. Williams 1934; Simpson 1956, 1980; Seaga 1969) have accomplished little in undermining this low status, in the main because the prevailing views saw the African connection as a thing of the past, which the people have since rejected, or outgrown. But by adopting a continuity approach, Jean Besson (Chapter 3) has elevated Revival from a simple African retention to cultural resistance on par with the Baptist and Rastafari religions. This suggests underlying values at work and she makes it quite clear that the role of women and the role of land are central. Whether or not these are some of the 'grammatical principles' (Mintz and Price 1976) we should be looking for, she has convincingly demonstrated the fruitfulness of the approach.

Thus, more can be gleaned from a reappraisal of Revivalism and other earlier forms of folk religion among the African populations of the Caribbean, not so much from the point of view of their organizational structure, rituals and beliefs as for the way they shaped the structuring of reality and legitimized social action. This, it seems to me, is what a number of scholars have begun to do from a historical point of view. The question is, though, what about the present? Here the full import of Besson's paper is to be understood, for her claims of cultural resistance are based not on history alone, but also on contemporary field work. So too is the fascinating work of van Wetering in the heart of Amsterdam, where Surinamese cling to *Winti*, despite their upward mobility, as a means of retaining their sense of identity. Thoden van Velzen and van Wetering (1988:61) report a similar process of ethnic integration among the Ndyukas of Suriname through a High God cult in the early years of Ndyuka independence, at about the same time that Myal emerged in Jamaica, in the 1760s. It is, thus, clear that the earlier classificatory approaches taken towards these 'African-derived' religions have less than exhausted all that needs to be gleaned from them.

The emphasis on continuity given in this collection, it could be argued, would seem also to revive the issue of African retentions long ago posed by the Herskovitses. This issue remains alive in Anglophone Caribbean anthropology and African-American studies in North America. One reason lies in the emergence of a more confident generation of Black scholars, who are utilizing the craft of history as well as anthropology to explore the questions of identity. Very few escape the methodological hurdles posed by Roland Littlewood in the present collection, however, and one that does (Warner-Lewis 1991) does so only by being able to trace living carriers of African continuity in Trinidad, namely third-generation descendants of nineteenth-century Yoruba indentured migrants, and to link their thoughts, philosophy and customs, as reflected in their retained language, to aspects of the wider Trinidadian culture, such as aesthetics, music, religion and language. Others, not at all bothered by methodological problems, have different agenda, such as the task of escaping being trapped in European discourse (Asante 1987). Theirs is a sort of 'intellectual decolonization'.[1]

Another reason for the persistence of so-called African retentionism derives, it seems, from the effort of anthropologists to deepen their understanding of Caribbean society and culture by exploring its inner workings, so to speak, the underlying patterns of thought and ideas, the values and ethics, which either determine or justify individual and social behaviour. There is much that Caribbean anthropology can gain from analysis of the deeper structure of thought and ideas beneath the surface of social action and social structure, both religious and secular.

But continuity, even at this level, need not be with Africa; or with Europe, for that matter. For some scholars the starting point of Caribbean culture is the historic struggles of its peoples against European slavery and colonialism. Thus, whether Africa, Europe or the Caribbean, or all, none of the chapters in this collection took up an explicit position on this issue, nor needed to take one. What the collection did was explore certain themes and ideas from a fresh angle. There is little doubt, however, that the issue looms in the background.

Approaching Caribbean culture in this way also makes it possible to understand cultural change. Indeed, it is impossible to study continuity without also studying change. To revert to the main focus of this collection, namely the Rastafari, the dynamism of this socio-religious movement within its Jamaican context stands out very clearly. The cumulative effect of the chapters by Besson, Homiak and Chevannes unequivocally establishes the Rastafari as a force of cultural continuity and change. A fuller understanding, however, would require encompassing the wider religious universe, in which we are witnessing the birth, growth and decline of religions. Jamaica and indeed the rest of the Caribbean and almost the entire Latin American region, is the scene of tremendous changes, as Pentecostalism makes steady, in some places phenomenal, inroads. Revivalism and the Rastafari are only two movements in this landscape. Even if they are, as I believe, critical to the understanding of the Jamaican worldview, they remain only a part of the greater picture which remains to be understood.

The dynamism of Rastafari, however, is, as Cashmore showed, not confined to Jamaica or even the Caribbean. The discussion of its presence in Britain raises questions about its presence in other parts of the world as well, Africa, Europe, Asia, Australasia and North America. Thus, even as we ask what specific contribution has been made by the Rastafari to Jamaican (and perhaps Caribbean) culture and how permanent it is, the question is also being posed: why has it gone global? Is its internationalization a function of the globalization of reggae music, and therefore, perhaps, a passing fancy? Or, could it be that Rastafari articulates certain universal values which make it possible for other ethnic and racial groups to identify with it? These and other questions remain in urgent need of answers.

Note

1. To borrow a term from Kenyan novelist Ngũgĩ Wa Thiong'o (*Decolonising the Mind*, 1988) and from the May 1991 symposium on the identity of the new Europe in relation to the Third World and minorities, hosted by the Centre for Race and Ethnic Studies of the University of Amsterdam.

References

Abrahams, Roger (1983) *Man-of-Words in the West Indies: Performance and the Emergence of Creole Culture*. Baltimore and London: Johns Hopkins University Press.

Abrahams, Roger D. and J.F. Szwed (eds) (1983) *After Africa: Extracts From British Travel Accounts and Journals of the 17th, 18th and 19th Centuries Concerning the Slaves, Their Masters and Custom in the British West Indies*. New Haven: Yale University Press.

Akers, Glenn (1981) *Phonological Variation in the Jamaican Continuum*. Ann Arbor, MI: Karoma.

de Albuquerque, Klaus (1977) *Millenarian Movements and the Politics of Liberation: The Rastafarians of Jamaica*. PhD dissertation, Virginia Polytechnic Institute and State University.

de Albuquerque, Klaus (1980) 'Rastafarianism and Cultural Identity in the Caribbean', *Revista/Review Interamericana*, 10(2): 230-47.

Alleyne, Mervyn (1988) *Roots of Jamaican Culture*. London: Pluto Press.

André, J. (1987) *L'Inceste Focal Dans La Famille Noire Antillaise*. Paris: Presses Universitaires de France.

Asante, Molefi Kete (1987) *The Afrocentric Idea*. Philadelphia: Temple University Press.

Asante, Molefi Kete (1990) 'African Elements in African-American English' in Joseph E. Holloway (ed.), *Africanisms in American Culture*. Bloomington and Indianapolis: Indiana University Press.

Austin, D.J. (1979) 'History and Symbols in Ideology: A Jamaican Example', *Man*, 14: 497-514.

Austin, Diane (1983) 'Social Class and Religious Experience: The Case of Jamaica', Paper presented at the Conference, New Perspective on Caribbean Studies: Toward the 21st Century. Hunter College, CUNY.

Bakhtin, Mikhail (1981) *The Dialogical Imagination: Four Essays by M.M. Bakhtin*. (Michael Holquist, ed.). Austin: University of Texas Press.

Barrett, Leonard (1968) *The Rastafarians: A Study in Messianic Cultism in Jamaica*. Rio Piedras, Puerto Rico: Institute for Caribbean Studies.

Barrett, Leonard (1977) *The Rastafarians: The Dreadlocks of Jamaica.* London: Heinemann.

Barrett, Leonard (1976 and 1979). *The Sun and the Drum: African Roots in Jamaican Folk Tradition.* Kingston: Sangsters/Heinemann.

Barth, F. (1969) *Ethnic Groups and Boundaries.* London: Allen and Unwin.

Bastide, Roger (1979) *The African Religions of Brazil: Towards a Sociology of the Interpretation of Civilizations.* Baltimore: Johns Hopkins University Press.

Beckwith, Martha (1929) *Black Roadways: A Study of Jamaican Folk Life.* Chapel Hill, NC: University of North Carolina.

Bernal, Martin (1987) *Black Athena: The Afroasiatic Roots of Classical Civilisation.* vol. 1. London: Free Association Books.

Besson, Jean (1974) *Land Tenure and Kinship in a Jamaican Village.* 2 vols. PhD dissertation, University of Edinburgh.

Besson, Jean (1979) 'Symbolic Aspects of Land in the Caribbean: The Tenure and Transmission of Land Rights among Caribbean Peasantries', pp. 86-116 in Malcolm Cross and Arnaud Marks (eds), *Peasants, Plantations and Rural Communities in the Caribbean.* Guildford: University of Surrey and Leiden: Royal Institute of Linguistics and Anthropology.

Besson, Jean (1981) 'Review of Schuler, Monica, *"Alas, Alas, Kongo": A Social History of Indentured African Immigration into Jamaica, 1841-1865'.* Baltimore: Johns Hopkins University Press, *Man,* 16(3): 505-6.

Besson, Jean (1984a) 'Family Land and Caribbean Society: Toward an Ethnography of Afro-Caribbean Peasantries', pp. 57-83 in Elizabeth M. Thomas-Hope (ed.), *Perspectives on Caribbean Regional Identity.* Monograph Series No. 11. Centre for Latin American Studies, University of Liverpool: Liverpool University Press.

Besson, Jean (1984b) 'Land Tenure in the Free Villages of Trelawny, Jamaica: A Case Study in the Caribbean Peasant Response to Emancipation', *Slavery & Abolition,* 5(1): 3-23.

Besson, Jean (1987a) 'A Paradox in Caribbean Attitudes to Land', pp. 13-45 in Jean Besson and Janet Momsen (eds), *Land and Development in the Caribbean.* Warwick University Caribbean Studies Series. London: Macmillan.

Besson, Jean (1987b) 'Family Land as a Model for Martha Brae's New History: Culture-Building in an Afro-Caribbean Village', pp. 100-32 in Charles V. Carnegie (ed.), *Afro-Caribbean Villages in Historical Perspective.* ACIJ Research Review No. 2. Kingston, Jamaica: African-Caribbean Institute of Jamaica.

Besson, Jean (1988a) 'Agrarian Relations and Perceptions of Land in a Jamaican Peasant Village', pp. 39-61 in John S. Brierley and Hymie Rubenstein (eds), *Small Farming and Peasant Resources in the Caribbean*. Manitoba Geographical Studies 10. Winnipeg: University of Manitoba.

Besson, Jean (1988b) *The Free Villages of Trelawny, Jamaica: Towards a Caribbean Cultural History*. Institute of Commonwealth Studies Occasional Papers (forthcoming).

Besson, Jean (1989a) 'Introduction', pp. 12-30 in Jean Besson (ed.), *Caribbean Reflections: The Life and Times of a Trinidad Scholar (1901-1986)*. London: Karia Press.

Besson, Jean (1989b) 'Review of OLWIG, Karen Fog, *Cultural Adaptation and Resistance on St. John: Three Centuries of Afro-Caribbean Life*. Gainesville: University Presses of Florida, 1985', *Plantation Society in the Americas*, 2(3): 345-8 (May).

Besson, Jean (1992) 'Freedom and Community: The British West Indies', in Seymour Drescher and Frank McGlynn (eds), *The Meaning of Freedom: The Anthropology and History of Post-Slavery Societies*. Pittsburgh: University of Pittsburgh Press, pp. 183-219.

Besson, Jean (1993) 'Reputation and Respectability Reconsidered: A New Perspective on Afro-Caribbean Peasant Women', forthcoming in Janet Momsen (ed.), *Women and Change: A Pan-Caribbean Perspective*, London: James Currey and Bloomington: Indiana University Press, pp. 15-37.

BHW (1985) *Berichen uit de(n) Heiden-Wereld*, (Journal of the Moravian mission) 12: 42.

Bilby, Kenneth (1985) 'Caribbean Crucible', in Geoffrey Heyden and Dennis Marks (eds), *Repercussions: A Celebration of African-American Music*. London: Century Publishing.

Bilby, Kenneth, and Elliott Leib (1983) 'From Kongo to Zion: Three Musical Traditions from Jamaica' (liner notes to the album) Heartbeat Records No. 17. Cambridge, MA: Heartbeat Recordings.

Bilby, Kenneth, and Elliott Leib (1986) 'Kumina, the Howellite Church and the Emergence of Rastafarian Traditional Music in Jamaica', *Jamaica Journal*, 19(3): 22-28.

Blyth, George (1851) *Reminiscences of Missionary Life*. Edinburgh: William Oliphant and Sons.

Bourdieu, Pierre (1982) *Lecon sur le leçon*. Paris: Minuit.

Brathwaite, Edward (1971) *The Development of Creole Society in Jamaica. 1770-1820*. Oxford: Clarendon.

Brathwaite, Kamau (1986) *Roots*. Havana: Casa de las Americas.

Brenneis, Donald (1987) 'Talk and Transformation', *Man*, 22: 499-510.

Bristol, M.D. (1985) *Carnival and Theatre: Plebeian Culture and the Structure of Authority in Renaissance England.* New York: Methuen.

Brodber, Erna (1986) 'Afro-Jamaican Women at the Turn of the Century', *Social and Economic Studies,* 35(3).

Brown, J. (1977) *Shades of Grey.* Cranfield: Cranfield Institute of Technology.

Buiks (1983) *Surinaamse jongeren op de Kruiskade: Overleden in een etnische randgroup.* Deventer, NL: Van Loghum Slaterus.

Burkhardt, G. (1898) *Die Mission der Brudergemeine in Missionsstunden: 2: Suriname.* Leipzig: Jansa.

Burridge, Kenelm (1969) *New Heaven and New Earth: A Study of Millenarian Activities.* New York: Schocken.

Buschkens, W.F.L. (1974) *The Family System of the Paramaribo Creoles.* Leiden: Royal Institute of Linguistics and Anthropology and The Hague: Martinus Nijhoff.

Campbell, Horace (1980) 'Rastafari: Culture of Resistance', *Race & Class,* 22(1): 1-22.

Campbell, Horace (1985) *Rasta and Resistance: From Marcus Garvey to Walter Rodney.* London: Hansib.

Cargill, Morris (1965) *Ian Fleming Introduces Jamaica.* New York: Hawthorn Books, Inc.

Cashmore, E. (1983) *Rastaman.* London: George Allen & Unwin. 2nd edn (first edn 1979).

Cashmore, E. (1987) *The Logic of Racism.* London: George Allen & Unwin.

Cashmore, E. (1990) 'The Functions of Social Conflict', *European Journal of Intercultural Studies,* 1(1).

Cassidy, Frederick (1961) *Jamaica Talk: Three Hundred Years of the English Language in Jamaica.* London: Macmillan.

Cassidy, F.G. and R.B. LePage (1980) *Dictionary of Jamaican English.* 2nd edn London: Cambridge University Press.

Chevannes, Barry (1971) 'Revival and Black Struggle', *Savacou,* 5: 27-37.

Chevannes, Barry (1976) 'The Repairer of the Breach: Reverend Claudius Henry and Jamaican Society', in Frances Henry (ed.), *Ethnicity in the Americas.* The Hague: Mouton.

Chevannes, Barry (1978a) 'Revivalism: a Disappearing Religion', *Caribbean Quarterly,* 24.

Chevannes, Barry (1978b) 'Social Origins of the Rastafari Movement', (unpublished) Institute of Social and Economic Research, Kingston, Jamaica.

Chevannes, Barry (1981) 'Rastafari and the Urban Youth', in Carl Stone and Aggrey Brown (eds), *Perspective on Jamaica in the Seventies*. Kingston: Jamaica Publishing House.

Chevannes, Barry (1986) *Jamaican Men: Study of Male Sexual Attitudes and Behaviour.* Kingston: National Family Planning Board (unpublished).

Chevannes, Barry (1989a) *The Social and Ideological Origins of the Rastafari Movement in Jamaica.* PhD dissertation, Columbia University, New York.

Chevannes, Barry (1989b) 'Drop Pan and Folk Consciousness', *Jamaica Journal,* 22(2).

Chevannes, Barry (1990) 'Healing the Nation: Rastafari Exorcism of Racism in Jamaica', *Caribbean Quarterly*, 36(3&4).

Clifford, James (1988) *The Predicament of Culture: Twentieth Century Ethnography, Literature and Art.* Cambridge, MA: Harvard University Press.

Cohen, David W. (1989) 'The Undefining of Oral Tradition', *Ethnohistory*, 36(1): 9-18.

Cohn, Norman (1975) *Europe's Inner Demons.* London: Heinemann.

Comaroff, Jean (1986) *Body of Power. Spirit of Resistance.* Chicago: University of Chicago Press.

Cooper, Wendy (1971) *Hair: Sex, Society, Symbolism.* London: Aldus Books.

Cross, Malcolm (1979) *Urbanization and Urban Growth in the Caribbean: An Essay on Social Change in Dependent Societies.* Cambridge: Cambridge University Press.

Cross, Malcolm and Hans Entzinger (eds) (1988) *Lost Illusions: Caribbean Minorities in Britain and the Netherlands.* London: Routledge.

Dalton, George (1967) 'Primitive Money', pp. 254-81 in George Dalton (ed.), *Tribal and Peasant Economies: Readings in Economic Anthropology.* Garden City, New York: Natural History Press.

Dalton, George (1971) 'Peasantries in Anthropology and History', pp. 217-66 in George Dalton (ed.), *Economic Anthropology and Development.* New York: Basic Books.

Dance, Darryl C. (1985) *Folklore From Contemporary Jamaicans.* Knoxville: University of Tennessee.

Davis, Stephen (1983) *Reggae Bloodlines: In Search of the Music and Culture of Jamaica.* New York: Anchor.

van Dijk, Frank Jan (1988) 'The Twelve Tribes of Israel: Rasta and the Middle Class', *New West Indian Guide*, 62(1&2).

Drummond, Lee (1987) 'The Cultural Continuum: A Theory of Inter-systems', *Man*, 15: 352-74.

Elkins, W.F. (1986) 'William Lauron DeLaurence and Jamaican Folk Religion', *Folklore*, 97: 215-18.

van der Elst, Dirk H. (1970) *The Bush Negro Tribes of Surinam, South America: A Synthesis*. PhD dissertation, Northwestern University, Chicago.

Faristzaddi, Millard (1982) *I-tations of Jamaica and I Rastafari*. New York: Grove.

Fernandez, James (1986) 'The Argument of Images and the Experience of Returning to the Whole', in Victor Turner and Edward Bruner (eds), *The Anthropology of Experience*. Chicago: University of Illinois Press.

Field, Margaret (1960) *Search for Security: An Ethnopsychiatric Study of Rural Ghana*. London: Faber.

Fischer, Michael J. (1986) 'Ethnicity and the Post-Modern Arts of Memory', in James Clifford and George E. Marcus (eds), *Writing Culture: the Poetics and Politics of Ethnography*. Berkeley: University of California Press.

Fishman, J.A. (1977) 'Language and Ethnicity', in H. Giles (ed.), *Language, Ethnicity, and Intergroup Relations*. London: Academic Press.

Forsythe, Dennis (1983) *Rastafari: For the Healing of the Nation*. Kingston: Zaika Publications.

Foucault, Michel (1980) *Power and Knowledge: Selected Interviews and Other Writings, 1972-1977* (Colin Gordon, ed). New York: Pantheon Books.

Gates, H.L. (1988) *The Signifying Monkey: A Theory of Afro-American Literary Criticism*. New York: Oxford University Press.

Gellner, Ernest (1964) 'Foreword' to I.C. Jarvie, *The Revolution in Anthropology*. London: Routledge and Kegan Paul.

van Gennep, Arnold (1960) *The Rites of Passage*. London: Routledge and Kegan Paul (first published in 1908).

Gill, Sam (1988) *Mother Earth: An American Story*. Chicago: University of Chicago Press.

Girvan, Norman (1988) 'The Political Economy of Race in the Americas: The Historical Context of Garveyism', in Rupert Lewis and Patrick Bryan (eds), *Garvey: His Work and Impact*. Kingston: Institute of Social and Economic Research, University of the West Indies.

Gould, J. (1964) 'Ideology', pp. 315-17 in Julius Gould and William L. Kolb, *A Dictionary of the Social Sciences*. New York: Free Press of Glencoe.

de Groot, Silvia W. (1969) *Djuka Society and Social Change: History of an Attempt to Develop a Bush Negro Community in Surinam, 1917-1926*. Assen: Van Gorcum.

Hall, Douglas (1989) *In Miserable Slavery: Thomas Thistlewood in Jamaica, 1750-1786*. London: Macmillan Caribbean.

Hall-Alleyne, Beverly (1984) 'The Evolution of African Languages in Jamaica', *African-Caribbean Institute of Jamaica Research Review*, (1): 21-46.

Halliday, M.A.K. (1978) *Language as Social Semiotic*. London: Arnold.

Hallpike, C.R. (1969) 'Social Hair', *Man*, 4.

Hanks, W. (1987) 'Discourse Genres in a Theory of Practice', *American Ethnologist*, 14: 668-92.

Hart, Richard (1989) *Rise and Organize*. London: Karia.

Hebdige, Dick (1979) *Subculture: The Meaning of Style*. New York: Methuen.

Henige, David (1982) *Oral Historiography*. London and New York: Longman.

Herskovits, M.J. (1951) 'The Present State and Needs of Afro-American Research', *Journal of Negro History*, 36: 123-47.

Herskovits, M.J. (1958) *The Myth of the Negro Past*. Boston: Beacon Press (first published 1941).

Herskovits, M.J. and F.S. Herskovits (1969) *Surinam Folklore*. New York: AMS Press (first published 1936).

Herskovits, M.J. and F.S. Herskovits (1947) *Trinidad Village*. New York: Alfred Knopf.

Hertz, Robert (1960) The Collective Representation of Death', in Robert Hertz, *Death and the Right Hand*. Cohen & West (first published 1907).

Hill, Christopher (1972) *The World Turned Upside Down: Radical Ideas During the English Revolution*. London: Temple Smith.

Hill, Christopher (1984) 'Radical Pirates', in M. and J. Jacob (eds), *The Origins of Anglo-American Radicalism*. London: Allen and Unwin.

Hill, Robert (1981) 'Dread History: Leonard P. Howell and Millenarian Visions in Early Rastafari Religion in Jamaica', *Epoche*, 9: 30-71.

Hill, Robert (1983) 'Leonard Howell and Millenarian Visions in Early Rastafari', *Jamaica Journal*, 16(1).

Hoetink, H. (1961) 'Gezinsvormen in het Caribisch gebied', *Mens en Maatschappij*, pp. 81-93.

Hogg, Donald (1960) 'The Convince Cult in Jamaica', in Sidney Mintz (ed.), *Papers in Caribbean Anthropology*. New Haven: Yale University Press.

Hogg, Donald (1964) *Jamaican Religions: A Study in Variations*. PhD dissertation, Yale University, New Haven CN.

Homiak, John P. (1985) *The 'Ancients of Days' Seated Black: Eldership, Oral Tradition and Ritual in Rastafari Culture*. PhD dissertation, Brandeis University, Waltham, MA.

Homiak, John P. (1987) 'The Mystic Revelation of Rasta Far-Eye: Visionary Communication in a Prophetic Movement', in Barbara Tedlock (ed.), *Dreaming: Anthropological and Psychological Interpretations*. Cambridge: Cambridge University Press.

Homiak, John P. (1989) 'The Half that's Never Been Told: Pa-Ashanti and the Development of Nyabinghi Music' (forthcoming in *Reggae and the African Beat*).

Honigmann, John J. (1964) 'Ethos', pp. 246-7 in Julius Gould and William L. Kolb, *A Dictionary of the Social Sciences*. New York: Free Press of Glencoe.

Hurbon, Laennec (1986) 'New Religious Movements in the Caribbean', pp. 146-76 in J.A. Beckford (ed.), *New Religious Movements and Rapid Social Change*. London: Sage.

Jah Bones (1985) *One Love: History, Doctrine, and Livity*. London: Voice of Rasta Publishing House.

Kerr, Madeleine (1952) *Personality and Conflict in Jamaica*. Liverpool: University Press.

Kitzinger, Shiela (1969) 'Protest and Mysticism: The Rastafari Cult of Jamaica', *Journal for the Scientific Study of Religion*, 8: 240-62.

Kitzinger, Shiela (1971) 'The Rastafarian Brethren of Jamaica', in Michael Horowitz (ed.), *Peoples and Cultures of the Caribbean*. New York: Natural History Press.

de Klerk, Leo, and Hans van Amersfoort (1988) 'Surinamese Settlement in Amsterdam 1973-1983', pp. 147-63 in Malcolm Cross and Hans Entzinger (eds), *Lost Illusions: Caribbean Minorities in Britain and the Netherlands*. London: Routledge.

Kluckholn, Clyde and Leighton, Dorothea (1947) *Children of the People: the Navaho Individual and His Development*. Cambridge: Harvard University Press.

Knibb Sibley, Inez (1965) *The Baptists of Jamaica 1793-1965*. Kingston: Jamaica Baptist Union.

Kruyer, G.J. (1973) *Suriname: Neocolonie in rijksverband*. Boom: Meppel.

Landman-Bouges, J. (1977) 'Rastafarian Food Habits', *Cajanus*, 9(4): 228-34.

Lanternari, Vittorio (1963) *Religions of the Oppressed: A Study of Modern Messianic Cults*. New York: Alfred Knopf, and London: Mac-Gibbon and Kee.

Leach, E.A. (1958) 'Magical Hair', *Journal of the Royal Anthropological Institute*, 88(2) (July-December).

Leib, Elliott (n.d.) *Film, Ethnography, and the Making of 'Rastafari Voices'*. Study Guide to accompany the film 'Rastafari Voices', Human Studies Film Archives, Smithsonian Institution, Washington DC.

Lenders, M. and M. van de Rhoer (1984) *Mijn god hoe ga ik doen?* Amsterdam: SUA.

Lewis, Oscar (1969) *La Vida*. London: Panther Books.

Lienhardt, Godfrey (1964) *Social Anthropology*. Oxford University Press.

Lovejoy, David (1985) *Religious Enthusiasm in the New World: Heresy to Revolution*. Cambridge, MA: Harvard University Press.

Mansingh, Ajai and Mansingh, Laxmi (1985) *Hindu Influences on Rastafarianism*. Caribbean Quarterly Monograph. Kingston: University of the West Indies.

Maude, Aylmer (1904) *A Peculiar People: The Doukhobors*. London: Grant Richards.

McGarrity, Gail. (n.d.) 'I-laloo, I-ney and I-tal I-ud in a Jamdown: The I-talist Movement in Jamaica in the 1970s' (unpublished paper).

McPherson, E.S.P. and Semaj, Leachim T. (1980) 'Rasta Chronology', *Caribbean Quarterly*, 26.

Mercer, P.M. (1979) 'Tapping the Slave Narrative Collection for the Responses of Black South Carolinans to Emancipation and Reconstruction', *Journal of Politics and History*, 25: 358-74.

Mercer, P.M. (1970) 'Creating Culture in the Americas', *Columbia University Forum*, 13: 4-11 (spring).

Miller, Errol (1969) 'Body Image, Physical Beauty and Colour', *Social and Economic Studies*, 18(1): 72-89.

Mintz, Sidney. W. (1971) 'The Caribbean as a Socio-Cultural Area', in M.M. Horowitz (ed.), *Peoples and Cultures of the Caribbean*. New York: Garden City.

Mintz, Sidney. W. (1974) *Caribbean Transformations*. Chicago: Aldine.

Mintz, Sidney. W. (1984) *From Plantations to Peasantries in the Caribbean*. Washington DC: The Wilson Center.

Mintz, Sidney. W. (1989) *Caribbean Transformations*. New York: Columbia University Press, Morningside Edition.

Mintz, S. and R. Price (1976) *An Anthropological Approach to the Afro-American Past: A Caribbean Perspective*. Philadelphia: Institute for the Study of Human Issues.

Momsen, Janet (1987) 'Land Settlement as an Imposed Solution', pp. 46-69 in Jean Besson and Janet Momsen (eds), *Land and Development in the Caribbean*. Warwick University Caribbean Studies Series. London: Macmillan.

Moore, Joseph Graessle (1953) *Religion of the Jamaican Negroes: A Study of Afro-American Acculturation*. PhD dissertation, Northwestern University, Chicago IL.

Nettleford, Rex (1970) *Mirror, Mirror: Identity Race and Protest in Jamaica*. Kingston: Collins-Sangster.

Nettleford, Rex (1978) *Caribbean Cultural Identity: The Case of Jamaica*. Kingston, Jamaica: Sangster.

Norris, Katrin (1962) *Jamaica: The Search for an Identity*. Institute of Race Relations. Oxford: Oxford University Press.

Northam, G. (1988) *Shooting in the Dark*. London: Faber & Faber.

Obeyesekere, Gananath (1981) *Medusa's Hair: An Essay in Personal Symbols and Religious Experience*. Chicago: University of Chicago Press.

Olwig, Karen Fog (1990) 'The Struggle for Respectability: Methodism and Afro-Caribbean Culture on 19th Century Nevis', *Nieuwe West-Indische Gids/New West Indian Guide*, 64(3&4): 93-114.

Ortner, Sherry (1974) 'Is Female to Male as Nature is to Culture?', in Michele Rosaldo and Louise Lamphere (eds), *Women, Culture and Society*. Stanford, CA: Stanford University Press.

Otto, Rudolf (1963). *Het heilige*. Hilversum: Paul Brand (first published 1917).

Owens, Joseph (1975) 'Literature of the Rastafari: 1955-1974, A Review', *Savacou*, (Sept.): 86-114.

Owens, Joseph (1976) *Dread: The Rastafarians of Jamaica*. London, Kingston and Port of Spain: Heinemann.

Paget, Hugh (1964) 'The Free Village System in Jamaica', *Caribbean Quarterly*, 10(1): 38-51.

Patterson, Orlando (1964) 'Ras Tafari: the Cult of Outcasts', *New Society*, 111 (12 November).

Patterson, Orlando (1970) 'Slavery and Slave Revolts: A Socio-Historical Analysis of the First Maroon War: Jamaica 1655-1740', *Social and Economic Studies*, 19(3): 289-325.

Patterson, Orlando (1973) *The Sociology of Slavery: An Analysis of the Origins, Development and Structure of Negro Slave Society in Jamaica.* London: Granada (first published 1967).

Peek, Philip (1981) 'The Power of Words in African Verbal Arts', *Journal of American Folklore*, 94: 19-43.

Pollard, Velma (1980) 'Dread Talk: The Speech of the Rastafarian in Jamaica', *Caribbean Quarterly*, 26(4): 32-41.

Pollard, Velma (1982) 'The Social History of Dread Talk', *Caribbean Quarterly*, 28(4): 17-40.

Pollard, Velma (1983) 'Word Sounds: the Language of the Rastafari in Barbados and St. Lucia', *Jamaica Journal*, 17(1): 57-62.

Post, K.W.J. (1970) 'The Bible as Ideology: Ethiopianism in Jamaica, 1930-1938', in C. Allen and R.E. Johnson (eds), *African Perspectives*. Cambridge: Cambridge University Press.

Post, K.W.J. (1978) *Arise ye Starvlings: The Jamaica Labour Rebellion of 1938 and its Aftermath.* The Hague, Boston and London: Martinus Nijhoff.

Powell, Dorian (1986) 'Caribbean Women and their Response to Familial Experience', *Social and Economic Studies*, 33(4)97-122.

Robotham, Don (1974) 'Agrarian Relations in Jamaica', in Carl Stone and Aggrey Brown (eds), *Essays on Power and Change in Jamaica*. Kingston: Institute of Social and Economic Research, University of the West Indies.

Robotham, Don (1977) *The Notorious Riot: The Socio-economic and Political Bases of Paul Boate's Revolt.* ISER Working Paper Series, Number 28. Kingston: Institute of Social and Economic Research, University of the West Indies.

Robotham, Don (1988) 'The Development of a Black Ethnicity in Jamaica', pp. 23-38 in Lewis Rupert and Patrick Bryan (eds), *Garvey: His Work and Impact*. Mona, Jamaica: ISER and Extra-Mural Dept., University of West Indies.

Rowe, Maureen (1980) 'The Women in Rastafari', *Caribbean Quarterly*, 26(4): 13-21.

Rubin, Vera and Comitas, Lambros (1975) *Ganja in Jamaica*. Paris and The Hague: Mouton.

Sahlins, Marshall (1987) *Islands of History*. London: Tavistock.

Seaga, Edward (1969) 'Revival Cults in Jamaica: Notes Towards a Sociology of Religion', *Jamaica Journal*, 3(2).

Semaj, Leachim (1980) 'Rastafari: From Religion to Social Theory', *Caribbean Quarterly*, 26(4): 22-41.

Schneider, H.G. 1893) *Die Buschneger Surinames.* Herrnhut: Warned (Reprint of articles from the *Allgemeine Missions-Zeitschrift*).

Schoonheym, P.E. (1980) *Je geld of . . . je leven.* Utrecht: ICAU.

Schuler, Monica (1979a) 'Afro-American Slave Culture', pp. 121-55 in Michael Craton (ed.), *Roots and Branches: Current Directions in Slave Studies.* Toronto: Pergamon Press.

Schuler, Monica (1979b) 'Myalism and the African Religious Tradition in Jamaica', pp. 65-79 in Margaret E. Crahan and Franklin Knight (eds), *Africa and the Caribbean: The Legacies of a Link.* Baltimore and London: Johns Hopkins University Press.

Schuler, Monica (1980) *'Alas, Alas, Kongo': A Social History of Indentured African Immigration Into Jamaica, 1841-1865.* Baltimore and London: Johns Hopkins University Press.

Schwimmer, E. (1972) 'Symbolic Competition', *Anthropologica*, 14: 117-25.

Simpson, George Eaton (1955) 'Political Cultism in West Kingston, Jamaica', *Social and Economic Studies,* 4(2): 133-49.

Simpson, George Eaton (1956) 'Jamaican Revivalist Cults', *Social and Economic Studies*, 5: 321-442.

Simpson, George Eaton (1980) *Religious Cults of the Caribbean.* Puerto Rico: Institute of Caribbean Studies.

Simpson, G.E. and P. Hammond (1960) *Discussion'*, in V. Rubin (ed.), *Caribbean Studies: A Symposium.* Seattle: University of Washington Press.

Smith, M.G. (1960) 'The African Heritage in the Caribbean', in Vera Rubin (ed.). *Caribbean Studies: A Symposium.* Seattle: University of Washington Press.

Smith, M.G., Roy Augier, and Rex Nettleford (1961) *Report on the Rastafari Movement in Kingston, Jamaica.* Kingston: Institute of Social and Economic Research, University of the West Indies, Mona.

Smith, R.T. (1988) *Kinship and Class in the West Indies: A Genealogical Study of Jamaica and Guyana.* Cambridge and New York: Cambridge University Press.

Spalburg, J.G. (1979) *De Tapanahoni Djuka rond de eeuwwisseling: Het dagboek van Spalburg (1896-1900).* Bronnen voor de Studie van Bosneger Samenlevingen 5. Utrecht: Department of Cultural Anthropology, State University of Utrecht.

Stephen, Henri J.M. (1983) *Winti, Afro-Surinaamse religie en magische rituelen in Nederland.* Amsterdam.

Stone, Carl (1974) *Electoral Behaviour and Public Opinion in Jamaica.* Kingston: Institute of Social and Economic Research, University of the West Indies.

Synnott, Anthony (1987) 'Shame and Glory: A Sociology of Hair', *British Journal of Sociology*, 38(3): 381-413.

Tafari-Ama, Imani (1989) 'Analysis of a Research Project: Gender Relations in Rastafari', The Hague: Institute of Social Studies (unpublished MA thesis).

Taussig, M.T. (1987) *Shamanism, Colonialism and the Wild Man: A Study in Terror and Healing.* Chicago, IL: University of Chicago Press.

Thoden van Velzen, H.U.E. and W. van Wetering (1988) *The Great Father and the Danger; Religious Cults, Material Forces, and Collective Fantasies in the World of the Surinamese Maroons.* Royal Institute of Linguistics and Anthropology, Caribbean Series No. 9, and Dordrecht/Providence, RI: Foris.

Thomas-Hope, Elizabeth M. (1978) 'The Establishment of a Migration Tradition: British West Indian Movements to the Hispanic Caribbean in the Century after Emancipation', pp. 66-81 in Colin G. Clarke (ed.), *Caribbean Social Relations.* Monograph Series No. 8. Centre for Latin American Studies, University of Liverpool: Liverpool University Press.

Turner, Mary (1982) *Slaves and Missionaries: The Disintegration of Jamaican Slave Society, 1787-1834.* Urbana: University of Illinois Press.

Underhill, Edward B. (1861) *The West Indies: Their Social and Religious Condition.* London: Jackson, Walford and Hodder.

Vansina, Jan (1973) *Oral Tradition: A Study in Historical Methodology.* Harmondsworth, Middlessex: Penguin.

Waddell, Hope Masterton (1863) *Twenty-nine Years in the West Indies and Central Africa: Missionary Work and Adventure, 1829-1858.* London and New York: T. Nelson and Sons.

Walvin, James (1983) *Slavery and the Slave Trade: A Short Illustrated History.* London: Macmillan.

Warner-Lewis, Maureen (1977) *The Nkuyu: Spirit Messengers of the Kumina.* University of the West Indies, Mona: Savacou Publications No. 3.

Warner-Lewis, Maureen (1991) *Guinea's Other Suns: The African Dynamic in Trinidad Culture.* Dover, MA: The Majority Press.

Webber, Thomas L. (1978) *Deep Like the Rivers: Education in the Slave Quarter Community 1831-1865.* New York: Norton.

Wedenoja, William (1978) *Religion and Adaptation in Rural Jamaica*. PhD dissertation, University of California.

Wedenoja, William (1989) 'Mothering and the Practice of "Balm" in Jamaica', in Carol Shepherd McClain (ed.), *Women as Healers: Cross Cultural Perspectives*. New Brunswick, NJ and London: Rutgers University Press.

Werbner, R.P. (1979) 'Totemism in History; the Ritual Passage of West African Strangers', *Man*, 14: 663-83.

van Wetering, W. (1973) *Hexerij bij de Djuka: Een sociologische benadering*. PhD dissertation, University of Amsterdam.

van Wetering, W. (1987) 'Informal Supportive Networks: Quasi-kin Groups, Religion and Social Order among Surinamese Creoles in the Netherlands', *Sociologia Nederlandica*, 23(2): 92-101.

van Wetering, W. (1988) 'Ritual Laundering of Black Money among Suriname Creoles in the Netherlands', in Philip Quarles van Ufford and M. Schoffeleers (eds), *Religion and Development*. Free University of Amsterdam.

Williams, Brackette (1987) 'Humor, Linguistic Ambiguity, and Disputing in a Guyanese Community', *International Journal of the Sociology of Language*, 65: 79-94.

Williams, Eric (1970) *From Columbus to Castro: The History of the Caribbean 1492-1969*. London: André Deutsch.

Williams, J.J. (1934) *Psychic Phenomena in Jamaica*. Westport, Connecticut: Greenwood Press.

Wilson, Bryan (1973) *Magic and the Millennium*. London: Heinemann.

Wilson, Peter J. (1969) 'Reputation and Respectability: A Suggestion for Caribbean Ethnology', *Man*, 4(1): 70-84.

Wilson, Peter J. (1973) *Crab Antics: The Social Anthropology Of English-Speaking Negro Societies of the Caribbean*. New Haven: Yale University Press.

Wood, Donald (1968) *Trinidad in Transition: The Years After Slavery*. Oxford: Oxford University Press.

Wooding, Ch.J. (1973) *Winti, een Afro-Amerikaanse Godsdienst in Suriname*. Meppel, NL: Krips Repro.

Wooding, Ch.J. (1981) *Evolving Culture: A Cross-Cultural Study of Suriname, West Africa and the Caribbean*. Washington DC: University Press of America.

Wooding, Ch.J. (1984) *Geesten genezen*. Groningen: Konstapel.

Wright, Christopher (1984) 'Cultural Continuity and the Growth of West Indian Religion in Britain', *Religion*, 14: 337-56.

Wright, Philip (1973) *Knibb, 'The Notorious': Slaves' Missionary 1803-1845*. London: Sidgwick and Jackson.

Yawney, Carole D. (1976) 'Remnants of All Nations: Rastafarian Attitudes Toward Ethnicity and Nationality', in Frances Henry (ed.), *Ethnicity in the Americas*. The Hague: Mouton.

Yawney, Carole D. (1979) 'Dread Wasteland: Rastafari Ritual in West Kingston, Jamaica', in R. Crumrine (ed.), *Ritual, Symbolism, and Ceremonialism in the Americas*. Greeley, CO: University of Northern Colorado Occasional Publications in Anthropology, Ethnology Series No. 33, Museum of Anthropology.

Yawney, Carole D. (1983) 'To Grow a Daughter: Cultural Liberation and the Dynamics of Oppression in Jamaica', in A. Miller and G. Finn (eds), *Feminism in Canada*. Montreal: Black Rose Books.

Yawney, Carole D. (1985a) 'Strictly I-tal: Rastafari Livity and Holistic Health', Paper presented at the 9th Annual meeting of the Society for Caribbean Studies, Hertfordshire, July 2-4.

Yawney, Carole D. (1985b) 'Don't Vex Then Pray: The Methodology of Initiation Fifteen Years Later', Paper presented at the Qualitative Research Conference, University of Waterloo, May 15-17.

Yawney, Carole D. (1987) 'Moving with the Dawtas of Rastafari: From Myth to Reality', in Ulrich Fleischmann and Ineke Thaf (eds), *The Caribbean and Latin America: Papers presented to the Third Interdisciplinary Colloquium about the Caribbean*. Berlin: Verlag Klaus Dieter Verwoerd.

Yawney, Carole D. (1990) 'Africa in the Caribbean: Ethiopian Themes in Rastafari Culture' (forthcoming in the published proceedings of the Second Interdisciplinary Congress of the Society of Caribbean Research, Vienna).

Glossary

akete (or kete)
Type of drum used by Rastafari for playing syncopated rhythms.
akra
Soul (Suriname).
Ampuku
Important forest demon which sometimes appears in dreams as an incubus (Winti).
Back 'O Wall
Kingston slum, also called Abacka, or Egypt by Rastas.
Bakru
Demons present in the daily lives of individuals (Winti).
balm yard
The yard or home of a Revival leader with healing powers, where such healing takes place.
binghi
See nyabinghi.
Black Baptist
See Myal.
Bobo
Rasta sect led by Prince Emmanual Edwards, living communally on the outskirts of Kingston.
Convince
African-derived Jamaican religious sect.
croton
Shrub, symbolic of the prophet Jeremiah, believed to keep duppies in their graves.
Doukhobor
Originating in the 1700s in Russia, the sect recognizes the supreme authority of inner experience and the embodiment of the spirit in prophets and religious leaders, and rejects all civil authority.
Dreadlocks
Members of the House of Dreadlocks.
dreadlocks
Matted hair, adopted as a symbol of Rastafarianism in the 1950s.

duppy
Spirit of the dead (Jamaican).

Earth People
small religious sect in Trinidad that practises nudity and adopts dreadlocks and certain other Rastafari practices.

Fifth Monarchy Men
Radical Christian sect in England in the seventeenth century who believed they were called to aid the arrival of the impending millenium by force.

funde
Type of Rastafari drum, played with the hands, in a steady, one-two beat; see nyabinghi.

Gaan Gadu
Religious cult (also called *Sweli*) originating among a rising class of boat owners in the inland areas of Suriname in the late nineteenth century, based around a powerful God called *Gaan Gadu*.

ghost dance
Purification ritual practiced on the North American plains in the late nineteenth century; the ghost dance prepared for a millenium that would banish the Whites and return the buffalo together with all the native people who had died in the White invasion.

Great Revival
Christian movement that spread from Ireland through North America and the Caribbean in the mid-nineteenth century, inspiring a revival of earlier African-based religious movements in Jamaica as well.

grounding, grounation
From 'to grounds', meaning 'to get along well'; activities such as nyabinghi and reasonings.

Higes-Knots
Rastafari group of the 1950s that went about barefoot, with matted hair, cloaked in sackcloth (crocus bags), and armed with large rods. 'Higes' derives from an archaic Jamaican term meaning 'to torment'.

House
Main divisions of Rastafari.

House of Combsomes
Rastafari who comb their hair.

House of Dreadlocks
Rastafari who wear dreadlocks.

House of Nyabinghi
The informal organizational unit of Rasta, run by an 'Assembly of

Elders' who plan events, settle disputes and appoint delegations should the need arise, with no formal membership as such.

Order of Sixty

Revival Zionists who worship only sky-bound spirits (Jesus, the prophets, etc.).

Order of Sixty-one

Revivalists who worship both the sky-bound spirits (Jesus, the prophets, etc.) and the earthbound (Satan, fallen angels, etc.); also Pukumina.

I-Gelic House

The same as Higes Knots.

International Unification Committee

Attempt to unify the Rastafari, led by attorney Michael Lorne.

Ital

Rastafari word for 'natural'.

I-talk

Rasta talk based on the pivitol concept of the first person pronoun; also known as I-ance.

I-tes

See Higes Knots.

I-tesvar

Higes Knots word for Rasta talk.

Jah or Jah-Jah

The Godhead (Rastafari).

JOS

Jamaica Omnibus Service, the company responsible for urban transportation in Kingston.

jump poko

Revival dance.

King of Kings people

Original self-designation of the Rastafari.

Kumina

African-derived Jamaican religious sect.

lyke-wake

Wake ritual to effect the safe transition of a duppy to join the spirits of the dead.

Maroons

Escaped slaves in Suriname and the West Indies, and their descendants (from 'marooned').

Myal, Myalism

Pan-African religious movement in Jamaica, dating from the mid-eighteenth century, which absorbed Christian (Baptist) teachings around the turn of the nineteenth century, and became known first as Native Baptist, and in the 1860s as Revival.

nyabinghi
Dances held to commemorate events sacred to the Rastafari; originally believed to mean 'death to white oppressors'; also, the drum rhythm peculiar to Rastafari and central to all Rastafari gatherings.

Native Baptist
See Myal.

obeah
Fetishes, oils and powders used to achieve personal goals; also, negative spirits (Suriname).

obeahmen
Experts in obeah (mainly called upon to cause damage).

oso sani
House rituals (Winti).

Pukumina
An African-derived sect linked historically to Myal, one of two Jamaican religious traditions that evolved from the Great Revival. Also misspelt 'pacomania'.

Ras Tafari
Ethiopian for Prince Tafari, crowned Emperor Haile Selassie I in November 1930.

repatriation
Rastafari concept of return by all diaspora Africans to Africa or Ethiopia.

repeater
Type of Rastafari drum, played with the hands, and used for variations on rhythms set by bass and funde drums; see nyabinghi.

Revival
Jamaican folk religion which evolved from Myal in the nineteenth century, taking its name from the Great Christian Revival of the early 1860s, and comprising Revival Zion (or Zion Revival) and Pukumina. See Myal.

Revivalism
The world view underlying Revival and common to the Jamaican folk.

Revival Zion
The Christianized variant of Pukumina; (also Zion Revival).

reasonings
Small, informal religious gatherings for discussion and the ritual

smoking of marihuana, with an importance comparable to that of Christian communion (Rastafari).

sankeys

Songs from the collection by Ira D. Sankey, sung at Revival meetings, read line by line as they are sung.

seal

Sacred spots scattered around a balm yard or near or in a church or tabernacle; indoors these usually consist of a three-tiered altar, outdoors they usually include a flag on a bamboo pole; other objects include sacred herbs and flowers, water; stones, bottled beverages, candles, pictures of Jesus, fruit and vases of flowers. The candles are lit at night.

Sheshamane

Area in Ethiopia made available to migrants by Haile Selassie, via the Ethiopia World Federation.

sounds

Rastafari pronouncements, usually critical or prophetic.

Table

Feast (Revival).

trumping

Groaning associated with spiritual possession.

Twelve Tribes (of Israel)

Dues-paying, middle class Ratafari sect headed by Prophet Gad.

Vodun

A pan-African religion in Haiti.

Winti

Surinamese folk religion.

yeye

Eye (pronounced 'yai' by Jamaicans).

Youth Black Faith

Rastafari grouping, founded in 1949, apparently to purge the faith of Revivalist practices; source of dreadlocks.

Zion Revival

One of two Jamaican religious traditions that evolved from the Great Revival that spread from Ireland through North America and the Caribbean in the mid-nineteenth century.

Index